CREATING a CULTURE
— of —

REFLECTIVE
PRACTICE

CREATING a CULTURE
— of —
REFLECTIVE PRACTICE

Capacity-Building for
Schoolwide Success

PETE HALL | ALISA SIMERAL

Alexandria, Virginia USA

1703 N. Beauregard St. • Alexandria, VA 22311-1714 USA
Phone: 800-933-2723 or 703-578-9600 • Fax: 703-575-5400
Website: www.ascd.org • E-mail: member@ascd.org
Author guidelines: www.ascd.org/write

Deborah S. Delisle, *Executive Director;* Robert D. Clouse, *Managing Director, Digital Content & Publications;* Stefani Roth, *Publisher;* Genny Ostertag, *Director, Content Acquisitions;* Julie Houtz, *Director, Book Editing & Production;* Jamie Greene, *Associate Editor;* Khanh Pham, *Graphic Designer;* Mike Kalyan, *Director, Production Services;* Cynthia Stock, *Typesetter;* Mike Podgorny, *Senior Production Specialist*

PAPERBACK ISBN: 978-1-4166-2444-8   ASCD product #117006   n8/17
PDF E-BOOK ISBN: 978-1-4166-2446-2; see Books in Print for other formats.

Quantity discounts are available: e-mail programteam@ascd.org or call 800-933-2723, ext. 5773, or 703-575-5773. For desk copies, go to www.ascd.org/deskcopy.

Library of Congress Cataloging-in-Publication Data

Names: Hall, Peter A., 1971– author. | Simeral, Alisa, author.
Title: Creating a culture of reflective practice : capacity-building for
    schoolwide success / Pete Hall and Alisa Simeral.
Description: Alexandria, Virginia : ASCD, [2017] | Includes bibliographical
    references and index.
Identifiers: LCCN 2017023399 (print) | LCCN 2017029818 (ebook) | ISBN
    9781416624462 (PDF) | ISBN 9781416624448 (pbk.)
Subjects: LCSH: Reflective teaching. | School improvement programs.
Classification: LCC LB1025.3 (ebook) | LCC LB1025.3 .H344 2017 (print) | DDC
    371.102—dc23
LC record available at https://lccn.loc.gov/2017023399

Dedication

To Myn, Reno, Junior, and PJ: You're my North Star. I love you.

—*Pete Hall*

To Gin: At 95 years, you haven't stopped learning—or teaching. I love you.

To my children J and O, without whom this book would have been completed months earlier (sorry, Pete!): You inspire me and make me so proud. Always be the best you can be.

—*Alisa Simeral*

Some of the forms and figures found in this book can be downloaded and customized for classroom use. To access these documents, please visit www.ascd.org/ASCD/pdf/books/HallSimeral2017.pdf

Use the password "HallSimeral117006" (no quotes) to unlock the files.

CREATING a CULTURE
— of —
REFLECTIVE PRACTICE

Preface

When we first wrote *Building Teachers' Capacity for Success: A Collaborative Approach for Coaches and School Leaders* (or *BTCFS* for short; Hall & Simeral, 2008), our work was more theoretical, based upon a strong case study (Anderson Elementary School in Reno, Nevada) and a few additional sample projects smattered about the United States. If you're interested in the Anderson School turnaround story, look up the *Educational Leadership* article "A School Reclaims Itself" (Hall, 2005). That's where Pete explains how the school went from being the lowest-achieving school in Nevada (the only school to have failed to make its Adequate Yearly Progress goals for four consecutive years) to the only Title I school in the state to earn a High Achieving designation just two years later.

Now, nearly a decade after the publication of *BTCFS*, the research is thorough, the implementations are widespread, and the jury is back: the philosophy, model, structures, and strategies within *BTCFS* are guilty of having a positive impact on student learning, through the capacity-building efforts of administrators, coaches, and educators worldwide. And we're not just looking at short-term results; indeed, this approach isn't fulfilled until we've established persistent, enduring, long-lasting, positive change in the belief systems, thought patterns, and collective results in schools and communities.

As one might expect, we have considerably refined our work over the past several years. We are Refinement-stage thinkers, after all, and there's no way our first product arrived as stain-free and streamlined as it could be! And while we thought these updates would serve as a 2nd edition of *BTCFS*, we quickly realized the breadth and depth of new, exciting, and extensive information herein truly amounts to a new tool, rather than a refurbished one. In fact, we believe this to be the *definitive* guide to building teachers' capacity.

Our experiences as in-the-trenches practitioners (Pete as a principal of two additional Title I schools; Alisa as a dean of students, instructional coach, turnaround specialist, and coach of coaches) and as in-the-field professional development agents (through years of concurrent consulting work in schools and districts internationally) have verified the impact that this work—this idea, this structure, this approach—has had upon legions of educators in elementary, middle, and high schools, in urban and rural settings, teaching every content imaginable.

If you're interested in exploring the implementations and their early (and long-term) results, you might look into some of the following locations:

- Washoe County (Nevada) School District
- Point Isabel (Texas) Independent School District
- Sarasota County (Florida) Public Schools
- Cypress-Fairbanks (Texas) Independent School District
- Page (Arizona) Unified School District
- Iowa City (Iowa) Community School District
- Gibbes Middle School (Columbia, South Carolina)
- Linn-Mar High School (Marion, Iowa)
- Brule Elementary School (Navasota, Texas)
- White Street School Elementary (Springfield, Massachusetts)

Our initial goal, as we launched this work, was to build a capacity model that truly affected the quality of the instruction delivered by our teachers, strengthened their reflective abilities in order to have a lasting impact, and encouraged collaboration between the administrator, the instructional coach, and other capacity-builders (peers, mentors, teacher-leaders, and others) in our teachers' lives.

Interestingly, in a lot of the early implementations, we encountered instructional leaders who were so hyperfocused on their own roles and strategies, they hadn't yet included their *teachers* in the work. As they strove to improve reflective practices and technical expertise across their campuses, and despite the best of intentions, they had accidentally excluded the very people whose capacity they were attempting to build! Soon we wrote and published our parallel teacher text, *Teach, Reflect, Learn: Building Your Capacity for Success in the Classroom* (Hall & Simeral, 2015), to ensure that teachers not only were a part of the conversation but also could take the reins of their own professional growth through the many self-directed options we provided.

At that point, we thought we had all our bases covered (be ready—that's just the first of many sports metaphors we've woven into this text). As we scrutinized the implementations and their effectiveness, it was clear that some settings were yielding stronger returns than others, despite the same professional development, resources, activities, and timelines. What made the difference? Well, many things: personnel, context, commitment of the leaders—and, more than anything else, the environment established by the leadership. Hence the "culture of reflective practice" that you'll read so much about in this book.

In the preface for *BTCFS*, we wrote something that still holds true today:

> What follows are the current results of our investigation.
> We write *current* because as education evolves, information
> expands, and experience accrues, our understandings of the
> work we do will continue to change and evolve as well. We'll
> never know everything we need to know, and we may never
> achieve our ultimate goal. But the beauty of this work is that
> while we strive, we make a difference. (p. x)

Throughout this text, we, the authors—one of us a veteran principal and the other a veteran instructional coach—add our individual two cents to the discussion. Sometimes telling an anecdote, sometimes going into a bit more detail, Pete Hall (in "Pete's Perspective") and Alisa Simeral (in "Alisa's Approach") share experiences and outlooks. Our hope is that these asides will add flavor and resonance to the text.

We also want to note that we have provided downloadable, fillable PDF versions of several of the book's tools, templates, forms, and protocols for your immediate use at www.ascd.org/ASCD/pdf/books/HallSimeral2017.pdf (password: HallSimeral117006).

As you read on, we challenge you to critically reflect upon your thinking and your work; we urge you to continuously strive for excellence; we encourage you to cultivate collaborative relationships; and we commend you for making a difference.

Truly, this work would not be possible but for the input and impact of the educators who shaped us, gave us opportunity, and helped to refine our approaches over the years. From the stout trunk of the Frank C. Garrity tree to the common sense of Derek Cordell, from the models of excellence from Kim Price and Lisa Johnson to the fearless leadership of Prim Walters, from the passion of Andre Wicks to the gorgeous lessons of Collette McIntyre, and from the nuanced coaching of Gia Maraccini to the persistent advocacy of Amanda Romey—this list could span to the moon and back, and we love and appreciate each of you that much.

As we've proceeded through the writing process with this project, we cannot say thank you enough to the wonderful folks at ASCD, namely, the incomparable Genny Ostertag and the persnickety editing of Jamie Greene—both of whom have made us not only feel like we know what we're doing but look like it, too. And to our families and pets—from spouses and kids to dogs, chickens, horses, cats, and hamsters—we owe a tremendous amount of appreciation for the love and support with which we are constantly warmed. You are why we do the work we do.

Part I: The Game

No one would ever mistake education for a game. The stakes are too high and the outcomes are too critical to be compared to simple fun and entertainment. However, when it comes to metaphors, nothing comes close to conveying the complexity, organization, relationships, and goal orientation of sports. And after much deliberation and contemplation, we've chosen the sports metaphor as the mode through which we share our work.

Launching this exploration is Part I, where we set the stage for the game itself. This introduction outlines four key ideas that compel us forth.

In Chapter 1, we present a pretty straightforward argument: our schools and education system are underperforming, and we can do better—and improving teacher quality is the key.

Going deeper, Chapter 2 reveals our thesis: the difference between mediocrity and excellence is our ability to engage in rigorous self-reflection about the task at hand, so in order to improve our educational outcomes, we must focus on building the reflective capacity of our teachers. We also introduce and explain the first of two important tools—the Reflective Cycle—to show how teachers reflect and to guide this process.

In Chapter 3, we update a classic tool—the Continuum of Self-Reflection—first published in *Building Teachers' Capacity for Success* (Hall & Simeral, 2008) to provide a playbook for developing our teachers as reflective practitioners. The Continuum of Self-Reflection is a two-pronged tool that helps capacity-builders (administrators, coaches, and teacher-leaders) identify how their teachers reflect and suggests strategies for supporting their growth.

Finally, in Chapter 4, we introduce the idea of a culture of reflective practice. Before we, as capacity-builders, can begin the exciting work of capacity-building, we must prepare the environment for this work. The first four fundamentals of a culture of reflective practice provide a blueprint for establishing a culture and building readiness for reflection, while the final three fundamentals share the collaborative, feedback, and coaching elements of deep and lasting capacity-building.

Play ball!

Demystifying the Surest
Path to Student Learning

One hundred percent. Is there any other number in education—or in any element of life, for that matter—that is more important? Wouldn't our communities breathe a little easier if 100 percent of our citizens were well educated, employed, and contributing members to society? Shouldn't our school districts aim for 100 percent of their students graduating prepared for college, careers, and life? Don't schools and teachers want 100 percent of their students to master 100 percent of key learning outcomes? We can guarantee you that all parents want 100 percent of their children to succeed, achieve, and meet 100 percent of their potential.

Unfortunately, educators have long been loath to promote goals that include the lofty, audacious figure of 100 percent. In the 2002 reauthorization of the Elementary and Secondary Education Act (commonly referred to as the No Child Left Behind Act, or NCLB), that very goal was set for 2014 student achievement rates. That "finish line" has come and gone, as has NCLB, but the effects are lasting: setting a goal of 100 percent proficiency has shifted the focus to *all* students, which by definition includes and emphasizes *each* and *every* individual student. Here's a mission—a philosophy, at least—we can all get behind.

In a lot of contexts, numbers other than 100 percent have been deemed sufficient. Many schools, districts, and teachers set goals to have 90 percent,

80 percent, 60 percent, or even a smaller percentage of students reach the proficiency level on academic achievement indexes. When would 90 percent be sufficient? When referring to the number of words one spells correctly on a spelling test? The number of students adequately supporting a thesis statement in an essay? The percentage of parents or families representing their children during parent-teacher conference week? The number of free throws made in a basketball game? The high school graduation rate?

Let's extend our thinking beyond education, just for argument's sake. Would 90 percent meet our needs for on-time flight arrivals? How about crash-free flights? Successful medical procedures? Accurate billing from your credit card company? The success rate of your own bungee jumps off the Rio Grande Bridge in Taos, New Mexico? Heavens, no!

One hundred percent is the *only* number that matters.

As educators, we engage every day in the most noble, the most impactful, and the most important act known to humankind: teaching. Ensuring the success, the learning, and the development of our community's young people is not a task to take lightly and certainly isn't one worthy of shucking off one-tenth of our clientele. We can, and we must, reach every single child, every single moment: 100 percent.

Are We There Yet?

Over the past two decades or so, we (the collective *we*) have pummeled our schools, lambasted our teachers, skewered our principals, and—worst of all—heaped anxiety upon piles of torment and stress on our kids—all in the name of explaining our collective lack of academic success and growth. We could look at PISA (Program for International Student Assessment) or TIMSS (Trends in International Mathematics and Science Study) scores (both of which—along with other international measures—are available for your scrutiny at https://nces.ed.gov/surveys/international/ide), homegrown assessment results such as the NAEP (National Assessment of Educational Progress, commonly known as the Nation's Report Card), or the reams of standardized test score data we've so eagerly collected to know this: it ain't pretty.

Let's just cut to the chase, shall we? If you teach, lead, or work in a school system—or if you're a member of our human society—you're quite aware that our schools are not functioning up to their potential. Never mind the unattainable (albeit admirable) goal of 100 percent across the board. The painful and plentiful reality is this: our students are not achieving as they could. We are stumbling along this path, churning out masses of young adults toting a remarkable disparity of knowledge, skills, and readiness for the *real* world, including some who are ill-prepared to the point of embarrassment. That's the bad news. Here's the good news: there's *plenty* of room for improvement.

Have We Gone Mad?

Because we have yet to encounter anyone who claims, "Our schools are fine; just leave them alone," it's safe to say there's consensus about the urgent need to improve our educational outputs. And now, for the $620 billion question (that was the total expenditure for public elementary and secondary schools in the United States in 2012–13, according to the most recent NCES data, available at http://nces.ed.gov/fastfacts/display.asp?id=66): *How* do we improve our schools? And where should we allocate our funds to get the biggest bang for the buck?

As a profession, and as a society, we decry the lack of funding in education. We lament the shortfalls, pummel our legislators, plead for increased spending, and even sue the states for their failure to adequately fund basic education needs (National Educational Access Network, available at http://schoolfunding.info/litigation/litigation.php3). To a certain extent, this is justifiable outrage. Then again, what mechanisms are in place to monitor and evaluate our allocation of the funds we *do* receive and the impact of those expenditures? Are we wise stewards of public funds? Or are we simply asking for more money to spend on doing more of the same thing, sowing the seeds of the status quo? Do we even know what to do to improve?

In our ardent quest to unravel the mysteries of effective teaching, we have swung from one end of that puckish educational pendulum to the other. Over and over again, we've embraced a "new" approach, banishing our previous practices as "old school" and claiming innovation as the key to improvement. We have sought the strategies that lead to higher levels of student learning, hoping that replicating them in our classrooms will produce better results. The consequence of this pursuit, noble as it may appear, is a frightful adherence to lock-step actions, teachers following a prescribed checklist monitored by zealous principals; and when the test results come back stagnant, we switch to a different set of instructional techniques, again hoping for different outcomes.

Plan A

What does the research say about what successful, effective schools and districts are doing to make their gains? How do high-performing schools and districts allocate their precious resources (time, money, energy, and personnel)? If we are going to focus on the educational growth and development of our students, where do we start? Where do we direct our energy in order to address education's public accountability charge? The answer is startlingly simple. We must improve teacher quality, because *teacher quality—and quality instruction—is the number-one determinant of student success.*

Teacher quality—and quality instruction—is the number-one determinant of student success.

Now, now. Before you cast this claim into the cacophony of prominent voices all across the educational landscape singing the same song, know this: we have an idea for how to do this in a rather simple, replicable, focused manner. More on that later. For now, let's validate the claim.

Research has long supported the assertion that better teachers lead to higher student achievement. A 70-year-old article in *Educational Leadership* identified an early perspective on the characteristics of effective teaching—with a rudimentary rubric distinguishing between the Teachers, the Gentlemen, the Conscientious Souls, and the Wastrels (Landsdowne, 1944)! More recently, Charlotte Danielson, creator of the indispensable Framework for Professional Practice, stated quite directly, "High-level learning by students requires high-level instruction by their teachers" (2007, p. 15). Not surprisingly, this is a global perspective, echoed by Barber and Mourshed in *How the World's Best-Performing School Systems Come Out on Top*: "The only way to improve outcomes is to improve instruction" (2007, p. 34). Education expert Linda Darling-Hammond studied the results of the 2013 Teaching and Learning International Survey (TALIS) to declare, "We cannot make major headway in raising student performance and closing the achievement gap until we make progress in closing the teaching gap" (2014–15, p. 18).

The message is the same closer to home. Bryan Goodwin, CEO of the research think tank Mid-continent Research for Education and Learning (McREL), concurred that "one of the most important ways that school systems can change the odds for students is to ensure that every child receives the benefit of a great teacher, every year, and in every classroom" (2011, p. 19). The reality, as expressed by renowned educational researcher Robert J. Marzano, is this: "It is clear that effective teachers have a profound influence on student achievement and ineffective teachers do not. In fact, ineffective teachers might actually impede the learning of their students" (2003, p. 75).

Based on this commonsensical idea, the Teacher Quality Roadmap series from the National Council on Teacher Quality has investigated the state of teacher quality in 13 school districts since its launch in 2009, offering findings in policy and practice that guide reform initiatives (for more information, go to nctq.org). John Hattie, whose mega meta-analysis *Visible*

Learning carries significant professional clout, acknowledges the variation in teacher quality, noting that "it is the differences in the teachers that make the difference in student learning" (2009, p. 236). Hattie proceeds to reveal the teaching actions and instructional strategies that have the greatest effect on student learning. With this profound research support, the mystery of effective instruction really has no business being a mystery anymore.

First off, let's be clear that our emphasis is on improving the learning outcomes for every child, every moment of every day, in every classroom in every school. That means 100 percent. This effort requires a concerted, laserlike focus on strengthening core first instruction, an argument that the Response-to-Intervention (RTI) movement has attempted to bring to light, but its particulars have obfuscated that emphasis. Experts such as Buffum, Mattos, and Weber remind us, "No intervention program can compensate for ineffective core instructional practices" (2008, p. 74); and the esteemed Douglas Fisher and Nancy Frey suggest, "Approximately 75 to 85 percent of students should make sufficient progress through core instruction alone. Schools where this is not the case should focus on improving core instruction" (2010, p. 24). We must remain beholden to this responsibility. First things first: we've got to have a strong Plan A.

The X Factor

In *Building Teachers' Capacity for Success* (Hall & Simeral, 2008), we asked you to consider the difference between a classroom with no learning tools and one devoid of a teacher within it. We now ask you to hone your envisioning skills a bit further.

Imagine, if you will, a garden-variety school classroom—any setting, any content, students of any age. Fill it with the best furniture, materials, curriculum, technology, and tools that money can buy. Load it up with everything from your wish list, as if you had just won the lottery and your first act was to better equip this single classroom with top-notch *everything*. Gorgeous, isn't it? The paint, the lights, the carpet, the tablets, the simulators, and the thousand-dollar unbreakable-tip pencils. What parents wouldn't want their kid in this classroom? And right on cue, let's load up the room with students, as many as can comfortably fit while maintaining the ideal student-teacher ratio.

And for the coup de grâce, bring in the teacher—and not just any teacher. No, for this classroom we're going to bring in a certifiably, thoroughly *mediocre* teacher.

What will the results be? What kind of learning is going to take place in this room?

Now let's shake things up a bit. First, turn off the electricity and eliminate all that technology—no computers, no panacean apps, no holographics, no Internet. Next, remove the books. Take out the desks, the paper, the ergonomically designed chairs, the lectern, and even the crayons. Picture the room barren of furniture and materials.

How will the students learn now? How will they develop their curiosity, grow and develop as thinkers, comprehend rules and exceptions to rules, understand the Earth's place in the universe, decipher poetry, conceive of ways to better the world, embrace the natural existence of mathematics, and make meaning of the events of World War II?

As a final touch, let's excuse that mediocre teacher. Quickly now—because a classroom without a teacher is ripe for some frightening situations—let's bring a different teacher into the room; someone exceptional, passionate, committed, engaging, and by all means extraordinary.

What will the results be now? What kind of learning is going to take place in this room? And how will the students learn?

Silly, isn't it, that it's that obvious, that straightforward, and that elemental? We're not overstating the point when we say that teachers matter. Effective teachers matter. The quality of the teacher is the "X factor." Everything in education depends on it.

The quality of the teacher is the "X factor." Everything in education depends on it.

It is doubtful that your response to this scenario includes exclamatory statements such as "Startling," "Revolutionary," or "No way! I'd never considered that before!" Even so, the questions remain: How much value are we really placing on teacher quality? If it's so important, what are we doing to unilaterally and unabashedly address it? In their report *The Widget Effect*, the New Teacher Project dug into our profession's tendency to hide poor performance and overinflate teacher evaluation ratings, finding a "culture of indifference about the quality of instruction" (2009, p. 2). Then, in their scathing follow-up, *The Mirage*, they uncovered an even uglier reality: despite expenditures of nearly $18,000 per teacher per year on various forms of professional development, nearly 70 percent of teachers did not improve or *declined* in their performance over a period of two to three years, suggesting a "pervasive culture of low expectations for teacher development and performance" (2015, p. 2). As a result, and not surprisingly, teacher morale is in a steady decline, with large numbers of educators leaving the profession. A recent report for the Alliance for Excellent Education (2014), a policy and advocacy organization, found that "roughly half a million U.S. teachers either move or leave the profession each year" (para. 1).

"The teaching workforce continues to be a leaky bucket, losing hundreds of thousands of teachers each year—the majority of them before retirement age," says a 2016 report from the Learning Policy Institute (Sutcher, Darling-Hammond, & Carver-Thomas, 2016, para. 7).

So a better question might actually be this: Why aren't we *developing* our teachers with consistent, effective *professional development* endeavors that *improve* teaching, positively *affect* student learning, and *build capacity* for enduring, long-term professional growth? Why aren't we (again, the collective *we*) providing PD that sticks?

PD That Sticks

Common sense tells us that in order to improve, we must change. Insanity, Albert Einstein told us, "is doing the same thing over and over again and expecting different results." Change, then, is a prerequisite of improvement. And in this case, change means learning more, thinking differently, altering practices, and improving student outcomes.

In his valuable publication *Professional Development That Sticks,* award-winning educator Fred Ende states a tenet we can't deny: "All of us, no matter what role we hold, no matter what organization we work for, no matter what profession we belong to, need to strive to keep getting better" (2016, p. 3).

For decades, we have erroneously focused our efforts on providing simple technical fixes to complex systemic problems. Our professional development still consists predominately of "sit 'n' git" sessions that lack relevance and tend to encourage a single course of action—usually the *correct* implementation of a tool, a strategy, a method, or a program—that the rank-and-file teachers, once back in their classrooms, use only as directed, checking off boxes accordingly. And we're surprised when (1) teachers fail to follow through as demanded, (2) student learning outcomes continue to lag, and (3) teachers rebel against such poorly designed, poorly executed professional torture exercises.

Oh, for heaven's sake, we know what to do! The research is plentiful—and even eloquent—in its blueprints for continued professional growth. Ende (2016, pp. 8–9) continues with four key characteristics of professional development that sticks: it is meaningful, it is highly engaging, the audience has ownership, and it has an impact on professional practice and student learning. Let's explore these commonsense items one at a time.

1. *It is meaningful.* Historically, educator PD has been rather hit-and-miss, something we do *to* teachers that may or may not have any relevance. With clear goals and a powerful vision, however, we can streamline all of our efforts. One of education's leading voices on effective professional development, Tom Guskey, implores us to begin with the end in mind: "We must first consider the specific student learning outcomes we want to attain" (2014,

p. 13). Bryan Goodwin, in *Simply Better* (2011, p. 10), compels us to then answer the question: "In light of the hundreds (if not thousands) of things we might do, are we doing what matters most?" By emphasizing learning experiences that focus on the few approaches that will have the greatest impact upon our progress toward the collective outcomes, the meaningfulness quotient skyrockets.

2. *It is highly engaging.* One of our biggest misconceptions about professional learning is that it's an event. Although workshops, seminars, and coursework certainly canvass the educational landscape, the notion of "inservice training" severely limits our perspective. In fact, the very term, *training,* causes a pseudo-gagging reflex in us, as it conjures images of seals with beach balls balanced atop their snouts, not the ongoing growth of professional educators. Instead, let's think of professional learning as an experience: it could be job-embedded (Hall & Simeral, 2008), a function of collaborative inquiry (David, 2008–09), spurred by curiosity (Goodwin, 2014), and structured in a format that participants—either at the table together in a workshop or in a classroom trying out a new strategy with a colleague—are eager to focus on, interact with, and reflect upon thoroughly (Ende, 2016). In their 2015 revision of the Standards for Professional Learning (available at https://learningforward.org/standards), Learning Forward reveals an undeniable truth: "Educators learn in different ways and at different rates." Our plans and delivery must respect this.

3. *The audience has ownership.* There's a subtle but monumental difference between "ownership" and "buy-in," which zealous principals and professional development facilitators often pursue. Doug Reeves, in *Transforming Professional Development into Student Results,* eschews the notion that staff "buy-in" is

an essential antecedent for positive change. Instead, he argues, we should be compelled by the *vision* and our focused goals—*those* are what should drive our professional learning ambitions, programs, and experiences (2010, p. 6). In his seminal work, *Drive*, author Daniel Pink details the impact autonomy has upon motivation, offering the view that we need less prodding and more choice in *how* to satisfactorily meet our vision and goals. We need to let our teachers *own* it (2009, pp. 88–90), rather than determining a course of action and then somehow trying to convince, bribe, or cajole teachers into "buying in." Ownership rules. This is the difference between *compliance* and *commitment*.

Ownership rules. This is the difference between *compliance* and *commitment*.

4. *It has an impact on professional practice and student learning.* Learning Forward's updated standards (referenced earlier) also express a need to provide professional development that is ongoing, differentiated, and addresses the knowledge, skills, and *dispositions* that lead to changes in educator practice, that lead to changes in student outcomes. This will require a significant amount of forethought in planning effective learning experiences that are related to the common vision and goals (Guskey, 2014). And, not to be overlooked, we must allocate a considerable investment in follow-up and follow-through: communicating expectations, monitoring implementation, providing just-in-time support, and maintaining focus and momentum on the goals (Hall, Childs-Bowen, Cunningham-Morris, Pajardo, & Simeral, 2016; Hall & Simeral, 2008; Marzano, Frontier, & Livingston, 2011). This isn't work that we can leave to chance, hope, or happenstance.

> If we want our PD to affect how we provide learning experiences for students, it's got to be intentionally crafted and delivered to meet that end.

In addition to Ende's clear blueprint for effective professional learning, we'd like to contribute our perspective on keeping the long-range vision in focus. In the fun and impactful leadership guide *Water the Bamboo*, author Greg Bell discusses the patience needed to see the full benefits of our capacity-building efforts. Although the growth rate of giant timber bamboo (a foot-and-a-half per day) is exciting, "what's even more amazing about giant timber bamboo is that once it's planted, it takes at least three years to break through the ground" (2009, p. 1). The farmers trust the process as they tend to their invisible crops, season after season. This observation offers a pretty vibrant metaphor for us as instructional leaders and professional developers.

We know what to do, so let's do it. Acting with deep knowledge, inescapable intentionality, and consistent support will undoubtedly have an impact—a lasting, powerful impact—and promises to strengthen the entire system. This is the essence of capacity-building: continued growth and ongoing development for the long haul.

$n + 1$

Perhaps there is a number as important as 100 percent, after all. It is this: $n + 1$. No matter what our present levels of performance are, no matter what our baseline is, and no matter where we are now (represented by data point n), we can always do better. We can always strive for more. We can always take that step forward. We can always aim for $n + 1$.

What if we altered the model, reduced the number of dollars we allocate to the *stuff* that comes in glitzy packages and touts success for all students and the *fluff* of PD that has strangled our profession, and instead extended our professional educators' daily and annual schedules to include ongoing, job-embedded professional learning opportunities? This could come in the form of extended collaboration time for teams, built-in time for research, PD with experts, data analysis, strategic planning, deepening content knowledge and pedagogical skill, and running instructional scrimmages. *Practice*. Let's pay our teachers more, invest our funds in the folks who truly determine the student learning outcomes, and get the biggest bang for the buck!

Pete's Perspective

I was recently working with a district that had a very adept grant writer on staff. This person, well versed in learning theories and recent research, successfully obtained over a million dollars' worth of grant funding for the district. With these funds, she purchased truckloads of educational tools: interactive whiteboards, piles upon piles of books, the latest and greatest PE equipment, laptops, subscriptions to websites with assessment tools and personalized learning pages, and a gazillion other items.

Needing to account for their whereabouts, she stored these tools in a central warehouse, available to teachers for checkout. She ran special training sessions to inform teachers of the tools and how to use them, she invited teachers to browse the inventory, and she offered bonus gifts to anyone who checked items out to use. Unfortunately, the incredible majority of these terrific tools remained in the warehouse, collecting dust and taking up space. Despite the best of intentions, this endeavor fell flat. No one took advantage of these items, so learning wasn't affected.

More dramatic was this: $1 million of grant funds had brought in stuff. What might have been the impact on that district's children if that money had been allocated to personnel, professional development, or—better yet—personnel who provided professional development, like instructional coaches?

Unfortunately, the district will never know.

Let's Put Our Money Where Our Research Is

Here's a thought: let's gain clarity about what will make the greatest impact on student achievement. That's easy. It's teacher quality, and we've been banging this drum for a while now. Then let's prioritize that fact in our practices, policies, and pocketbooks. Let's reallocate the funds that get derailed at the online marketplace toward enhancing teacher quality. Paying teachers for the full days they're working anyway, let's reconfigure the work day to include regular teacher collaboration, job-embedded professional development, the pursuit of action research projects, data analysis, and regular opportunities for extending their professional learning endeavors. What if teaching became a true profession, in every sense of the word, and we paid our teachers to learn, grow, collaborate, reflect, and augment their performance *every day*, thereby increasing their positive impact on student learning? What if we truly put our money where our research is?

Let's put the person at the front of the classroom at the top of the list for funding. It isn't necessarily the number of dollars we spend in education that's the issue; rather, it's how we're spending those dollars. Let's get it right. And let's build a culture of reflective practice.

The Culture of Reflective Practice

What is a culture of reflective practice, you ask? Here is our operational definition:

> A culture of reflective practice is an organization that embraces reflective growth as the primary driving force behind continuous, lasting improvement. In such an organization, members speak the language of reflection, engage in rigorous metacognitive tasks, and earnestly support their individual and collective growth. The entire organization oozes self-reflection.

In short, a culture of reflective practice describes the conditions that enable all our strength-based, adult-differentiated, student-learning-focused efforts to be successful. It is composed of the factors that embrace change, that clarify the vision and goals, that communicate openly and transparently, that work together to make steady progress toward organizational outcomes, and that facilitate deep reflection that leads to ongoing, steady, enduring professional growth.

The foundation of a culture of reflective practice is built upon seven fundamentals. These Building Teacher Capacity (BTC) Fundamentals are the foundational pieces necessary to support and guide schools and districts through the process of shifting school culture and climate, growing a reflective mindset, and establishing a culture of reflective practice:

1. Relationships, Roles, and Responsibilities

2. Expectations and Communication

3. Celebration and Calibration

4. Goal Setting and Follow-Through

5. Strategic PLC and Teacher-Leadership Support

6. Transformational Feedback

7. Differentiated Coaching

In Chapters 5 through 13, we will explore these BTC Fundamentals in more depth. But first, we've got to address that spongy gray matter between our ears.

Think about it.

Reflections on Self-Reflection and the Reflective Cycle

"Think about it." That's the sentence we used to wrap up Chapter 1, and for a very specific reason, we repeat it here. Our thinking is perhaps the most important key to unlocking the black box of continuous improvement. As René Descartes famously uttered, "Cogito, ergo sum." *I think, therefore I am.*

Let's take a moment to make sense of this. Our definitive, undeniable, and obvious goal is to improve student learning outcomes. Students learn because of what they do—the activities they engage in, the tasks they complete, the problems they solve. In the school setting, student learning tasks are overwhelmingly the result of teacher actions, in the form of lessons, assignments, scenarios, lesson plans. And teachers *do* what they *do* because of what they think about: their focus, their objectives, their plans, their expertise. Looking at this train of thought from a cause-and-effect perspective, we get something like what you see in Figure 2.1. And if how we think drives what we do, then developing and refining strong habits of thought is at the heart of all capacity-building work and, ultimately, both teacher and student success.

As we mentioned in Chapter 1, it's not *what* we do that truly matters—it's *how* we do what we do that makes the difference. And to be perfectly clear, let's consult John Dewey: "It's not the doing that matters; it's the thinking about the doing" (quoted in Archambault, 1974, p. 321). Dewey's writings,

FIGURE 2.1

Reflection-to-Learning Cause and Effect Flowchart

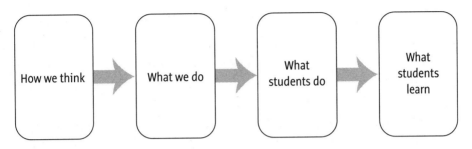

including his seminal *How We Think* (1910), have been instrumental in our work, leading us beyond the standards, the curriculum, the strategies, the structure, and the walls of the classroom to the mind of the teacher standing at the front of it. The way we think, and the manner in which we reflect on our practice, determines the effectiveness of our actions. The key to increasing our impact—to raising student achievement—lies in our ability to engage in frequent, accurate, and deep self-reflection.

From Mediocrity to Excellence

Consider the two teachers we placed at the front of the classroom in our hypothetical scenario in Chapter 1, when we introduced the concept of the teacher being the "X factor." What is the difference between a *mediocre* teacher and an *excellent* teacher? To answer that question, we could probably brainstorm a list of adjectives and consult with some noted research experts on the characteristics of effective educators, and that would certainly get the conversation started. But here's the real challenge for us as instructional leaders: How do we move teachers from mediocrity to excellence? What are the approaches, the secrets, the maneuvers, and the leverage points to facilitate that transformative growth?

Our hypothesis is rather simple: *Our ability to reflect frequently, accurately, and deeply about our actions is what sets apart the excellent from the mediocre.*

Technical expertise, as we all know, is an important component of effective instruction. Knowing how to implement a particular teaching strategy, such as reciprocal teaching, is a prerequisite for putting it into place. However, emphasizing *only* technical expertise is where most professional development models fall short. Weaving in the elements of self-reflection allows a teacher to address *why* reciprocal teaching is an appropriate choice for this particular learning outcome; *which* students should be grouped together; *when* this strategy is best applied; *how* it should be launched, monitored, and modified; and *whether* a different strategy might work more effectively before, after, in addition to, or instead of reciprocal teaching.

Expertise is not something a chosen few are endowed with at birth; it does not arrive neatly packaged on our porch; nor is it commensurate with years of experience. Developing a skill takes time, yes, as well as effort, energy, and practice. In fact, we've commonly come to embrace the "10,000 hours" rule, popularized by Malcolm Gladwell in *Outliers* (2008); and it's not just quantity—it's got to be high-quality "deliberate practice" (Ericsson, Krampe, & Tesch-Römer, 1993, whose research Gladwell borrowed to create the 10,000-hour rule, by the way). It's this deliberate, intentional, strategic approach that signifies the importance of the key ingredient for excellence: a healthy dose of self-reflection. The difference between learning a skill and being able to implement it effectively resides in our capacity to engage in deep, continuous, rigorous thought about that skill. Technical expertise is one thing; practical expertise is another thing altogether.

Back to Dewey and his amazing insights. "We do not learn from experience," he stated. "We learn from reflecting on experience" (1916, p. 139). In *The Reflective Practitioner,* author Donald Schön discussed the importance of both reflecting *after* an act, calling this "reflection-on-action," or in the midst of the experience, referring to this as "reflection-in-action" (1983, p. 26). Both are important, and both yield insights that might affect student learning and teacher growth in the long term or immediately, if the teacher uses such reflections to guide future decision making and planning. According to Lortie (2002), failing to do so results in teaching by imitation rather than with intentionality—individuals may act like teachers and do what teachers do, but they lack the understanding of *why* to do it and *how* to do it better. This approach is not a recipe for success.

The thought processes that lead to greater levels of understanding, intentionality, and assessment are critical to long-term reflective growth. The difference lies in having a "disposition toward reflection," versus "expert teachers adjust their thinking to accommodate the level of reflection a situation calls for" (Danielson, 2009). It doesn't take an elaborately modified bell schedule, additional preparatory periods, a meditation chamber, or any other external factor to build and sustain one's reflective habits (though we'll describe the conditions that are most essential to a viable culture of reflective practice throughout this book). In fact, John Hattie's research offers a statement explaining the overarching keys to excellence in education, highlighting teachers' engagement in "critical reflection in light of evidence about their teaching" (2009, p. 239), regardless of resources, structure, subject, working conditions, student demographics, and a host of other variables. The ability to self-reflect is based in our brain, not in any specific content, skill, strategy, or approach. Self-reflection is independent of context.

What do we make of all this research and theory? Our colleague and pal Bobby Marzano, globally known as a modern master of educational research, sums it up quite succinctly: "Reflective practice is critical to expertise" (2012, p. 5). The consensus in the research realm confirms our hypothesis: our reflective habits are really, really important.

In short, we say this: *The more reflective we are, the more effective we are.*

A Definition of Self-Reflection

So what do we mean, precisely, when we use the term *self-reflection?*

Dewey defined reflection as "active, persistent and careful consideration of any belief or supposed form of knowledge in the light of the grounds that support it and the further conclusion to which it tends" (1910, p. 9). Moon, meanwhile, focuses more on the role of reflection in learning and embeds reflection into the learning process. She describes reflection as "a form of mental processing with a purpose and/or anticipated outcome that is applied to relatively complex or unstructured ideas for which there is not an obvious solution" (1999, p. 23).

In Stephen Covey's *Principle-Centered Leadership* (1990), one of the traits of effective leaders he identifies involves continuous learning and the relationship between increased skills and increased thinking about such improvement. In Covey's words, principle-centered people "are constantly educated by their experiences," and "they are curious, always asking questions." Perhaps most powerfully, "They discover that the more they know, the more they realize they don't know; that as their circle of knowledge grows, so does its outside edge of ignorance" (p. 33).

If you think this sounds considerably like the "growth mindset" that Stanford researcher Carol Dweck detailed for us in *Mindset*, you're not alone. If indeed we believe in the expansiveness of our potential, if we have the efficacy to effect change, and if we consider every challenge as a possibility, then our willingness to "stretch ourselves" will determine the successes to come (2006, p. 6). In short, Dweck might paraphrase our catchphrase: our reflectiveness determines our effectiveness.

Our working definition of *self-reflection* includes an overarching concept (i.e., the act of exerting mental energy about our professional responsibilities) and a series of very specific reflective behaviors:

- Gaining awareness of our educational surroundings (students, content, and pedagogy).

- Planning deliberately to take action with intentionality.

- Assessing the impact of our decisions and actions.

- Adjusting our course of action based on the feedback we receive from those assessments.

This thought process is best depicted using the Reflective Cycle (Figure 2.2), a tool we first shared with educators in our book *Teach, Reflect, Learn: Building Your Capacity for Success in the Classroom* (Hall & Simeral, 2015). It portrays the connectivity of thought first described by Dewey thus: "Reflection involves not simply a sequence of ideas, but a *con*sequence—a consecutive ordering in such a way that each determines the next as its

FIGURE 2.2

The Reflective Cycle

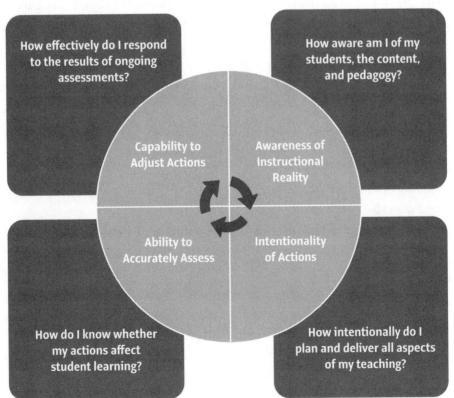

How effectively do I respond to the results of ongoing assessments?

How aware am I of my students, the content, and pedagogy?

Capability to Adjust Actions

Awareness of Instructional Reality

Ability to Accurately Assess

Intentionality of Actions

How do I know whether my actions affect student learning?

How intentionally do I plan and deliver all aspects of my teaching?

proper outcome, while each in turn leans back on its predecessors" (1910, p. 3, emphasis in original). Daudelin and Hall (1997) describe reflective learning as "the process of stepping back from an experience to ponder carefully and persistently its meaning . . . to reflect on the learning that is occurring" (p. 13). The examination is only part of the equation, as Jennifer York-Barr and her colleagues found: self-reflection is "aimed at understanding and subsequent improvement" of practice (2006, p. 4).

Taken as a whole, one might choose a very simple definition to answer this question: Want to know what self-reflection really is? *Think about it.*

In unending succession, reflective practitioners progress through the four components of the Reflective Cycle (which are the four specific reflective behaviors embedded in our working definition and shown in the bulleted list): they build awareness of learning goals, student needs, and instructional strategies; they create plans and act intentionally upon that information; they accurately assess the results of their efforts and the student learning outcomes; and they respond appropriately to the changing needs of their students, based on the results of that assessment. Let's take a closer look at the four components, as well as a fifth related to frequency of reflection.

The Reflective Cycle

Readers of *Teach, Reflect, Learn* will recognize the following description of the Reflective Cycle (Hall & Simeral, 2015, pp. 39–41).

Reflective practitioners have awareness of their instructional realities. *How aware am I of my students, the content, and pedagogy?* Teachers with awareness are knowledgeable about each and every student in their class, including the students' individual academic levels, interests, learning profiles, and instructional needs (Tomlinson, 2014). Having awareness means possessing a deep understanding of the content, including prerequisite relationships, connections across content and subject areas, and common misconceptions that will need to be addressed. Such teachers know how to facilitate learning in a manner that students understand; in other words, individual learning styles are connected to the right pedagogical approach in order to maximize retention. These are practitioners who are acutely aware of every aspect of classroom instruction. Charlotte Danielson (2007) describes awareness as an attribute that allows a teacher to comprehensively "see" what's going on in the classroom, in the plan book, and in all measures of learning.

Reflective practitioners are intentional in their actions. *How intentionally do I plan and deliver all aspects of my teaching?* The next step in the Reflective Cycle consists of a teacher taking intentional steps to affect student learning. With awareness of the instructional reality, a teacher can better select learning goals, curricula, materials, instructional strategies, student groupings, learning activities, and management strategies to meet the needs of specific students in the classroom. This is done, most assuredly, on purpose. Implementing research-based best practices is a solid strategy, though there is a big difference between a teacher who performs a specific teaching act and one who does it well. According to Hattie (2009), "What 'some' teachers do matters—especially those who teach in a most deliberate and visible manner" (p. 22).

Reflective practitioners accurately assess their impact. *How do I know whether my actions affect student learning?* Once a teacher engages in intentional, calculated actions, it is imperative to determine whether or not the specific actions resulted in the intended outcomes. Implementing some form of assessment is the next step in the Reflective Cycle, informing teachers of the impact of their actions (Danielson, 2009; Lortie, 2002; Marzano, 2012). Assessment tools are varied and must be matched to the task and purpose: student observations, performance assessments, surveys, quizzes, and other methods of data collection inform the teacher of the degree to which Teaching Strategy A resulted in Student Learning B.

Reflective practitioners adjust their actions on the fly. *How effectively do I respond to the results of ongoing assessments?* What a teacher does with assessment data often determines the outcome of a particular unit, lesson, or instructional strategy. In the Reflective Cycle, teachers armed with real-time assessment data can immediately adapt their approach, modify their lesson, or even stop and regroup. These decisions—based on ongoing, formative assessment information—help clarify misconceptions, address holes in learning, recalibrate energy, increase engagement, and provide an alternative method for helping students access their learning. Highly reflective teachers know that they have a powerful and immediate effect on student learning, and if students are struggling, then they can swiftly get them back on track by intervening in calculated and meaningful ways (Danielson, 2009; Hattie, 2009).

Reflective practitioners engage in ongoing reflection. *How often do I reflect about my teaching and student learning?* Reflection is a habit; as such, it must be developed. Engaging in the Reflective Cycle requires practice, diligence, and focus. Reflective practitioners have mastered this process and seem to engage in ongoing reflection almost intuitively. They do not wait for someone to pose a reflective prompt or to suggest that they attend to something. Rather, they are constantly alert to the reality of their classrooms, they make decisions intentionally, they assess the impact of those decisions, and they take immediate actions to correct their course as necessary. Reflective practitioners engage in metacognition—the practice of being aware of one's own thinking—in order to direct their thoughts toward more effective actions (Costa & Kallick, 2008).

 The Reflective Cycle is a predictable pattern of thinking that we all pursue as we build our skills, develop expertise, and progress toward excellence.

All teachers progress through this Reflective Cycle to some extent, and highly reflective teachers do so relentlessly. Such practitioners have cultivated their habits of thought with great intentionality, resulting in reflections that are deep, accurate, and continuous. In short, reflective practitioners proceed through the Reflective Cycle dozens, if not hundreds, of times in a single school day. Their minds are always at work.

Pete's Perspective

It's been my observation that greatness isn't an accident. Consider some of the all-time greats in the sporting world: Michael Jordan, Usain Bolt, Billie Jean King, Ted Williams, Jackie Joyner-Kersee, Muhammad Ali—whoever is on your list, they're not only talented—they possessed an inscrutable work ethic and a keen mind for their discipline. They worked their way to greatness because they thought and strategized their way to greatness.

In the words of the immortal UCLA basketball coach John Wooden, "Winning takes talent. To repeat takes character." And he would know: his teams won 10 national championships, including 7 in a row.

Teaching is no different, except we needn't possess much in the way of physical gifts to excel in the classroom—just character, which is found in our hearts and our minds.

Consider the current standard for excellent, "accomplished" teaching performance: National Board Certified Teachers (NBCTs). Take a moment to read the following list of the Five Core Propositions that describe what all NBCTs should know and be able to do (for more information, visit the National Board for Professional Teaching Standards website at www.nbpts.org):

- Proposition 1: NBCTs are committed to students and their learning.
- Proposition 2: NBCTs know the subjects they teach and how to teach those subjects to students.
- Proposition 3: NBCTs are responsible for managing and monitoring student learning.
- Proposition 4: NBCTs think systematically about their practice and learn from experience.
- Proposition 5: NBCTs are members of learning communities.

Now examine these characteristics in light of the Reflective Cycle that we have proposed. Where do you see overlap? Are there commonalities? We believe strongly in the thinking behind the doing—a perspective that is echoed within the rigorous, demanding requirements of achieving National Board Certification. Just ask any of your colleagues who have been through the excruciatingly challenging process (successfully or unsuccessfully).

And if the highest level of teacher certification in the United States expects teachers to reflect deeply, accurately, and frequently about the impact of their practice in order to achieve greater results, who are we to argue?

As a principal, I always sought teachers who had acquired National Board Certification. Why? Because it symbolized their deep commitment to the profession and gave me insight into their highly reflective nature. In the words of Lisa Jones, an NBCT with whom Alisa and I both worked, "Once you go through the NBCT process, you'll never go back. Reflection becomes embedded in who you are as a teacher."

Benefits of Self-Reflection

Besides the causative flowchart we depicted in Figure 2.1 (see p. 19), the benefits of growing as reflective practitioners are bountiful. Why, we can even harken back to a quote by a prominent educational thinker from the 1970s, Madeline Hunter: "If what a teacher does is consonant with what is now known about cause-effect relationships in learning, and *if* that teacher's decisions and actions reflect awareness of the current state of the learner and the present environment, then learning will predictably increase" (1979, p. 62).

The capacity-building model we propose is based on the idea that individuals who are self-reflective will exhibit these characteristics:

- They will think about their thinking, developing metacognitive awareness and "critical thinking" skills (Costa, 2001; Costa & Kallick, 2008; Dewey, 1933; Schön, 1983).

- They will demonstrate a growth mindset (Dweck, 2006).

- They will be more discerning, analytic, and insightful about their practice (Danielson, 2007).

- They will have more heightened sensitivity to their students' moods, engagement, understanding, and confusion (Medina, 2008).

- They will have an increased awareness of personal strengths and weaknesses, becoming more effective and efficient as professionals (Dewey, 1933; Kolb, 1984).

- They will be increasingly intentional in their instruction—they will know what they are doing and why they are doing it (Perry, 1998; Schön, 1983).

- They will better integrate new knowledge and information in order to make sound decisions when confronted with unfamiliar situations (Marzano, 2012).

- They will demonstrate more sensitivity to how their instruction affects their students (McCarthy, 1996; Schön, 1983; Wolcott & Lynch, 1997).

- They will be more open to mandated changes from within their building, district, and state (Dewey, 1933; Furlong & Maynard, 1995; Reeves, 2009).

- They will be more collaborative and actively participate in professional learning communities (Eyler, Giles, & Schmeide, 1996; Guskin, 1994; Reeves, 2010).

- They will be intrinsically motivated to continue learning and empowered to seek new ways to better themselves (Dewey, 1933; Kolb, 1984).

Now, who wouldn't want their child's teacher to possess these habits of mind, approaches, and professional characteristics? We are reminded of the answer to the question we posed near the beginning of this chapter: What is the difference between a *mediocre* teacher and an *excellent* teacher?

 The skill of self-reflection transcends all other skills, strategies, and teaching approaches. In fact, it *strengthens* us in all areas.

The skill of self-reflection transcends all other skills, strategies, and teaching approaches because it can grow over the course of a career and enable teachers to cultivate and solidify all of their professional learning. And the beauty of it all? We're in charge of our thoughts, not vice versa. To illustrate this reality, remember the words of Norman Vincent Peale, whose book *The Power of Positive Thinking* continues to influence millions of readers today:

> You can actually think yourself into or out of situations. You can make yourself ill with your thoughts and by the same token you can make yourself well by the use of a different and healing type of thought. Think one way and you attract the conditions which that type of thinking indicates. Think another way and you can create an entirely different set of conditions. (1952, p. 169)

Self-Reflection and Teacher Evaluation Systems

It stands to reason, then, that as teachers grow in their reflective abilities and habits, they will perform more effectively in the classroom, and as a related consequence, will fare more favorably in their teacher evaluation ratings. Although there may indeed be a causative relationship between reflectiveness and effectiveness—and we've argued fervently so far that there is—we don't feel that self-reflection can be evaluated.

Consider this: The idea of developing one's self-reflection is rather nebulous. It's fluid, artistic, hidden, messy. Talk about a "soft skill"! Identifying and quantifying what teachers *do* is one thing; trying to categorize and evaluate a teacher's *thinking*—what is happening inside that teacher's mind—is akin to photographing a mythological beast, like a bandersnatch or a yeti. Teachers face immense pressure (both within the education system and among the greater public) to demonstrate accountability for their performance. The public wants results, and a renewed emphasis on high-stakes teacher evaluation systems adds a daunting element to the profession. So how does self-reflection fit in?

First, let's reiterate. Self-reflection, in itself, should not be measured within a teacher evaluation system. The tools we introduce and use in this book (and in our other publications) and in our workshops and tailored professional development services worldwide should never be used to evaluate teachers. Is that clear?

Now that we have clarified that point, it is understandable that many teacher evaluation tools assess reflective *behaviors,* such as whether a teacher reflects after a lesson, considers a response to administrative feedback, or investigates ways to improve practice. Interestingly, almost every teacher evaluation model we surveyed includes some element of self-reflection. Each of the three most popular instructional frameworks—Bob Marzano's *The Art and Science of Teaching* (2007), Charlotte Danielson's *Enhancing Professional Practice* (2007), and McREL's *Teacher Evaluation System* (2013)—includes specific domains allocated for reflecting on teaching. Others mention self-reflection in one form or another, dotting the landscape with a peripheral emphasis on the idea that intentional thought contributes to effective teaching.

With all due respect to the experts just cited, we believe that self-reflection warrants more than a nod toward a short list of behaviors near the end of an evaluation tool. Rather, the practice of self-reflection ought to be embedded into our everyday professional responsibilities. Deliberate and focused thinking should be considered a *driving* skill that operates constantly, below the surface level, in a manner that directly affects every single action a teacher takes in a classroom. Everything. In fact, we'd be hard-pressed to find anything teachers *ought* to be doing that they wouldn't do better through intentional, consistent *reflection* upon that action!

Reflection fits nicely into the acquisition of any skill, the application of any material, and the accomplishment of any goal. Regardless of the instructional framework in use in your school or district, the ability to consider thoughtfully the technical aspects of instruction offers our teachers a wide base upon which to build their expertise. Across all content areas, within any grade level or age of students, despite changes in curriculum, materials,

standards, and district initiatives, and irrespective of schedules, demographics, neighborhoods, or teaching assignments, the ability to be thoughtful,
intentional, and reflective will lead to unambiguous success across the board.
Let the puckish pendulum swing, say our reflective educators. *We'll thrive in
any environment.* Self-reflection, as we mentioned earlier, is independent of
context. It's a transferrable skill—the linchpin, the key cog, the critical link.

And to our instructional leaders, supervisors, and assessors, we say this:
let's continue to observe, assess, and evaluate teachers' performance based
on the observable actions that clear criteria and tangible evidence so help-
fully support. And during the other 99 percent of the time that we're interacting with our teachers—"talking teaching," exploring options, planning,
analyzing assessments, and debating theoretical application of pedagogical
approaches—let's focus on supporting our teachers' reflective skills, habits,
and tendencies. If we do that well (and we'll offer a thorough model for that
soon enough), our teachers' success in their classrooms—and in the evaluation process—will surely follow.

Reflecting Toward Excellence

Clearly, self-reflection is a vital skill for teachers to possess. As instructional
leaders, in our various jobs and roles, it's of paramount importance to be
aware of this fact and act accordingly. After all, if our teachers are going to
grow as reflective thinkers, they'll need our unyielding help, support, encouragement, feedback, and confidence. Sounds daunting and exhausting, you
say? No, no. It's just a matter of professional prioritization and the allocation
of our gray matter toward a pursuit of excellence. Remember the best news
of all: reflection is a skill that we can nurture and develop. And because every
teacher is unique and reflects a little bit differently, we'll need a tool to help
us (1) identify *how* our teachers currently reflect, and (2) provide the right
type and amount of support to *match* their individual needs. That's where
the Continuum of Self-Reflection—the topic of Chapter 3—comes in.

3

The Continuum
of Self-Reflection

We all reflect differently. The frequency, accuracy, and depth with which we engage in the four components of the Reflective Cycle vary from person to person. We probably all know colleagues who seem to reflect all the time, selectively addressing and ignoring countless events during a single classroom lesson. Alternatively, we probably can name a teacher who seemingly reflects just once a year, and only when prompted by the year-end meeting with the principal to update goals. There are folks who are incredibly attuned to the nuances of their classrooms and those who seem out of touch with reality. Some teachers are capable of describing events and outcomes with incredible precision and detail, whereas others can just scratch the surface with their perceptions. And, of course, there are all of us in between.

With the importance of self-reflection already noted and acknowledged, it would be important to have access to a tool that allows us to simultaneously (1) identify the manner in which each of our teachers currently reflect and (2) guide us to provide the personalized, differentiated support that each of our teachers needs to grow as a reflective practitioner.

Fortunately, the Continuum of Self-Reflection is here.

What Is the Continuum of Self-Reflection?

The Continuum of Self-Reflection is a tool—one of the most powerful, influential, and usable tools in the arsenal of instructional leaders. First published in our book *Building Teachers' Capacity for Success: A Collaborative Approach for Coaches and School Leaders* (Hall & Simeral, 2008), the Continuum of Self-Reflection presented in this book is the revised, updated edition—based on the data that we've collected from schools and districts across the globe over the past decade or so.

Figure 3.1 shows the continuum at a glance: four developmental stages through which teachers generally progress as they become skilled in the art of self-reflection. To be clear, these stages are really states of mind, levels of self-awareness, and phases in the self-reflective process that ultimately leads to our teachers becoming reflective practitioners. We've chosen the term *stage* to emphasize that self-reflection is a progressive process. We do *not* mean to suggest a categorical definition. In fact, an individual may demonstrate characteristics of more than one stage simultaneously and be in different stages while teaching different subjects or courses. As teachers learn to reflect with greater frequency, accuracy, and depth, their reflections have greater impact—and along the continuum they progress.

 The Continuum of Self-Reflection is the Swiss Army knife of capacity-building—an indispensable tool for establishing a culture of reflective practice.

FIGURE 3.1

Continuum of Self-Reflection at a Glance

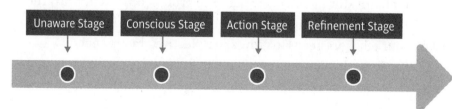

As the more detailed overview in Figure 3.2 illustrates, each of the four stages denotes gains in self-reflective abilities, which then correspond to growth in knowledge, expertise, experience, and motivation. And because self-reflection is a skill we can nurture and develop, the Continuum of Self-Reflection offers specific strategies for capacity-builders (those with instructional leadership responsibilities, regardless of role or title) to do just that: nurture and develop the self-reflective abilities in teachers. Within a culture of reflective practice, this precise approach to providing on-site, job-embedded professional development can yield tremendous benefits as teachers become more aware, more intentional, more accurate, and more responsive as they grow increasingly self-reflective. Let's examine the tool one chunk at a time.

Teacher's Reflective Tendencies

The first column in our tool simply describes *how* a teacher tends to think about her professional responsibilities within each stage of the Continuum of Self-Reflection. The characteristics listed in each stage are a *general approximation* of a teacher's reflective habits of mind. Remember, because this is a continuum and we're all unique thinkers, any individual teacher may demonstrate characteristics from multiple stages—and there's certainly no guarantee that any teacher will demonstrate all the reflective tendencies within one particular stage. This compilation of descriptions addresses the first of the two goals of this tool: to describe how teachers currently reflect. Our intent is for you to view the reflective characteristics associated with each stage more as reference points than as a list of behaviors that need to be "checked off" before a teacher can "advance" to the next stage.

To apply this tool when considering a given teacher's reflective tendencies, we use the legal term *preponderance of evidence* to help us identify that teacher's *dominant* stage on the Continuum of Self-Reflection. The dominant stage is the stage in which more of the bulleted descriptions in this first column appear to match the teacher's reflective behaviors. This information, coupled with a handy Reflective Self-Assessment Tool that we've created for teachers—published in our book *Teach, Reflect, Learn* (Hall &

FIGURE 3.2

The Continuum of Self-Reflection (2nd edition)

Unaware Stage

Capacity-Building Goal: To build deeper awareness of students, content, and pedagogy

Teacher's Reflective Tendencies	Leadership Roles	Strategic PLC and Teacher-Leadership Support	Transformational Feedback (Directive statements)	Differentiated Coaching Strategies
• Demonstrates little or no awareness of instructional reality in the classroom. • Engages in little or no self-initiated reflection. • Defines problems or challenges inaccurately. • Sees surface-level events and classroom elements. • Collaborates infrequently with colleagues. • Focuses on routine. • Exhibits the best of intentions. • Expresses confusion about own role in learning. • Focuses on the *act* of teaching.	**Administrator:** Director **Instructional Coach:** Unconditional Partner	• Assign a specific task during team meetings. • Front-load the upcoming content/meeting with an article, video, or one-on-one discussion. • Debrief immediately following the meeting to support understanding and next steps. • Facilitate collegial idea sharing through professional learning protocols. • Strategically partner this teacher with a colleague (in particular, one in the Action stage) to build reflective capacity.	• When you did this ____, the students did this ____. It worked because ____. Do that again! • I noticed you used ____, and it was effective because ____; use it whenever you want your students to ____. • When you did this ____, the students did this ____. Tomorrow try ____, and tell me what happens. • Your lesson was successful today because ____. • You (or your students) struggled today because ____. Next time that happens, try this ____, and tell me what happens. • You appear frustrated with ____, and I noticed you ____ several times. Tomorrow, try to take note of how many times you ____. Then let's chat further. • I observed ____, which is not what you/we were going for in that lesson; try ____ to get the lesson back on track. This usually works because ____.	• Make frequent contact, checking in often to talk about goals and progress toward them. • Build confidence through short-term goal setting. • Celebrate successes immediately. • Model a strategy or lesson. • Whisper-coach while co-observing another teacher's class. • Write lesson plans together. • Coteach a lesson. • Debrief a lesson together. • Record a lesson, provide clear look-fors, and debrief the video together. • Engage in side-by-side reflective journaling.

Conscious Stage

Capacity-Building Goal: To work with greater intentionality in addressing student needs, content, and pedagogical practices

Teacher's Reflective Tendencies	Leadership Roles	Strategic PLC and Teacher-Leadership Support	Transformational Feedback (Leading prompts)	Differentiated Coaching Strategies
• Demonstrates a consistent "knowing-doing" gap. • Reflects when prompted by others. • Offers external explanations for problems or challenges. • Makes generalizations in observations about classroom reality. • Collaborates inconsistently with colleagues. • Tends to operate with strong habits and comfortable practices. • Becomes easily distracted from goals. • Disregards others' ideas. • Focuses first on self.	**Administrator:** Navigator **Instructional Coach:** Motivator and Strategist	• Emphasize the use of data (pre and post) to clarify cause-and-effect relationships. • Analyze student work samples as a team. • Promote team lesson planning. • Facilitate collegial observations to see strategies at work in various settings. • Use protocols to guide discussion and promote engagement. • Strategically partner this teacher with a colleague (in particular one in the Refinement stage) to grow reflective capacity.	• Your goal is ___. How can I help you keep that focus and support your efforts? • I see you were using ___ today. Keep that focus! What worked well today? • Tell me about the purpose of today's activity. What is your evidence of success? • Today, your students were successful at ___. What did you do that directly led to their success? • I noticed ___ today. How might the outcomes change if you tried ___? Give it a shot and let me know how it goes. • Yesterday I observed your students ___; today, they are ___. How do you determine your daily lesson structure? • Tell me more about the planning that went into today's lesson. Why did you select the strategy you chose for this lesson? • How do you use what you know about your students to drive lesson planning each day? • When you did ___ today, I observed several students ___. How will you shift tomorrow's lesson to change the outcomes? • How does this lesson connect to prior and future student learning objectives? • What misconceptions might students have during tomorrow's lesson? How will you address that in your planning?	• Make daily contact, checking in often to talk about goals and progress toward them. • Build confidence through short-term goal setting. • Celebrate successes immediately. • Meet weekly for collaborative planning. • Engage through interactive journaling. • Invite participation in small-group discussions around a common problem of practice. • Model a strategy or lesson in the teacher's classroom. • Coplan, coteach, and debrief a lesson together. • Provide opportunities to observe in other classrooms—using clear look-fors. • Record a lesson, provide clear look-fors, and debrief the video together.

(continued)

FIGURE 3.2

The Continuum of Self-Reflection (2nd edition) *(continued)*

Action Stage

Capacity-Building Goal: To build on experience and help strengthen expertise through accurate assessment of instructional impact

Teacher's Reflective Tendencies	Leadership Roles	Strategic PLC and Teacher-Leadership Support	Transformational Feedback (Open-ended prompts)	Differentiated Coaching Strategies
• Commits to taking steps to affect student learning outcomes. • Engages in reflection before and after teaching. • Evaluates problems or challenges objectively. • Notices trends and themes in student performance and classroom elements. • Collaborates on a limited basis with colleagues. • Seeks to incorporate research-based concepts and strategies. • Gravitates toward a particular structure or strategy. • Struggles to identify solutions to long-term problems. • Craves feedback from trusted partners. • Focuses on the science of teaching.	**Administrator:** Prompter **Instructional Coach:** Mentor	• Provide opportunities for all teachers to share methods in team meetings. • Engage in healthy debate about the pros and cons of various pedagogical strategies. • Maintain a focus on data analysis during team meetings. • Incorporate professional learning (new and deeper instructional strategies) as a regular component of team meetings. • Strategically partner this teacher with colleagues (in particular, those in the Unaware stage) to build leadership capacity.	• What was the purpose of today's activity? Was it successful? How do you know? • Which parts of today's lesson went well? Which parts didn't? Why? • What was the goal of today's lesson? How did you determine that goal? • Today I observed you ___. Did that contribute to your goal? How can you tell? • Why did you choose to ___ today? Was that strategy effective? How do you know? • What other strategy could you have used today to achieve your goals? • How do you predetermine what your evidence of success will be for a lesson? • Do your anecdotal observations of student learning align with more formal assessment data? • If you could teach this lesson again, what would you do differently? Why? • Which students were successful achieving today's learning target? Which students struggled? Why was that so? • What does the student work from today's lesson tell you about ___ as a learner? • What can you tell me about ___ as a learner? How can you find out more?	• Analyze data together. • Analyze student work samples together. • Collaboratively engage in diagnosis and action planning based on beliefs of how students learn. • Provide research from which to construct meaning. • Invite participation in small-group discussions around a common problem of practice. • Foster idea sharing through collegial observations. • Model new strategies in a gradual-release model. • Record lesson and discuss video analysis. • Model open-mindedness toward multiple approaches and perspectives. • Encourage participation in a professional book club. • Engage in interactive journaling.

Refinement Stage

Capacity-Building Goal: To encourage long-term growth and continued reflection through responsiveness to ongoing assessments

Teacher's Reflective Tendencies	Leadership Roles	Strategic PLC and Teacher-Leadership Support	Transformational Feedback (Challenging prompts)	Differentiated Coaching Strategies
• Accepts responsibility for the success of each student and for ongoing personal growth. • Reflects before, during, and after taking action. • Modifies lessons and plans to meet students' varied needs. • Dissects lessons and learning to reveal options for improvement. • Pursues opportunities to work and learn with colleagues. • Maintains a vast repertoire of instructional strategies. • Recognizes that there are multiple "right" courses of action. • Thinks globally, beyond the classroom. • Focuses on the *art* of teaching.	**Administrator:** Challenger **Instructional Coach:** Collaborator	• Assign or encourage formal leadership roles within the team or department structure. • Encourage sharing and modeling of the thinking behind this teacher's decisions and actions in the classroom during team meetings. • Encourage leadership of a team action-research project. • Strategically partner this teacher with colleagues (in particular, those in the Conscious stage) to build their reflective capacity.	• Today your students did __, and you immediately responded with __. How did you plan to address that misconception? • In the middle of today's lesson, you abruptly changed course. What led to that decision? Was it a successful move? How do you know? • How do you know when students are learning in the middle of a lesson? What do you look for? • How do you identify specific learning styles of the students in your room? • Explain the thinking that went into planning a lesson like this. How do you know which strategies to select? How do you decide which activities to choose? • To what extent are you collaborating with your colleagues to plan and deliver your lessons? How can you become more intentional in partnering with your teammates? • Your lesson today reminded me of a recent article I read in *Educational Leadership*. I'll put a copy in your box. I would love to hear your thoughts.	• Analyze data and student work samples together. • Analyze schoolwide data together. • Stimulate discussions of personal vision and educational philosophy. • Serve as devil's advocate to challenge thinking. • Record lesson and discuss video analysis. • Facilitate idea sharing through collegial observations. • Encourage leadership of small-group discussions around a common problem of practice. • Encourage book club facilitation or leadership. • Arrange for student-teacher hosting opportunities. • Encourage conference participation and publication submission. • Engage in interactive journaling.

Simeral, 2015) and available online as a free download at www.ascd.org/ ASCD/pdf/books/HallSimeral2017.pdf (password: HallSimeral117006)— then provides a roadmap for the support, guidance, and capacity-building that best matches this teacher's current reflective state of mind.

Alisa's Approach

"How do we determine how our teachers reflect?" This question is common and one that Pete and I asked ourselves years ago in our work at Anderson Elementary School in Reno, Nevada. Since reflection is something that occurs in the confines of our own minds, it can be quite difficult to discern. Essentially, we're seeking to understand how someone thinks—we're looking to identify a person's metacognitive habits. So how do we go about this task? Robert Baden-Powell, British Army officer, writer, and famous founder of the Boy Scouts, once said, "If you make listening and observation your occupation, you will gain much more than you can by talk."

So we start there. We listen and we observe. We ask questions, then listen more carefully and observe. We engage in conversation, then listen and observe. We listen and observe as we walk the hallways, spend time in classrooms, and eat in the staff lounge. We listen and observe as we sit in staff meetings. Listening and observing becomes, as Powell puts it, our primary occupation.

If we want to determine how our teachers reflect, we ask questions to elicit talk of metacognition; we dig at the whys, hows, and what-nows. We begin to collect information around their reflective habits. Then we grab highlighters and, using the first column on the Continuum of Self-Reflection, we begin to note reflective tendencies. This will lead us to ask more questions. And we listen. Listen and observe.

Capacity-Building Goal

Armed with some information about the stage on the Continuum of Self-Reflection at which the teacher is currently operating (do you recognize the language of Dweck's [2006] "growth mindset" in that phrasing?), capacity-builders can prepare to partner with the teacher to set a goal to grow as a reflective practitioner. Each stage of the Continuum of Self-Reflection has a unique capacity-building goal, listed across the top of the stage's five columns and answering the question "If our teacher is currently reflecting in this manner, what is our goal for growing that teacher's reflective capacity?" The capacity-building goal should genuinely command our attention for each individual teacher—and if it does, it truly guides all the work that follows.

Leadership Roles

To best provide the tailored, personalized support teachers need to reach their particular capacity-building goal, the administrator and the instructional coach assume specific, complementary roles, as shown in the second column of the Continuum of Self-Reflection. We'll explain the roles in greater detail in Chapter 5 when we outline the roles and responsibilities of the capacity-builders in a culture of reflective practice, but for now suffice it to say that providing differentiated assistance to teachers requires a slightly different approach for each teacher. The roles we've identified for administrators and instructional coaches have been constructed to go hand-in-hand with one another—and just as there are many ways to brace a growing tree, so are there varied ways for leaders to support the growth of their teachers.

> Just as there are many ways to brace a growing tree, so are there varied ways for leaders to support the growth of their teachers.

Strategic PLC and Teacher-Leadership Support

Over the past two decades or so, the popularity and utility of professional learning community (PLC) concepts have exploded—and rightly so. Teaching is a profession that cries out for collaboration and collective pursuits of common goals. No longer can we leave the widespread learning outcomes for millions of children to the luck of individual teachers. So, in the third column of the Continuum of Self-Reflection, we provide ideas for teacher teams, PLCs, departments, and schoolhouse colleagues to support the reflective growth of their peers within a collaborative environment. In a culture of reflective practice, togetherness, interdependence, partnerships, transparency, and a common pursuit of deeper, more accurate, and more frequent professional reflections own the day. If it takes a village to raise a child, it may well take an entire schoolhouse to raise a teacher.

Transformational Feedback

We wouldn't be breaking new ground if we asserted that feedback can indeed transform the thinking—and, by extension, the instructional impact— of teachers across the board. And, because every teacher reflects differently, the feedback that will inspire reflective growth, transform thought, and revolutionize professional practice must be differentiated and individual- ized based on each individual teacher's needs and readiness. The language that capacity-builders use to prompt, suggest, nurture, challenge, and pique teachers varies from individual to individual, and from stage to stage along the Continuum of Self-Reflection. In the fourth column we provide exam- ples of the right language to use with the right teacher at the right moment to meet the right goal. You may notice that there's a different parenthetical subheading in this column for each stage. Take a moment to connect the transformational feedback prompts to the subheading, and then connect the dots between the feedback prompts and each stage's capacity-building goal.

Differentiated Coaching Strategies

Just as a doctor wouldn't dream of performing the same procedures and prescribing the same treatment for every patient, regardless of the reason for the office visit, anyone in an instructional coaching role wouldn't dream of providing coaching support in the same manner to every teacher on staff. Because every teacher reflects differently and is a unique human being with particular strengths and needs, every teacher will require coaching strate- gies that match those needs and lead most directly and successfully to the accomplishment of the capacity-building goal. With a focus on reflective growth, coaches should select strategies listed in the fifth column within each stage of the Continuum of Self-Reflection to develop a differentiated coaching plan. There is no room for "one size fits all" in the capacity-building world.

The Stages Along the Continuum of Self-Reflection

The Continuum of Self-Reflection, as both Figures 3.1 and 3.2 depict, is composed of four stages: Unaware, Conscious, Action, and Refinement. What follows is a general overview of each stage, which we invite you to unpack as you flip between Figure 3.2 and the descriptions that follow. Rest assured, we will provide abundant detail, scenarios, and a picture of each stage *in real life* in Chapters 10 through 13.

We encourage you to remember that the Continuum of Self-Reflection is a tool that capacity-builders use to help identify *how* teachers think and to guide the development of their reflective abilities in order to enable them to become more effective decision makers and practitioners in the classroom. There is no value—no "better than" or "worse than"—assigned to any of the stages on the continuum; there are just descriptions and strategies.

 The Continuum of Self-Reflection is not evaluative; the stages have no value, per se. They are characteristics that describe the manner in which we reflect so we'll know how to deepen our reflective habits.

The Unaware Stage

Teachers operating in the Unaware stage on the Continuum of Self-Reflection tend to personify the expression "doing the best they can with what they've got." For a host of reasons, including (but not limited to) lack of experience, change in teaching assignment, underpreparedness, or simply the sheer magnitude of the demands on their plates, such teachers allocate their attention to the act of teaching and getting their job done. They have not yet developed the reflective abilities to truly know their students, to understand the role of content, and to build a repertoire of teaching skills. At the Unaware stage, teachers simply haven't yet developed the skills to reflect on their instructional reality in a way that effects positive change.

The Conscious Stage

Teachers operating in the Conscious stage on the Continuum of Self-Reflection have acquired some additional knowledge, are aware of certain elements in their classrooms, and possess at least some expertise—though they are challenged to put what they know into place with consistency and intentionality. Often teachers in the Conscious stage will demonstrate some reflective abilities when prompted, and many can express what they *should* be doing differently. Most telling, their (intentional or subconscious) focus is on choosing strategies and approaches that they are more comfortable or familiar with, but they haven't yet developed the disciplined thought to guide them toward implementing practices for the good of their students.

The Action Stage

Teachers operating in the Action stage on the Continuum of Self-Reflection are motivated to change and begin to consistently integrate their knowledge with classroom instruction. As the title of the stage implies, they are ready, willing, and able to take action—all in the name of improving the learning outcomes for their students. The Action stage is home to a new degree of commitment, as teachers concentrate their energy on finding solutions to problems, learning new and different methods of instruction, implementing curriculum and materials appropriately, and acting with a sense of purpose.

The Refinement Stage

Teachers operating in the Refinement stage on the Continuum of Self-Reflection assume personal responsibility for the learning that does or does not occur in their classrooms. Highly reflective and constantly considering ways to tweak lessons to increase student learning outcomes, Refinement-stage teachers maintain an open mind about all possibilities, never accept anything at face value, and are known to "play with ideas" about what factors into student learning, adult learning, and school success (Hall, 2011). What truly sets apart a teacher in the Refinement stage is the ability to notice when a student is struggling and why, and to modify the lesson, question, assignment, discussion, or learning experience right there, *in the moment.*

A Professional Case Study: Peyton Manning

To help us understand the stages of the Continuum of Self-Reflection in a professional capacity, let's analyze the case of Peyton Manning, arguably one of the greatest quarterbacks in National Football League (NFL) history. Has he always been that great? Has his performance as a football player always matched his potential? As you read the following vignette, compare it with the descriptions and action steps listed on the Continuum of Self-Reflection. How did Manning progress as a professional athlete and as a reflective practitioner throughout his career?

As a rookie out of Ole Miss, Manning was surrounded by a lot of hype. He arrived in the NFL with the Indianapolis Colts with high expectations, great enthusiasm, terrific skills, and a strong arm. He threw more passes that first season than any other quarterback in the league—and he led the league with 28 interceptions while his team lost 13 of their 16 games. Despite his physical abilities and extraordinary effort, he was not achieving the results he or his team desired. He didn't know what he didn't know yet. He needed to change the way he operated—and reflected on his work—in order to improve. He was in what we call the Unaware stage.

So he began studying. He sat with his coaches and analyzed his play calling, the defensive alignments he faced, and the choices he made on the field. He analyzed the plays his team was running and what happened when things went wrong; and because he wasn't yet able to consistently and intentionally implement his learnings, things still went wrong. Over the next four years, he threw 819 passes that weren't caught, including 72 more interceptions. He was experiencing limited success; he threw a lot of touchdowns as well, but he was also sacked 86 times and had 24 fumbles. He had entered what we call the Conscious stage.

And then he started really putting it together. Through analysis of video, constant collaboration with his coaches and teammates, and determination, he learned the art of the audible—changing things up when they weren't working. His recognition of defenses and his knowledge of his teammates' tendencies compelled him to take deliberate actions—sometimes right at the line of scrimmage. And his team really started winning. He wasn't just a super player; he was a Super Bowl champion. As the top-ranked passer in the NFL, he was leading his team and enjoying terrific success. He had definitely reached the Action stage, where he was "in it to win it."

And did he rest on his laurels? Heck, no—not even after an apparent career-ending injury to his neck, which caused him to miss an entire season, and the only team he'd ever played for (the Colts) let him go. He was signed by the Denver Broncos and reinvented himself. He watched game film all the time, practiced with game-level intensity, and studied meticulously. And he continued to add to his legacy and his team's success. Over a period of 11 years, his teams were 137-39, an astonishing 78 percent winning percentage. He won the NFL's Most Valuable Player award five times. He set more league records than any other quarterback. He was selected to the Pro Bowl (the NFL's all-star game) 14 times, and the Broncos won the Super Bowl again in his final season in 2016. And he'd be the first to tell you he was neither the most athletic nor gifted player on the field— ever. He was, however, the most studious, thoughtful, and reflective. He had progressed to the Refinement stage.

> We can all grow, learn, and improve throughout our careers. It starts by putting our minds to it.

Our teachers are no different than Peyton Manning. Regardless of background knowledge, experience, teaching acumen, or that innate teaching "sense" that some claim is endowed at birth, all can grow as educators. Teaching is a profession (just like NFL football, except without helmets), one composed of equal parts science and art—and reflection is both the lab and the canvas that allows for continuous, positive, transformative growth.

The Continuum of Self-Reflection Bell Curve

The ultimate goal of our capacity-building efforts is to nudge, encourage, and support our teachers as they grow as reflective practitioners, progressing along the Continuum of Self-Reflection from Unaware to Conscious to Action and, finally, to Refinement. Because we've already acknowledged that all teachers reflect differently and we can expect a wide range of reflective abilities to present themselves along the continuum, it's reasonable to wonder how often we might encounter teachers who are currently operating at each stage.

To our colleagues steeped in statistics, we offer a nod to the foremost of mathematicians, Carl Friedrich Gauss, by sharing that, by and large, the scattering of teachers along the Continuum of Self-Reflection is a rather symmetrical, bell curve–like Gaussian distribution (Zeidler & Hunt, 2004). This means there are few teachers who are truly operating in the Unaware stage and few who are consistently operating in the Refinement stage, leaving the overwhelming majority to confirm the measure of central tendency by clustering around the Conscious and Action stages (see Figure 3.3).

This is important information for three reasons: (1) it explains some of the interpersonal dynamics of a district, a school site, or a team; (2) it offers ample opportunity for partnering teachers together and for

FIGURE 3.3

Continuum of Self-Reflection Bell Curve

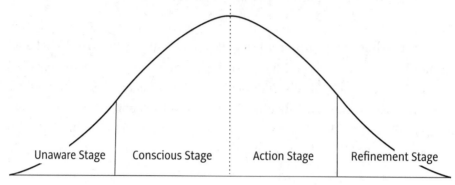

capacity-builders to attempt similar strategies with multiple teachers simultaneously; and (3) it shows how ripe the profession of education is for meaningful, impactful, long-lasting change. By building reflective capacity and moving all our teachers to the right on the continuum (toward the Refinement stage), we can replace the bell curve with the J curve. Imagine the possibilities with an army of verifiably reflective educators!

Directions for Application

At this point, you may be asking yourself, *Who uses this tool? When and where is it used? And how will we get the biggest, longest-lasting bang for the buck out of it?* Those are terrific questions, and the answers to those questions—and more—are presented in the next chapter, as we explore the inner workings of a culture of reflective practice.

A Culture of Reflective Practice

What is a culture of reflective practice? A culture of reflective practice is an organization that embraces reflective growth as the primary driving force behind continuous, lasting improvement. In such an organization, members speak the language of reflection, engage in rigorous metacognitive tasks, and earnestly support their individual and collective growth. The entire organization oozes self-reflection.

Oozing self-reflection across an entire school or district sounds enticing, doesn't it? We agree, and we've seen the benefits in schools and districts in every kind of locale, in all demographic settings, at all levels. So we aren't surprised if you find yourself asking any (or all) of the following questions as you attempt to make sense of this idea:

- How does a culture of reflective practice come to exist?
- What are the conditions that enable a culture of reflective practice to flourish?
- Why would we need to create such conditions?
- How is this different from what we're already doing?
- How does this fit into the work and priorities that we currently have on our plates?
- How would we go about strengthening a culture of reflective practice?
- Where do we start?

We'll answer these questions and more as we begin a deeper exploration into the inner workings of a culture of reflective practice.

The BTC Fundamentals

The foundation of a culture of reflective practice, as we introduced it to you briefly at the end of Chapter 1, is built upon seven fundamentals (see Figure 4.1). The following Building Teacher Capacity (BTC) Fundamentals are the foundational pieces necessary to implement a culture of reflective practice:

1. Relationships, Roles, and Responsibilities
2. Expectations and Communication
3. Celebration and Calibration
4. Goal Setting and Follow-Through
5. Strategic PLC and Teacher-Leadership Support
6. Transformational Feedback
7. Differentiated Coaching

FIGURE 4.1

The Seven Fundamentals of a Culture of Reflective Practice

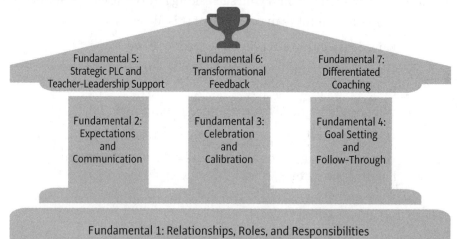

Together, these fundamentals guide schools and districts through the process of shifting school culture and climate, growing a reflective mindset, and strengthening their impact on student learning outcomes.

Each of the seven fundamentals is further broken down into a series of *factors* that, together, are the most vital elements of that particular fundamental. What follows is a brief overview of each of the seven fundamentals and their contributing factors. Please notice that the fundamentals are generally in priority order. Chronologically, a school or a district must have Fundamental 1 pretty well established before attempting to strengthen Fundamental 2, and 2 before 3, and so on. At the end of this chapter, we provide a simple, useful site assessment to help you gauge your school's or district's status and readiness to establish and strengthen a culture of reflective practice. For now, here they are.

Fundamental 1: Relationships, Roles, and Responsibilities

There are four categories of capacity-builders in a culture of reflective practice: teachers, administrators, instructional coaches, and PLC team members/colleagues. How they work together—collaboratively, interdependently, and collegially—will greatly influence the climate in which everyone operates. A vital piece of the professional atmosphere of a culture of reflective practice includes the capacity-builders' relationships. "No significant learning," stated Yale professor Dr. James Comer, "occurs without a significant relationship" (Comer, 1995). To effectively work together, all capacity-builders must have a clear understanding of their own and the others' roles and responsibilities. Among the phrases used by professional learning community pioneer Becky DuFour in her keynote addresses at PLC conferences, our favorite is "Clarity precedes competence." With that in mind, the factors within Fundamental 1 are the following:

a. Administrator and staff have rapport and trustworthy relationships.

b. Coach and staff have rapport and trustworthy relationships.

c. Administrator and coach discuss their roles and responsibilities, the nature of their professional partnership, and their common goals as capacity-builders.

d. Staff have a clear understanding of the role and responsibilities of coach—and can articulate how they are distinct from those of administrator in order to encourage reflective growth, support effective teaching, and promote student learning.

Fundamental 1: Relationships and clarity of roles form the strong foundation upon which all following work is stabilized.

Fundamental 2: Expectations and Communication

Once the positive professional relationships are established and all the capacity-builders understand their roles, responsibilities, and the interrelatedness of their work, it's time to identify the expectations for their work together. Now the big questions the school must face include the following: "What are our expectations within a culture of reflective practice?" and "How will we maintain open, transparent, and ongoing communication about these expectations and our vision?" As we have seen over and over in education, initiatives are launched with great fanfare and enthusiasm—and then die in the trenches of the day-to-day grind, buried by shovelfuls of forgotten promises.

This situation, fortunately, is avoidable. With constant, regular communication, a dedication to the goals of a culture of reflective practice, and some intentionality in the use of reflective language in all interactions, the implementation of a culture of reflective practice can remain at the forefront of our minds—the place where things get done. As researchers Nwogbaga, Nwankwo, and Onwa share, a tremendous amount of conflict and crisis can arise from within an organization stemming from "grapevine, gossip, and rumors"—which we can replace (at least to a certain extent) through formal, intentional, controlled communication planning (2015, p. 33). The factors that make up Fundamental 2 are the following:

a. School has a written plan for implementing a culture of reflective practice.

b. Staff understand their expectation is to seek ways to grow as reflective practitioners and effective instructors utilizing the Reflective Cycle.

c. Administrator has set the expectation that all teachers will work with a coach to meet their professional goals.

d. Administrator articulates the vision for implementing a culture of reflective practice to staff on a regular basis.

e. Coach communicates the role of coach and various supportive services available to staff on a regular basis.

f. Administrator or coach shares assessment and implementation data with staff and solicits feedback to inform the plan for implementing a culture of reflective practice.

Fundamental 2: Embed reflective dialogue into every nook and cranny of the organization. This is where it oozes.

Fundamental 3: Celebration and Calibration

The sternwheelers on the Mississippi River often have to travel upstream to their desired location. To combat the river's flow, these beautiful ships must maintain momentum and trajectory accordingly—any lapse and they'll lose ground and run off course. And so it is with our establishment of a culture of reflective practice. Positive momentum begins with that enthusiastic launch and continues through short-term accomplishments and the celebration of those "small wins." Success breeds success, generates additional enthusiasm connected with personal and organizational efficacy, and gets the flywheel spinning (Collins, 2001). In Fundamental 3, two big questions arise: "How do we celebrate when things go well?" and "How do we calibrate when things go awry?" Capacity-builders see the value in both acknowledging successes and in refocusing all stakeholders—keeping their eyes on the prize, as it were—before the ship goes adrift. The factors within Fundamental 3 are the following:

a. Time is routinely set aside for small and big celebrations of teacher capacity growth, progress toward goals, and other successes.

b. Staff review tools (instructional framework, research, data, site assessment and implementation plan, etc.) on a regular basis to calibrate understanding, expectations, vocabulary, and professional practices.

 Fundamental 3: Navigating the waters of a culture of reflective practice requires diligence and continuous alertness to the "WOW!" and "YIKES!" moments.

Fundamental 4: Goal Setting and Follow-Through

In a culture of reflective practice, the organization's mission is to accomplish its previously established student-learning goals while simultaneously growing as a *thinking* organization. Individual teachers and the teams in which they operate, likewise, must set goals to grow as reflective practitioners while increasing their technical teaching proficiency and bolstering student learning outcomes. As we'll explain in further detail in Chapter 8, this effort transforms a SMART goal into a SMART-R goal (spoiler alert: the second *R* is for *Reflection*). And this doesn't happen by chance. As the saying goes, "Life without goals is like a race without a finish line." Our ability to remain resolutely and unequivocally focused on the outcomes—or, as we like to say, remaining "mission-driven"—will determine the level of success we experience.

 Fundamental 4: Relentless pursuit of our common goals will drive us toward ongoing, repeatable, uncompromising success.

Capacity-builders then must ensure they follow through by providing the level of support necessary for each team and teacher to accomplish their respective goals. For teachers, that means diligently focusing on and working toward their goals. For administrators, coaches, and PLC teammates, that means circling the wagons around individual teachers to guide and nurture their reflective growth within the context of their teaching and learning focus. Follow-through really addresses our ability to be strategic and stick with what's important, emphasizing the key actions that most directly lead to our goals and eschewing the notion that we must do everything. "Simplexity," says Michael Fullan, is about "finding the smallest number of high-leverage, easy-to-understand actions that unleash stunningly powerful consequences" (2010, p. 16). The factors within Fundamental 4 are the following:

a. Administrator meets with each teacher at the beginning of the year to set SMART student achievement goals.

b. Staff take the Reflective Self-Assessment Tool to identify their current reflective stage on the Continuum of Self-Reflection.

c. Staff identify a personal—SMART-R—goal to grow as reflective practitioners, using the Reflective Cycle.

d. Staff work diligently toward their individual goals and strategic action steps in order to continuously grow as reflective practitioners.

e. Administrator intentionally follows up with staff on a regular basis to discuss progress toward goals and professional growth.

Fundamental 5: Strategic PLC and Teacher-Leadership Support

For decades—centuries, even—teaching firmly entrenched itself as a profession of individuals engaging in the über-important work of educating children *all by themselves*. For students, this approach has resulted in a series of visits to each teacher's private practice to receive a fragmented education, with content and experience varying from one classroom to another. We can turn that ideology on its ears—and we're well on our way to doing so with the expanse of the collaborative practices espoused within the professional learning community philosophy. And now, we'd like to add this: teachers can—and must—support one another as reflective practitioners. In Fundamental 5, we've identified five factors that contribute to the development of collaborative, interdependent partnerships and teams that create opportunities to learn, grow, and support one another very intentionally. If the whole is indeed greater than the sum of its parts, then it behooves us all to seek out our colleagues to offer—and accept—the outstretched hands of teamwork. The factors that make up Fundamental 5 are the following:

a. Administrator, coach, and teacher-leaders provide differentiated support for grade-level/department teams, using the Continuum of Self-Reflection.

b. Staff support one another in the collective pursuit of reflective practice and effective instruction.

c. Staff have formal and/or informal opportunities to provide peer-based feedback to one another.

d. Teacher-leaders assume a wide range of roles to shape the culture of their school, improve student learning, and influence practice among their peers.

e. Teacher-leaders engage in professional learning opportunities that support their professional growth.

Fundamental 5: We are in this together, so let's be all-in together.

Fundamental 6: Transformational Feedback

Ask any expert for a list of the influences that contributed to his or her acquisition of that expertise, and one item is sure to be on the list every time: feedback. Numerous educational experts, such as Goodwin and Hubbell (2013); Marzano et al. (2011); Hattie (2009); and Brookhart (2017), have long touted the impact of effective feedback—upon student learning. Feedback that augments professional practice and supports the ongoing development of teaching skill *and reflective abilities* is no different. Whether the feedback is provided in written, oral, nonverbal, or electronic formats, two characteristics seem to be critical: its very presence and the degree to which it matches the recipient's needs. The five factors of Fundamental 6 offer guidance to the nourishment of effective, impactful feedback practices for capacity-builders. Ultimately, this is an endeavor steeped in "talking teaching" with teachers, and what's better than that? The factors are the following:

a. Administrator provides regular feedback to staff to build their reflective tendencies and strengthen technical skill.

b. Coach provides regular feedback to staff to build their reflective tendencies and strengthen technical skill.

c. Clear look-fors, based on best practices, are established at the individual teacher, team/department, and schoolwide levels.

d. Feedback matches individual staff members' needs as reflective practitioners, linked to current stage on the Continuum of Self-Reflection.

e. Feedback is growth-oriented, part of a continuous process, accurate, relevant to individual teacher goals, and timely (within 24 hours).

Fundamental 6: The words we use with our teachers are critical if we're to transform the *thinking* that leads to transformed practices.

Fundamental 7: Differentiated Coaching

When we first published *Building Teachers' Capacity for Success* in 2008, instructional coaching was still a relatively new, rather untested, clever innovation that showed quite a bit of promise. Since then, coaching has grown in popularity and application. The Bureau of Labor Statistics reported that in 2014 there were over 150,000 instructional coaching jobs in the United States, with that number projected to increase by 7 percent within 10 years (Bureau of Labor Statistics, n.d.). We have begun to collect reams of data supporting the positive impact coaches can have on teachers (Marsh, McCombs, & Martorell, 2012; Thomas, Bell, Spelman, & Briody, 2015; among others) and the students they serve (Eisenberg & Medrich, 2013; Matsumura, Garnier, & Spybrook, 2013; among others).

With such an overwhelming influence, it might surprise you to find "Differentiated coaching" way down the list as Fundamental 7. Well, truth be told, this is where we'd all like to start—and many schools and districts eschew the first six fundamentals in order to hurry up and get to this headline-grabbing, "sexy" part of capacity-building. We've seen far too many such initiatives leap out of the box, ill prepared for the grind of reality that awaits, and fall flat. Sadly, schools and districts often toss their coaching plans into the rubbish bin rather than question and refine the environment in which they attempted this work in the first place. With the first six fundamentals in place, coaching can have an immense, powerful, lasting impact on individual teachers, teams, and organizations as technically strong, reflectively savvy practitioners. We'll share more on coaching, including in-depth examples, in Chapters 10 through 13. In the meantime, here are the key factors for Fundamental 7:

a. Administrator provides regular coaching support to staff to build their reflective tendencies and strengthen technical skill.

b. Coach provides regular coaching support to staff to build their reflective tendencies and strengthen technical skill.

c. Coaching strategies match individual staff members' needs as reflective practitioners using the Continuum of Self-Reflection.

d. Coaching strategies are growth-oriented, part of a continuous process, relevant to individual teacher goals, and provided in a timely manner.

e. Staff seek out coach for coaching support of their instructional goals.

Fundamental 7: All other influences being equal, teachers with coaches will have a greater positive impact on student learning.

Who Needs to Create and Cultivate a Culture of Reflective Practice?

In *Start with Why,* author and professional thinker Simon Sinek (2009) implores us to connect with our purpose first, before getting consumed by the nitty-gritty details of *how* and *what.* We're big believers in this theory of action, which is why you'll hear us talk ad nauseum about being "mission-driven." In that vein, we now will answer the question proposed in the heading for this section, tapping into the purpose that propels this work.

Who needs to create and cultivate a culture of reflective practice? Our simple response is this: every school, every district, and every educational organization should strive to establish and nurture a strong, viable culture of reflective practice. That said, there are certain scenarios that might motivate a school to pursue this concept with particular vigor, including the following:

- To construct or refine an instructional coaching model.
- To strengthen instructional leadership practices.
- To develop and use teacher-leaders.
- To strengthen collaborative/peer support systems.
- To enhance systemwide leadership.
- To cultivate a corps of reflective practitioners.
  - » ... to bolster instructional practices.
  - » ... to increase student achievement.

How Is a Culture of Reflective Practice Different from a Typical School?

A school that has a culture of reflective practice differs from a typical school in the following ways.

A culture of reflective practice creates a shift from compliance to commitment. Oh, how we lament the traditional hierarchy of so many of our schools and education systems. They are breeding grounds for line authority, orders, mandates, and industrial requirements. Unfortunately, classic organizational charts often serve to promulgate the perception of leadership, though the reality is that compliance and fidelity become the pervasive results. When management's focus is on what the labor force is doing, how often it's being done, to what degree it's done, and how effectively it's done, we don't require an advanced degree to recognize that folks will *do* in order to appease their supervisors. In education, that's not why we should do anything! Checking boxes rarely gets us to our goals, especially when those goals include the healthy growth and development of young people, academic growth and achievement, and meeting the diverse needs of the students within our communities. Rather, when we're truly "mission-driven," we commit ourselves to the accomplishment of the greater good, the identified and agreed-upon vision, and we pull out all the stops to achieve it. Aligning our *thinking* to the vision ensures that our *doing* is properly targeted to that same focus.

A culture of reflective practice is simultaneously collaborative (building collective capacity) and differentiated (building individual capacity). Education is no longer a profession characterized by isolationism. We cannot retreat to our own classes and ignore the collective knowledge and wisdom of our peers, especially when the stakes are so high. We rise or we fall together. This is the nature of collaboration, and in a culture of reflective practice, we support the growth of the collective *we*. Teachers encourage, motivate, enrich, expand, and support one another to achieve common goals. Also, a theme you may have noticed emerge in our exploration of the Continuum of Self-Reflection is *differentiation*. This is the notion that it's our responsibility to provide the resources, support, motivation, and influence that match *each individual teacher's* needs. In one of our favorite leadership texts, *First, Break All the Rules*, former Gallup Organization researchers Marcus Buckingham and Curt Coffman identified the behaviors and approaches of successful leaders whose branches or offices outperformed their peers. One of their key takeaways? Great managers "consistently disregard the Golden Rule" (1999a, p. 11). Now, this has nothing to do with treating people respectfully—that's the Platinum Rule. Rather, this approach could be paraphrased in this manner: Rather than doing unto others as *you* would have done unto *you*, our charge is to do unto others as *they need to be done unto*.

A culture of reflective practice is strength-based and growth-oriented. As noted earlier, Stanford researcher Carol Dweck (2006) captivated us with talk of the growth mindset and our willingness to embrace the potential impact we can have upon ourselves and others. This sense of personal and professional efficacy is at the heart of a culture of reflective practice. Identifying our strengths provides a solid foundation upon which we can then build professional capacity, motivates us to apply those strengths more consistently, and encourages us to bolster our other practices simultaneously—by helping us to recognize and *think* deliberately about those practices. This is an arena rich with optimism, after all. Rather than lamenting what we lack or the obstacles we face, our emphasis is on the goal and the myriad paths we might follow to reach it. The discourse one might overhear in a culture of reflective practice includes "What can we do?" and "Let's try ___" instead of "We can't" or "That won't work here." And in an overt nod to the growth mindset, we add the word *yet* to comments about our reality: "We haven't had successes yet" and "We haven't reached our goals yet."

A culture of reflective practice weaves reflection into every other current initiative. This is perhaps the most profound and singularly energizing characteristic of a culture of reflective practice. Self-reflection is not a beast unto itself; rather, it's an approach that supports, deepens, and expands the effectiveness of whatever we set our (individual or collective) minds to. No matter what other initiatives, adoptions, mandates, or changes are imposed upon us (by others or by ourselves), our cultivation of a culture of reflective practice strengthens our capacity to embrace the new, to learn, and to engage in rich professional growth simultaneously. In this manner, building a culture of reflective practice allows us to be very strategic about our technical focus and our long-term reflective development. We all have worked in schools or districts that have eloquent, wordsmithed vision and mission statements and a strategic multiyear plan that might actually exacerbate our confusion (Schmoker, 2006), and we've heard rumors (wink-wink) about districts awash with a cascade of initiatives. Well, these can live hand-in-hand with a culture of reflective practice. In fact, every aspect of our professional sphere is enhanced within a culture of reflective practice.

 Every aspect of our professional sphere is enhanced within a culture of reflective practice.

How Do We Start? Where Should We Focus?

As you might expect, our advice is simple: start at the beginning. And because the fundamentals of a culture of reflective practice are in prioritized, chronological order (1 precedes 2, 2 precedes 3, and so on), we suggest you look at Fundamental 1 first. Which of the factors within Fundamental 1 need your focus and attention? Are there strengths within that fundamental? Are there items that could use some touch-up work and refinement?

The answers to those questions, and more, are awaiting you as you analyze the state of affairs in your school by completing the BTC Site Assessment (Appendix A). This is a formative assessment tool designed to provide you with feedback on the strengths and needs of your campus and professional environment as you strive to establish and nurture a robust culture of reflective practice. In the Site Assessment, you'll assign a "score" for each of the factors within the seven fundamentals using the rubric.

Once you're familiar with the rubric and its vocabulary, you may proceed with your analysis of the state of affairs in your school. We recommend that you read carefully Chapters 5 through 9 to get a more robust understanding of the fundamentals and their associated factors before attempting to "score" your school's status or readiness with the Site Assessment. Remember Becky DuFour's words: Clarity precedes competence.

Another recommendation is to engage key stakeholders (fellow capacity-builders, an entire school staff, a leadership team, or any other configuration of interested and invested individuals) in critical analysis of the vocabulary, ideas, and practical applications in order to achieve consensus. Doing so can go a long way toward opening communication and ensuring everyone is working from the same playbook.

Alisa's Approach

Questions about timeline inevitably crop up at this point in the conversation. In our work with schools and districts all across the country, folks often ask, *How long does this work take? What's a realistic timeline to shoot for, for success in all of this work?*

With all due respect, we'd like to point out that these aren't the questions that will provide the scope and sequence we're in search of. In a candid article about school improvement, Richard Elmore, professor of educational leadership at the Harvard Graduate School of Education, and Dr. Elizabeth City, director of the Doctor of Education Leadership Program, address it this way: "How long does it take? Educators know deep down that this is not the right question because it implies a finish line or summit that we will someday reach. That's not how improvement works." Instead, they say, "The discipline of school improvement lies in developing strong internal processes for self-monitoring and reflection—*not* in meeting an artificially imposed schedule of improvement. That existing accountability systems don't reflect this reality is one of the great political tragedies of current education policy." (Elmore & City, 2007, p. 3)

So what does this mean for us? Instead of planning for a nonexistent finish line, we direct our timeline questions to the launch, development, and sustaining of our culture of reflective practice: *How many fundamentals should be rolled out at a time? How do we know when to introduce the next fundamental? How do we know when our staff is ready to move forward? How do we build on previous work?* In other words, the focus is the journey. The journey *is* our destination.

With that in mind, we offer a different timeline—one that focuses not on end results, but on the development of strong internal processes to move a staff from corporately unaware to corporately operating in the Refinement stage. There is no finish line.

Stage	Characteristics	Approximate Time Frame
Unaware	Initial launch, establishing the foundational pieces of Fundamental 1 (and possibly 2)	0–6 months
Conscious	Gaining clarity and building knowledge of the practices within Fundamentals 1, 2, and possibly 3	6 months–1 year
Action	Putting knowledge into practice (Fundamentals 1, 2, 3, and 4) and implementing Fundamentals 5, 6, and 7	1–3 years
Refinement	Consistent application of all fundamentals with continuing refinement of practices	3–unlimited years

The big idea is this: each school will be starting from a slightly different point, due to the strength of the relationships within the building, the history with coaching, and the understanding of the importance of reflective thought. So although some steps may be implemented immediately and some early returns may come in very soon, it takes time, effort, consistency, and persistence to truly establish a culture of reflective practice. Stick with it! The positive results will arrive if we approach this work with urgency, patience, and diligence—and keep our eyes on the journey rather than a nonexistent destination.

Final Thoughts

In a 2004 *Educational Leadership* article, Andy Hargreaves and Dean Fink shared the results from a 30-year leadership study of change in eight different U.S. and Canadian schools. They summarized the article with the following statement:

> Most leaders want to accomplish goals that matter, inspire others to join them in working toward those goals, and leave a legacy after they have gone. Leaders don't usually let their schools down; the failure often rests with the systems in which they lead. The results of our study indicate that sustainable leadership cannot be left to individuals, however talented or dedicated they are. If we want change to matter, to spread, and to last, then the systems in which leaders do their work must make sustainability a priority. (Hargreaves & Fink, 2004, p. 13)

Part II:
The Players and the Playing Field

In Part I, we laid out the rationale for creating a culture of reflective practice, and we introduced its various components, including seven fundamentals. In Part II, we explore the first four fundamentals in depth.

If self-reflection is indeed the ticket that allows us entry into the arena of continuous professional growth and offers us an opportunity to increase student learning, then it would behoove us to concentrate our efforts on engaging our teaching staff in robust self-reflection. Supporting teachers' reflective growth requires coordination, collaboration, and communication. Those involved in this process (the *players*) are described in Chapter 5, which explores Fundamental 1: Relationships, Roles, and Responsibilities.

Chapters 6 through 8 describe the *playing field*—the specific conditions necessary for our capacity-building efforts to take hold and succeed. The playing field for a culture of reflective practice consists of three closely related fundamentals.

Fundamental 2: Expectations and Communication establishes the rules of the game. Setting up these ground rules beforehand gives the organization a much better chance of ensuring that all the players play within the desired parameters, and clear and consistent communication will help the game run smoothly.

Fundamental 3: Celebration and Calibration is comparable to keeping score, but the intent here is not to determine winners and losers but rather to establish a scoring system that enables the organization and its members to determine when they've accomplished any measure of success, tallied small wins, or achieved a goal. It also allows players to identify when things have gone awry so they can huddle and calibrate their understanding of any part of the experience that needs clarification.

Fundamental 4: Goal Setting and Follow-Through is akin to the efforts that players in a sporting contest make to identify their ideal result (winning the match, capturing a championship, or improving on last season's performance), commit to being mission-driven, and follow through with whatever it takes to achieve the mission.

5

Fundamental 1: Relationships, Roles, and Responsibilities

Fundamental 1 Theory of Action: *If* we cultivate strong professional relationships and obtain clarity around the roles and responsibilities of the various capacity-builders in our school, *then* we will have prepared a sturdy, solid foundation upon which to build the essential fundamentals of a culture of reflective practice.

Sports metaphors have a way of bringing to life some of the more eloquent descriptions of the human experience. And here, as we embark upon a discussion of Fundamental 1 in a culture of reflective practice, we call upon the interactions, relationships, and common understandings of the United States women's national soccer team to help make our case.

Since July 2003, the U.S. women's national soccer team has been ranked either number one or number two in the world, accumulating more international championships than any other team. Of note: the U.S. women's squad has taken three Women's World Cup titles (this event has occurred only seven times, starting in 1991) and collected four of the past six Olympic gold medals, perhaps explaining why the 2015 World Cup Final was the most-watched soccer game in U.S. history (Sandomir, 2015).

Of course, each of these teams is composed of excellent athletes with superior knowledge of the game, deft footwork, mythological endurance, and a keen sense for performing under pressure. However, it's the connection between players, the relationships on and off the field, and the teamwork that come together to make this team a modern dynasty.

The U.S. women's team undergoes rigorous practice sessions and meticulous preparation before its matches. Players not only understand their roles in a generic sense—who are the defenders, who are the midfielders, who are the strikers, and who is the goalie—but also clarify the particular areas of the field they will cover, their roles during game-specific plays such as corner kicks, and their collaborative strategies for attacking and defending throughout each match. For players on the team, the left foot definitely knows what the right foot is doing at all times, because they've talked about it, clarified it, practiced it, and performed it. And when they make a mistake, they fix it—together.

In the Schoolhouse

The broad, unyielding foundation of a culture of reflective practice begins with the establishment and nurturing of positive, professional relationships between all the members of the school. It's critical to emphasize that the relationships are not an *end* in themselves; rather, they are a *means* to an end. Having strong relationships enables the rest of the work to proceed unfettered. Adding to this strong base is the clarity of roles and relationships between the capacity-builders within the system, to ensure that they all know the parameters of their own work and that of their peers, and where there might be overlap. These three concepts (relationships, roles, and responsibilities) require the immediate and ongoing attention of those in leadership roles if a culture of reflective practice is to flourish.

The primary responsibilities in a culture of reflective practice rest on the shoulders of those in instructional leadership roles at the school level: administrators and coaches. Because their job descriptions contain language and obligations directly related to supporting individual teachers' professional growth, we'll refer to these two roles as "official" capacity-builders. These responsibilities are shared with others, however, as shown in our Triad Diagram (Figure 5.1), where you'll note that there are actually *four* specific roles designated: the administrator, the coach, the PLC/teammates, and the teacher. In the following paragraphs, we'll provide a brief overview of these four; later in the chapter, we'll provide some guidelines for how the roles partner in their collaborative endeavor to build teachers' capacity.

FIGURE 5.1

Triad Diagram

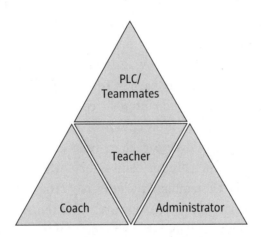

Administrators include principals, assistant principals, and those in any other site-based administrative position responsible for the supervision and evaluation of teachers. Although administrators' feedback inherently packs more wallop, those embracing our capacity-building model will ensure the establishment of a trusting relationship bent on maximizing teacher potential and having a positive impact on student learning. Administrators establish the tone and tenor of a school's capacity-building efforts, and their involvement is absolutely critical to the overall success of this venture.

Coaches make up a category headlined by actual instructional coaches, those who are hired to provide job-embedded professional development at the site level. This is a position and role introduced several decades ago by Joyce and Showers, who stated, "Like athletes, teachers will put newly learned skills to use—if they are coached" (1982, p. 5). For simplicity, we use the term *coach* throughout this text, though we're also referring to literacy coordinators, content coaches, department chairs, grade-level representatives, mentors, teacher-leaders, and any other site-based staff developers. They possess the ability to approach each teacher as a peer, providing nonevaluative, nonthreatening, meaningful support in an individualized collaborative coaching model.

The *PLC/teammates* group includes other teachers with assignments within that teacher's discipline, such as fellow grade-level, department, or content teachers. This category may also include members of a teacher's learning network, professional learning community, or anyone else with "skin in the game"—that is, an interest in achieving an interdependent student learning goal in partnership with a given teacher. Teammates have a unique leverage point: as colleagues with common interests, common assignments, and common challenges, they're fantastically poised to provide realistic, valid, and credible perspectives that help develop teachers' reflective and technical expertise.

Teachers, lest we forget, are the central focus of our work. As we've said before, the teacher is "the center of the universe" (Hall & Simeral, 2015, p. 2). Teachers are a vital part of this equation and should be included at every step in the process. Effective collaborative support, differentiated feedback, and personalized coaching are not things done *to* teachers; they're things done *with* teachers. Partnering early with our teachers is a wise step in building a robust capacity-building model that transforms the entire school community.

Relationship Triangulation

In data analysis, the term *triangulation* refers to the technique for drawing a defensible conclusion based on multiple data points from various measurement sources. In capacity-building, *triangulation* refers to the technique for strengthening a teacher's reflective tendencies based on multiple relationships between the teacher and the various sources of support in this process. Growth and progress require change, and change is often difficult. The *significant* relationships will ease the strains associated with lasting, meaningful, productive change.

Consider Figure 5.1 (p. 71). With the teacher in the center of the triad diagram, we note three clear sets of connections: (1) the teacher's significant relationship with the administrator; (2) the teacher's significant relationship with the coach; and (3) the teacher's significant peer relationships, grounded in the foundation of the PLC framework.

We also recognize three other important relationships: (1) the administrator's significant relationship with the coach; (2) the coach's significant relationship with teacher teams; and (3) the teacher teams' significant relationship with the administrator. All these players—these key capacity-builders—must work in a coordinated, intentional, and collaborative manner to support teacher growth.

Having all these relationships in place virtually ensures that the teacher will be bent on learning, be keyed into self-reflection, and interdependently receive support that leads to continuous professional growth. These three unyielding elements constitute the support network that is critical to building teachers' capacity.

Our overarching goal within this triad is to deepen teachers' reflection, to help teachers grow as reflective practitioners—to modify, amend, open, and strengthen their thought processes. Each of the various sources of support provides a specific venue for augmenting the teacher's reflective tendencies:

- The teacher-administrator relationship allows for clear expectations, regular reflective feedback, and accountability for making consistent progress.

- The teacher-coach relationship provides the job-embedded learning opportunities to meet the expectations and to deepen thinking.

- The teacher-team relationship ensures a collaborative, interdependent setting for practicing, sharing, and diversifying ideas and approaches.

To move effectively from *compliance* to *commitment*, we must shift the teacher's mindset—slightly or significantly—to get beyond the *doing* and into the messy and critical world of *thinking*.

Characteristics of Effective Capacity-Builders

As mentioned earlier, "official" capacity-builders include those in administrative or coaching positions, those who share the bulk of the responsibility for encouraging individual teachers' reflective growth. Members of each teacher's collaborative team (department, grade-level, content, or otherwise) do not ordinarily engage in direct, intentional capacity-building efforts, unless specified in their job descriptions or in the school's charter. So, for our purposes here, references to "capacity-builders" include those in the administrator and coach corners of the triad. Individuals seeking to thrive in this realm must possess and cultivate a slew of other interpersonal and professional skills. Let's look at the characteristics that tend to yield success.

An effective capacity-builder is mission-driven. The mission, should you choose to accept it, is crystal clear: build the capacity of each and every teacher within the scope of your influence. Effective capacity-builders identify the particular goals that each teacher is working toward, and they pull out all the stops to help the teachers achieve their goals. When the mission is embraced as the driving force behind all decisions and actions, and the capacity-builder is determined to work relentlessly to support each and every individual teacher, then the likelihood of success is increased dramatically. That's being mission-driven.

Effective capacity-builders pull out all the stops to help their teachers reach their goals. That's being mission-driven.

An effective capacity-builder is highly self-reflective. Well, this seems like a no-brainer, doesn't it? If we are to be successful in supporting a teacher's reflective growth, the least we can do is to model the expected approaches ourselves, right? This is a keystone skill, habit, strength, tendency—whatever you'd like to call it, capacity-builders *must* possess it. And demonstrate it. Our teachers deserve the very best role modeling, especially with this complicated and important skill.

An effective capacity-builder is service-oriented. One of the first things we realize about effective capacity-builders—all effective educators, really—is that they are givers. They give to others of their time, their knowledge, their support, their love, their resources, their energy, and their hope. This selfless, make-the-world-a-better-place approach enables capacity-builders to consider the "bus question," one we first posed in *Building Teachers' Capacity for Success* (Hall & Simeral, 2008). If you were to be struck by a bus on the way to work tomorrow (don't worry, you'll be fine; you just won't be able to report to work for about a year), how will you have prepared your teachers to be successful in your absence? How have you built their capacity? How are they better off after having worked with you all this time?

We gauge the effectiveness of capacity-builders by how much capacity they build in their teachers.

An effective capacity-builder is strength-focused. If we are to truly build capacity, we must have a foundation upon which to *build*. What better than strengths? Pete refers to our individual strengths as "little green stars," and we all have them. Do you notice the little green stars that each of your teachers brings to the schoolhouse every day? Do you use the growth mindset (once again, we thank Carol Dweck [2006] for introducing this term to the popular vernacular) in your thoughts, words, and actions with teachers? Do you bring positive energy to every interaction with your teachers and encourage them to use their strengths as frequently as possible? Staying focused on strength means believing in your teachers—every one of them—and building in them a sense of efficacy that they *will* be successful with their students.

Relationships, Roles, and Responsibilities Within a Culture of Reflective Practice

The following four factors contribute to the successful development and implementation of Fundamental 1, contributing to a robust and successful culture of reflective practice:

a. Administrator and staff have rapport and trustworthy relationships.

b. Coach and staff have rapport and trustworthy relationships.

c. Administrator and coach discuss their roles and responsibilities, the nature of their professional partnership, and their common goals as capacity-builders.

d. Staff have a clear understanding of the role and responsibilities of coach—and can articulate how they are distinct from those of administrator in order to encourage reflective growth, support effective teaching, and promote student learning.

We invite you, the capacity-builders, to engage your school staff in dialogue and explore your understanding of these factors, each of which is described in greater detail throughout this chapter. More important than falling entirely in line with what *we* (the authors) mean when we use certain terms or why we've included something and omitted something else is your consensus and the process by which you build it. Feel free to add, delete, or modify the factors in this list to better meet your particular school's contextual needs. We ask only that you keep in mind the spirit and big ideas of this fundamental—minding the related Theory of Action at all times!—and to think very critically about your collective rationale for making any changes before doing so.

A familiar tool, the Reflective Cycle, can help us refine our thinking about the strength of the interpersonal, working relationships within the school and the common understanding of the roles and responsibilities of the capacity-builders as they work together to fortify the culture of reflective practice. The questions in Figure 5.2 provide a macro-level (10,000-foot) perspective about Fundamental 1 as a whole. As you continue to read about the factors that make up this fundamental, you will be able to drill deeper, develop a more detailed understanding, and generate a more specific (micro-level) approach to refine your thinking—and your practices.

To help you apply the Reflective Cycle to focus your thinking on each factor, we provide explanations that should help all capacity-builders (administrator, coach, leadership team, and school staff) identify how to

FIGURE 5.2

The Reflective Cycle Within Fundamental 1: Relationships, Roles, and Responsibilities

Building Awareness	*How aware are we of the importance and strength of our professional relationships and the defined roles and responsibilities of the capacity-builders within our school?*
Working with Intentionality	*How intentionally do we work to cultivate those relationships, communicate with each other to clarify our roles and responsibilities, and connect with all staff to ensure a strong foundation for the culture of reflective practice? Do we have a plan for this?*
Assessing Our Impact	*How do we know to what extent all staff members are committed to the professional relationships within the school and understand the roles and responsibilities of the capacity-builders? How—and how frequently—do we check in?*
Becoming Responsive	*How do we adapt and adjust our practices and professional relationships as a result of our assessments in order to meet the shifting needs of the staff?*

build awareness. For each factor, you'll also find a corresponding figure with some guiding questions to get you started. The rest is up to you and will be determined by your goals, context, and identified areas of emphasis.

Factor 1a: Administrator and staff have rapport and trustworthy relationships. Establishing relationships is a critical piece of a healthy working environment in any field; in an arena such as education, which is heavy with interpersonal interactions between various human beings *all the time*, those relationships become even more important. Administrators have an immense responsibility to connect, build, and maintain positive professional relationships with every person on staff in order to begin the process of establishing a culture of reflective practice. It all starts in the principal's office.

Positive professional relationships, mind you, are different than getting along (being collegial) and working together without outward strife (being cooperative). Administrators and their teachers needn't always agree with each other, seek out each other's company, or even like each other as fellow travelers on the planet! However, when it comes time to work together for the benefit of students and the greater good, the relationship must be strong enough to enable everyone to buckle down and collaborate with purpose and professionalism.

Administrators must get to know and understand their teachers—their interests, their skills, their "little green stars," their fears, their dreams, and their ambitions. Trust and mutual respect are characteristics that cannot be overstated—this is especially important because the "elephant in the room" is that administrators also evaluate their teachers, making their high-stakes relationship fraught with anxiety.

However, by properly tending to the relationship; communicating clearly, specifically, and consistently; and following through with whatever is said, administrators can bolster the working environment and create a trusting, positive, mutually respectful atmosphere for professional learning, risk taking, dialogue, and collaboration. To move from a culture of compliance to one of commitment, we must all embrace and live in accordance with this fact: we're all in this together and we must row in unison, even if we're sitting in different seats in the boat. See Figure 5.3 for a set of guiding questions for capacity-builders related to the Reflective Cycle for Factor 1a.

FIGURE 5.3

Reflective Cycle for Factor 1a

Building Awareness	Does the administrator have positive working relationships with the staff?
	Does the administrator have a positive working relationship with each individual staff member?
	What characterizes the administrator-staff relationships? Trust? Mutual respect? Common interests? Fear?
	Do the administrator and staff members believe in each other's abilities to achieve their responsibilities toward the agreed-upon goals?
Working with Intentionality	What is our plan for addressing this?
Assessing Our Impact	How will we assess the impact of our actions?
Becoming Responsive	How will we respond to the shifting needs of the staff?

Factor 1b: Coach and staff have rapport and trustworthy relationships. Not surprisingly, the strength of the coach's relationships with every teacher in the building plays a significant role in the development and maintenance of a powerful culture of reflective practice. The coach is a highly influential, visible member of the staff, often interacting with many—if not all—of the teachers in a particular department, grade, or the entire faculty.

As a means to an end, we must ask: Are the coach's relationships with each teacher strong enough to support the roles that the coach must play to support teachers' reflective growth—unconditional partner, motivator/ strategist, mentor, and collaborator? (You'll read more about these specific roles in Chapters 10 through 13.)

One critical difference between the coach's relationships with teachers and the administrator's relationships with teachers is the absence of an evaluative role in the coach's responsibilities. Because the coaching position is characterized by nonevaluative, fully supportive, in-your-corner peer relationships with teachers, there *should be no concern* about whether or not what a coach observes or sees is reported to the evaluating administrator. To solidify that trusting component of the relationship, this point must be clarified (see Factor 1c below), communicated overtly to staff (see Factor 1d after that), and lived genuinely at all times. See Figure 5.4 for a set of guiding questions for capacity-builders related to the Reflective Cycle for Factor 1b.

FIGURE 5.4

Reflective Cycle for Factor 1b

Building Awareness	*Does the coach have positive working relationships with the staff?*
	Does the coach have a positive working relationship with each individual staff member?
	What characterizes the coach-staff relationships? Trust? Mutual respect? Common interests? Fear?
	Do the coach and staff members believe in each other's abilities to achieve their responsibilities toward the agreed-upon goals?
Working with Intentionality	*What is our plan for addressing this?*
Assessing Our Impact	*How will we assess the impact of our actions?*
Becoming Responsive	*How will we respond to the shifting needs of the staff?*

Factor 1c: Administrator and coach discuss their roles and responsibilities, the nature of their professional partnership, and their common goals as capacity-builders. One of the major themes of *Building Teachers' Capacity for Success* (Hall & Simeral, 2008) concerned the partnership between the administrator and the coach—hence the

subtitle of the book: *A Collaborative Approach for Coaches and School Leaders*. These two positions are often the most influential, active, and impactful capacity-builders in a teacher's life, so it's crucial that each understands his or her own role, the other person's role, and how they can partner to best support each individual teacher on staff. This isn't something that happens magically. It takes work.

In particular, administrators and coaches must commit to engaging in frequent, honest, and hearty conversations about these very topics. The more they talk and communicate with one another, the stronger *their* working relationship will become, and the greater clarity they'll both obtain about the particulars of their working assignments. How frequent is often enough? That's up to the parties involved. In our experience, ne'er a week should go by without a face-to-face dialogue between these two critical roles.

During these conversations, it's important to understand—and talk about directly—what's *on* the table and what's *off* the table between the two roles. To help with this, we've provided some descriptive guidelines in this Q & A:

Q: What should coaches and administrators talk about when discussing individual teachers?

A: Two things are *on* the table: (1) each teacher's current stage on the Continuum of Self-Reflection and (2) each teacher's individual goal. With those two pieces of information in hand, both know how the other will be approaching the capacity-building work.

Q: Can coach and administrator discuss individual teacher performance?

A: This is not advised. If either wants to gather more information about how a teacher runs a classroom, implements a strategy, plans lessons, or otherwise teaches, we suggest that person go ahead and stop by the classroom to see it directly. Otherwise, any discussion about performance is *off* the table.

Q: What else is *off* the table during these conversations?

A: Anything that has to do with the teacher evaluation process, rubric scores, observation feedback, and performance concerns are "no-go" areas. Nothing good comes from venturing here unless your goal is to create a culture of destructive practice—which it's not. So stay out.

One of the most prominent philosophical foundations of this work is simply this: the administrator and the coach are partners in this venture. And like teammates in any sport, their roles are sometimes distinct, sometimes quite similar, and sometimes overlapping; however, the goal is always the same.

And what is the overarching goal in our capacity-building efforts? We expect we've made this abundantly clear, though it's worth repeating nonetheless. The goal is twofold, with the two parts woven intricately together:

1. To support our teachers' growth as reflective practitioners, enabling them to think more deeply, accurately, and frequently about their impact upon student learning; and

2. To support our teachers' growth in technical expertise, positioning them to meet each and every one of their students' needs, thereby increasing student learning along all measurable achievement outcomes.

In short, the coach and the administrator share the ultimate goal of *effecting positive change*. Meaningful, positive change—a necessary condition for school improvement—is only possible within a framework of cooperation and collaboration. The coach and the administrator are partners through and through as they undertake this critical work.

As partners, the particular roles of administrator and coach are built to complement one another as they strive to build capacity in teachers across the Continuum of Self-Reflection. Figure 5.5 is a quick guide to the complementary roles undertaken to support teachers' reflective growth. Figure 5.6 is a set of guiding questions for capacity-builders related to the Reflective Cycle for Factor 1c.

Factor 1d: Staff have a clear understanding of the role and responsibilities of coach—and can articulate how they are distinct from those of administrator in order to encourage reflective growth, support effective teaching, and promote student learning. Not only do

FIGURE 5.5

Complementary Roles of Administrators and Coaches

Unaware Stage

Administrator's role: *Director*
Instructional coach's role: *Unconditional partner*

Conscious Stage

Administrator's role: *Navigator*
Instructional coach's role: *Motivator/Strategist*

Action Stage

Administrator's role: *Prompter*
Instructional coach's role: *Mentor*

Refinement Stage

Administrator's role: *Challenger*
Instructional coach's role: *Collaborator*

the coach and the administrator need clarity around their roles, but the teachers also need to know where the two positions are similar, are distinct, and overlap. This is particularly important when dealing with a relative unknown. Instructional coaches aren't yet commonplace in every school; often the positions are new and part of a larger initiative; and for schools that do not have coaches, there are other players (department chairs, mentors, etc.) who assume that responsibility. So clarity matters.

The understandings surfaced during coach-administrator conversations are repeated (in a concise and direct manner) with the teaching staff. This is no time to assume that teachers already know or that the role is "obvious." So whether the message is communicated via e-mail, presented in faculty meetings, reiterated in team meetings, shared in face-to-face conversation, posted on the staff room bulletin board, inserted in a newsletter, broadcast on the PA system, or mass-texted, the point is that it's

FIGURE 5.6

Reflective Cycle for Factor 1c

Building Awareness	Do the administrator and the coach understand the similarities and differences in each other's roles and responsibilities?
	Have the administrator and the coach discussed this together?
	How often do the administrator and the coach converse about their professional relationship and the nature of their collaborative work?
	Are the administrator and the coach clear about their mission and their complementary roles for supporting teachers' reflective growth?
	Have the administrator and the coach achieved clarity about which topics they can address and which topics they cannot discuss together?
Working with Intentionality	What is our plan for addressing this?
Assessing Our Impact	How will we assess the impact of our actions?
Becoming Responsive	How will we respond to the shifting needs of the staff?

shared, repeated, and clarified as necessary. All teachers should be able to answer the following questions with confidence:

- Why do we have a coach?
- What is the coach's goal in working with teachers?
- How can a coach support my growth as a professional?
- What are some ways I can connect with a coach?
- Will a coach contribute to my formal evaluation?

See also Figure 5.7 for a set of guiding questions for capacity-builders related to the Reflective Cycle for Factor 1d.

FIGURE 5.7

Reflective Cycle for Factor 1d

Building Awareness	Do all staff members understand the role and purpose of coach?
	Do staff members know the options available to them for partnering with a coach?
	How often (and in what manner) does this communication occur?
Working with Intentionality	What is our plan for addressing this?
Assessing Our Impact	How will we assess the impact of our actions?
Becoming Responsive	How will we respond to the shifting needs of the staff?

Bringing Fundamental 1 to Life

In the following two scenarios, you'll read about some capacity-builders' efforts to implement Fundamental 1 within their schools. Though the characters are fictional, they're amalgams of real human beings, compiled from case studies within schools we have worked and consulted with over the past several years. After the scenarios, we'll offer some discussion to distill a few of our key learnings for this fundamental.

Scenario 1

The principal of School 1 was excited to launch the district's instructional-coaching initiative, and the district had hired a fantastic teacher-leader to serve in this new role. Wanting to be sure that the position quickly had significant impact, the principal met with the incoming coach and outlined his expectations for her, explaining that she would be working with struggling and new teachers in the areas where they needed the most support.

At the back-to-school meetings before the first day, the principal introduced the coach and invited her to share a little about herself with the staff. Knowing that her responsibilities were focused mostly on a small group of teachers, the principal did not revisit the coaching conversation beyond this first meeting, opting to not clutter up the teachers' plates with information they really didn't need. If and when the time came for a teacher to be coached, there would be time for that discussion.

Over the course of the school year, teachers wondered aloud exactly how this coach was earning the same paycheck as they were, since she didn't have students, lesson plans, report cards, or homework to grade. The principal defensively supported the position and suggested that they all focus on improving their own classroom practices before they worry about others. Needless to say, there was much worry to follow.

Scenario 2

In School 2, the principal and the assistant principal invited the new instructional coach to lunch to discuss their roles and responsibilities. Over the course of an hour and a soup-and-sandwich combo, the three leaders built the foundation of the work that would guide their relationships and their interactions with each other for the year. They drafted some statements on operational norms and agreed to finesse them, and then sign them, when they got back to the building.

Over dessert, they sketched out a rough game plan for how they would approach each week: a Monday afternoon meeting was put on the books, followed by some outlines for visiting classes, connecting with teachers, and engaging in intentional coaching and feedback practices. And, very important, they discussed their "safe word." If one of them overstepped the boundaries or asked one of the others to overstep the boundaries, either party could say the safe word. For them, it was simple: "Time out." That would cue them to have a conversation about something that was going awry before it turned catastrophic.

Back at the building, the trio planned their back-to-school welcome, set aside some time to talk "coaching" with the staff, and brainstormed some ways to keep the coaching conversations in the front of the teachers' minds all year long. With a solid handshake, they agreed that this was going to be one fabulous year.

What's Really Going On?

Both schools in these scenarios are launching brand-new coaching initiatives, so there's ample opportunity to set things up in a way that exudes confidence, clarifies the concepts, and prepares the entire staff for success. In School 1, the principal appears to be keeping the reins taut, holding on to the key information and unilaterally making some decisions about the allocation of coaching support. With the intent of affecting teacher quality—and therefore student learning—the focus is on the weaker, or newer, teachers. For the most part, the rest of the staff is left in the dark, leading to skepticism and bitterness toward the coach. Unfortunately, with a poor launch, this initiative doesn't show much promise.

School 2 offers much more promise, however, as the principal, the assistant principal, and the coach connect, communicate openly, and create a collaborative plan for bringing the teachers into the fold. Their commitment to the success of the venture is never more evident than in their agreement on a "safe word," equipping everyone on the team with a way to call out each other's behaviors before a situation gets out of hand. By talking openly and planning in advance, the likelihood that the coaching initiative will succeed is much greater.

Wrapping Up

The fact is, we can't skip the first step. Even though talking about roles and responsibilities and doing yeoman's work to establish positive relationships isn't headline-grabbing, exciting stuff, it's essential. Fundamental 1 is the foundation upon which the rest of our culture of reflective practice is built. Success in the long haul—supporting the reflective growth of everyone in the building—hinges upon the quality and consistency of the work done at the onset. That's why it's Fundamental 1.

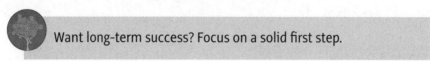

Want long-term success? Focus on a solid first step.

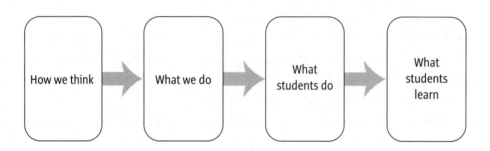

As capacity-builders, it's incumbent upon us to address this fundamental in a way that accounts for all aspects of the Reflective Cycle. We must become aware of what we need to do, we must implement it with intentionality and consistency, we must assess to what degree it's working, and we must be willing to adapt and adjust as events warrant.

Fundamental 2: Expectations and Communication

Fundamental 2 Theory of Action: *If* we clearly and regularly communicate our expectations for all staff to grow as reflective practitioners, *then* we will elevate the effectiveness and professional excellence of our schools.

"Wearing the same shirts doesn't make a team," once said Boston Red Sox pitcher Clay Buchholz. Leadership author Phil Rabinowitz agrees: "A *team* is a group of people with a commitment to one another, to the team, to a high level of achievement, to a common goal, and to a common vision. They understand that team success depends on the work of every member" (Rabinowitz, n.d.). In that regard, the name on the *front* of the jersey has to matter more to each team member than the name on the *back*.

So how do you shift from looking like a team on the *outside* to working as a team on the *inside*? High-performance teams attribute much of their success to the presence of explicit expectations and exemplary communication. Departing from the sports theme momentarily but sticking with a team known for its athleticism, let's examine the United States Navy's Sea, Air and Land teams, better known as the Navy SEALs. Commissioned in 1962 by President Kennedy, this elite military force is "organized, trained, and equipped to conduct a variety of Special Operations missions in all operational environments" (www.military.com/special-operations/about-the-navy-seals.html). You've probably heard or read about them. Although their daring raids, hostage extractions, and wartime missions are often glorified in the press, the great majority of their work is done in clandestine, subtle, and footprint-less stealth.

How are they so consistently successful in their missions? Known for their ability to perform with coordinated tactical precision, the effectiveness of these units is rooted in a carefully designed and comprehensive system of leadership and teamwork. Within that system, clearly defined expectations and objectives define the goal and motivate the team to follow. Without these elements in place, the team runs the risk of misunderstanding, failure, and ultimately putting lives at stake.

Not surprisingly, effective communication is at the heart of every mission. "There are three things you have to do well to be a SEAL operator," says former Navy SEAL combat veteran Brent Gleeson. "Move, shoot, and communicate. While all three are important, communication is the most crucial. When the team understood the big picture and everyone knew their specific roles in accomplishing the mission, we were always set up for success" (*Inc.*, 2014). In military lingo, this is known as communication synchronization: the coordination of people or events to operate in unison, and it's "critical to mission accomplishment," according to the U.S. Joint Forces Command (2010).

 Synchronization: *the coordination of people or events to operate in unison*

The secret to high-performing teams? Explicit expectations and communication synchronization on the *inside*. A SEAL might phrase it like this: "Pass the word." Key information must flow to all involved parties, ensuring uniform understanding, trust, and a shared sense of purpose.

Sure, incredible physical fitness, exceptional mental grit, high-caliber intelligence, and a deep commitment to special operations conducted under dark cover in some of the most hostile and unforgiving environments are helpful. But wait! Come to think of it, those characteristics would also work for educators! And although teacher preparation programs aren't in the same ilk as Navy SEAL training on Coronado Island near San Diego, the need for clear, specific, consistent communication remains the same.

Connecting to Schools

The essence of being a leader is defining a vision and compelling others to pursue and achieve that vision. Educators, not terribly unlike Navy SEALs, must be "mission-driven" (Hall et al., 2016) and unabashedly committed to their common goals. The expectations we set for our buildings, or lack thereof, have a direct impact on the results we receive. A report from Mid-Continent Research for Education and Learning (McREL) speaks to the importance of expectations set by school leadership: "Effective school leaders know how to focus the work of the school on the essential. They have a clear mission or purpose for the school and identify goals that align with that mission. They communicate the purpose and goals in a meaningful way such that all stakeholders understand what they need to do" (McIver, Kearns, Lyons, & Sussman, 2009, p. 12).

Our esteemed colleague, the late Rick DuFour (2004), wrote, "Humans have a fundamental longing to believe we are successful in what we do—our need to achieve. Educators are typically denied this sense of success. Bombarded with too many state, national and district standards for students to master . . . , teachers are often unclear as to what they are supposed to accomplish" (p. 67). DuFour puts it bluntly: without expectations, we are denied a sense of success and hinder our own progress forward. The way leaders define and communicate their vision, expectations, and goals will directly lead to the success or failure of the organization.

The way leaders define and communicate their expectations will directly lead to the success or failure of the organization.

The Perils Along the Way

Too often, great confusion and disappointment occur when the expectations we set don't seem to make the difference we anticipate, when the expectations we have seem to compound failure instead of revealing success, and when meeting expectations seems more of the exception than the rule.

According to long-time leadership researcher and author Robert H. Schaffer (1991), "Setting expectations that actually evoke maximum performance is executives' single weakest skill." Other experts agree. In 2012, *Forbes* ran a popular article, "Seven Mistakes Leaders Make in Setting Goals," in which the author asserted that the way leaders set expectations and goals determines their success. "Most managers struggle to find the right balance between being too tough or too easy, and when they overcompensate either way it can cause unintentional complexity" (Ashkenas, 2012). Leadership, at any level, certainly isn't easy; but unclear, vague, roller-coaster pronouncements make many leadership jobs infinitely more difficult than they need to be. Certainly, setting expectations matters. Setting them the right way and communicating them comprehensively matters even more.

Expectations and Communication Within a Culture of Reflective Practice

Leadership expert Michael Fullan, in *Leading in a Culture of Change* (2001), espouses that in order to lead sustainable change, we must set our sights—and expectations—on nothing less than developing the professional excellence and effectiveness of the teachers in our building. We have to address the "inside" workings of our teams. With this in mind, the vision and expectations that we set in a culture of reflective practice are focused on exactly that: asking all teachers to grow as professionals through the refinement of their thinking.

"No part of the work of consistent effective performance is static," states Fullan. "In the midst of any action, there is constant learning, whether it consists of detecting and correcting common errors or discovering new ways to improve" (2001, p. 80). In a culture of reflective practice, we place high value on the ability to think, learn, and grow professionally as educators. Our expectations convey this message, and our communication explicitly articulates this as well. Learning *is* the work we expect teachers to be engaging in every day.

The following six factors contribute to the successful development and implementation of Fundamental 2, which in turn contributes to a robust and successful culture of reflective practice:

a. School has a written plan for implementing a culture of reflective practice.

b. Staff understand their expectation is to seek ways to grow as reflective practitioners and effective instructors utilizing the Reflective Cycle.

c. Administrator has set the expectation that all teachers will work with a coach to meet their professional goals.

d. Administrator articulates the vision for implementing a culture of reflective practice to staff on a regular basis.

e. Coach communicates the role of the coach and various supportive services available to the staff on a regular basis.

f. Administrator or coach shares assessment and implementation data with staff and solicits feedback to inform the plan for implementing a culture of reflective practice.

In a culture of reflective practice, learning *is* the work we expect teachers to be engaging in each day.

We invite you, the capacity-builders, to engage your school staff in dialogue and explore your understanding of these factors, each of which is described in greater detail throughout this chapter. More important than falling entirely in line with what *we* (the authors) mean when we use certain terms or why we've included something and omitted something else are your consensus and the process by which you build it. Feel free to add, delete, or modify the factors in this list to better meet your particular school's contextual needs. We ask only that you keep in mind the spirit and big ideas of this fundamental—minding the related Theory of Action at all times!—and to think very critically about your collective rationale for making any changes before doing so.

Again, the Reflective Cycle can help us refine our thinking about the type of expectations we want to invest our time and energy in for the purpose of creating and communicating with frequency and precision in an ongoing fashion. The questions in Figure 6.1 provide a macro-level (10,000-foot) perspective about this fundamental as a whole. As you continue to read about the factors that make up this fundamental, you will be able to drill deeper, develop a more detailed understanding, and generate a more specific (micro-level) approach to refine your thinking—and your practices.

To help you apply the Reflective Cycle to focus your thinking on each factor, we provide explanations that should help all capacity-builders (administrator, instructional coach, leadership team, and school staff) identify how to build awareness. For each factor, you'll also find a corresponding figure with some guiding questions to get you started. The rest is up to you and will be determined by your goals, context, and identified areas of emphasis.

Factor 2a: School has a written plan for implementing a culture of reflective practice. In some ways, an implementation plan is a "heroic"

FIGURE 6.1

The Reflective Cycle Within Fundamental 2: Expectations and Communication

Building Awareness	*How aware are we of our expectations for staff to grow as reflective practitioners and how to effectively communicate those expectations?*
Working with Intentionality	*How intentionally do we communicate our expectations to staff about our mission to grow as a culture of reflective practice? Do we have a plan for this?*
Assessing Our Impact	*How do we know to what extent the communication of our expectations is having a positive impact on reflective practices in our school? How—and how frequently—do we check in?*
Becoming Responsive	*How do we adapt and adjust our communication plan as a result of our assessments and the shifting needs of the staff?*

act, helping to turn dreams into reality. It not only details our vision but is also a way to make sure that vision is tangible and concrete. Such a written plan should be developed after taking the BTC Site Assessment (Appendix A). After determining the specific strengths, goals, needs, and priorities of your site, the next step is to plan intentionally to strengthen your culture of reflective practice.

This plan will look different in different schools, as there is no fixed formula to follow; every school will need to determine its own areas of emphasis. Capacity-builders in a culture of reflective practice might use a professional protocol to help the staff identify a fundamental on which to focus and then determine the corresponding factors that will lead to growth. By connecting this with the Reflective Cycle, stakeholders can help craft a culture of reflective practice written plan, replete with goals, strategies, timelines, measures of success, and persons responsible for making it happen. It is often said, "What gets planned gets done," and this statement is true here. By bringing all interested parties together to craft the plan, capacity-builders can engage the staff in both *tactical actions* and *purposeful thinking* about their prioritized fundamental. See Figure 6.2 for a set of guiding questions for capacity-builders related to the Reflective Cycle for Factor 2a.

FIGURE 6.2

Reflective Cycle for Factor 2a

Building Awareness	*Do we have a written plan for implementing a culture of reflective practice?*
	Do all staff know what it contains?
	Does every staff member understand the goal and subsequent plan to develop a culture of reflective practice?
	Does every staff member consider their individual contribution to the accomplishment of this plan?
Working with Intentionality	*What is our plan for this?*
Assessing Our Impact	*How will we assess the impact of our actions?*
Becoming Responsive	*How will we respond to the shifting needs of the staff?*

Factor 2b: Staff understand their expectation is to seek ways to grow as reflective practitioners and effective instructors utilizing the Reflective Cycle. It if hasn't been stated clearly enough, the Reflective Cycle is the backbone to our work as reflective practitioners. There was a reason for its introduction in Chapter 2 of this book. This tool provides the frame with which we develop and grow our habits of thought. So it would be a logical next step to provide this resource to teachers as we communicate expectations around this work.

In a culture of reflective practice, there are three characteristics that define effective communication: it is clear, specific, and consistent.

Clear. What point are you trying to get across? Be understandable. Make sure your message includes adequate information and is complete. Ask for clarifying questions when finished. Do teachers understand the purpose for the Reflective Cycle? Do teachers know they are being asked to build their reflective capacity while simultaneously addressing their professional practice?

Specific. Specific and concrete communication makes it easy for teachers to respond. Does your message focus on a single objective? Are people clear that we're asking them to address their *thinking* while *doing*? Do they understand that the focus is on metacognition? Do they understand that they're being asked to become more aware of their reflective habits, to talk about their thinking in PLCs, and to reflect both during *and* after the action using the Reflective Cycle frame?

Consistent. Effective communication in a culture of reflective practice requires leadership to maintain a timely and consistent flow of information. Do you provide intentional and deliberate follow-up and reminders for staff to engage in the work? Are you referencing the quadrants on the Reflective Cycle? Are you reinforcing expectations on a regular basis through conversation, questioning, feedback, and other means?

These three elements—clarity, specificity, and consistency—are essential if we are to ensure that all staff members understand that their overarching expectation is to grow as reflective practitioners utilizing the Reflective Cycle. See Figure 6.3 for a set of guiding questions for capacity-builders related to the Reflective Cycle for Factor 2b.

FIGURE 6.3

Reflective Cycle for Factor 2b

Building Awareness	Do all staff understand that their expectation is to grow as reflective practitioners?
	To what extent does every staff member consider his/her reflective-growth focus when engaging in the "daily grind"?
Working with Intentionality	What is our plan for this?
Assessing Our Impact	How will we assess the impact of our actions?
Becoming Responsive	How will we respond to the shifting needs of the staff?

Factor 2c: Administrator has set the expectation that all teachers will work with a coach to meet their professional goals. The big idea here is that the coach is an invaluable resource. A partner! And if we're going to have a coach, the expectation is that all teachers will use that resource on a regular basis. That part is tight. The loose part is how your partnerships with the coach actually play out. So how do we communicate this to staff clearly, specifically, and consistently? Here are some examples:

Clearly: "The expectation this year is that you will use the coach as a resource for your professional growth on a regular basis—by both initiating requests for support and accepting offers of support from the coach. Throughout the year I will be asking you to share how the coach is partnering with you in your venture to grow as reflective practitioners."

Specifically: "Hello, Mr. Guider. Tell me about your partnership with our coach. How have you been using her lately? What types of conversations are you having? In what ways have you grown professionally with her as your support?"

Consistently: "Good morning, Mrs. Laster. I wanted to follow up after our conversation last week. Were you able to seek out the coach and get him into your classroom for support this week, as we talked about? How did that go? What are you learning through your work with him? What are your next steps? When would be a good time to check in again with you?"

For additional guidance, see Figure 6.4 for a set of questions for capacity-builders related to the Reflective Cycle for Factor 2c.

Factor 2d: Administrator articulates the vision for implementing a culture of reflective practice to staff on a regular basis. The culture of reflective practice is real. It lives and breathes—oozes, as we like to say—in all the nooks and crannies of the school. We speak the language

FIGURE 6.4

Reflective Cycle for Factor 2c

Building Awareness	*Has the administrator communicated the (tight) expectation that all staff are to work with the coach in order to build their own reflective capacity?*
	Has the administrator communicated the (loose) expectation that each teacher-coach relationship can be uniquely pursued in order to best meet each individual teacher's needs?
	Is the administrator aware of the degree to which each staff member seeks out and works with the coach?
Working with Intentionality	*What is our plan for this?*
Assessing Our Impact	*How will we assess the impact of our actions?*
Becoming Responsive	*How will we respond to the shifting needs of the staff?*

of reflection with each other at all times. Reflection isn't an add-on; it's woven into everything we do and every professional conversation we have.

So how do we communicate that expectation? We do so in a variety of ways: verbal, nonverbal, oral, written. We convey our beliefs about what's important by what we celebrate (see Fundamental 3, covered in Chapter 7) and how we allocate our time. When our actions meet our words—when we walk the walk instead of just talking the talk—observers, followers, peers, supervisors, and other stakeholders all understand the true measure of our commitment.

Although we communicate with people every day, it's not often that we adjust our communication style to the audience or the situation. We're experts at differentiation when it comes to classroom instruction, but not so much when it comes to communicating with adults. Consider your methods of communication. If differentiating instruction means creating multiple paths so that students with different abilities, learning styles, and interests can be successful in learning and demonstrating what they have learned, how can we create multiple paths of communication so that teachers can be successful in learning and demonstrating the vision, expectations, and reflective practice we want them to develop? That is what Factor 2d is all about: continuous alignment and refinement around the essentials. See Figure 6.5 for a set of guiding questions for capacity-builders related to the Reflective Cycle for Factor 2d.

FIGURE 6.5

Reflective Cycle for Factor 2d

Building Awareness	Is there a plan for regular communication regarding the concepts of reflective practice and continuous growth?
	To what extent does every staff member engage in reflective dialogue with one another?
Working with Intentionality	What is our plan for this?
Assessing Our Impact	How will we assess the impact of our actions?
Becoming Responsive	How will we respond to the shifting needs of the staff?

"When we expect certain behaviors of others, we are likely to act in ways that make the expected behavior more likely to occur" (Rosenthal & Babad, 1985).

Factor 2e: Coach communicates the role of coach and various supportive services available to staff on a regular basis. With the responsibility to support the school through the professional growth and development of staff, the coach must be skilled in many ways. In addition to the professional qualifications and experiences that prepare a coach for the rigors of this work, an effective coach also possesses certain interpersonal skills and internal dispositions. Above all, one might say, the first qualification listed under any instructional coach job description should be "initiator."

As an initiator, the coach must be able to launch, spark, pioneer, insti-gate, commence, kick off, fire up, and get the ball rolling when it comes to the duties assigned to the role. The big idea is simply this: the coach doesn't sit back and wait. The coach initiates conversations, recruits, offers options for service, and openly seeks opportunities to engage with staff. And there are many ways to do this: through a newsletter, visits to team meetings, one-on-one conversations, postings on the staff room bulletin board, quick promotional videos posted on YouTube—you name it. The end result is that *all* staff members clearly understand the benefits from working with their coach and know how to make that connection happen. See Figure 6.6 for a set of guiding questions for the coach and other capacity-builders related to the Reflective Cycle for Factor 2e.

FIGURE 6.6

Reflective Cycle for Factor 2e

Building Awareness	Has the coach clarified the position and its potential benefits to all staff?
	Does every staff member understand how the coach can support his/her reflective growth?
Working with Intentionality	What is our plan for this?
Assessing Our Impact	How will we assess the impact of our actions?
Becoming Responsive	How will we respond to the shifting needs of the staff?

 Effective coaches don't sit back and wait. They make it happen.

Factor 2f: Administrator or coach shares assessment and imple-mentation data with staff and solicits feedback to inform the plan for implementing a culture of reflective practice. In a culture of reflective practice, we seek commitment over compliance. Therefore, as

we work through the BTC Site Assessment (Appendix A), unpacking the fundamentals and their factors, we engage in continuous dialogue with staff around the work. Everyone contributes to the plan, which leads to *commitment* (which is 100 times more powerful than simple *buy-in*) to the entire process and goal.

Again, there is no exact formula that must be followed here. This is leadership inviting the staff to participate in authentic communication and corporate reflection guided by the fundamentals of reflective practice. When the involved stakeholders look at the data, analyze their situation, and contribute to the plan, the likelihood that (1) the plan is solid and (2) those stakeholders are fully "in it to win it" increases immensely. Figure 6.7 provides a set of guiding questions for capacity-builders related to the Reflective Cycle for Factor 2f.

FIGURE 6.7

Reflective Cycle for Factor 2f

Building Awareness	Do all staff have the opportunity to provide input into the plan for implementing a culture of reflective practice?
	To what extent is every staff member's voice heard in the ongoing revisions of the implementation plan?
Working with Intentionality	What is our plan for this?
Assessing Our Impact	How will we assess the impact of our actions?
Becoming Responsive	How will we respond to the shifting needs of the staff?

Bringing Fundamental 2 to Life

In the following two scenarios, you'll read about some capacity-builders' efforts to implement Fundamental 2 within their schools. Though the characters are fictional, they're amalgams of real human beings, compiled from case studies within schools we have worked and consulted with over the past several years. After the scenarios, we'll offer some discussion to distill a few of our key learnings for this fundamental.

Scenario 1

Members of the leadership team in School 1 have just finished writing their school performance plan for the year. To create it, they looked at school data, identified the lowest scores and subgroups, set new percentage goals, reallocated some resources, and submitted it to the district. The following week, the leadership team shares the plan with everyone at the staff meeting.

The principal starts off by stating, "Schoolwide, our lowest-performing subgroup last year was our ELLs, with a 24 percent achievement rate. We have to work to bring that number up. So this year, we're going to target our ELLs throughout all subjects and grade levels. I'm going to provide support through heavy accountability, making sure we're all working toward this goal as best as we can this year. All grade levels and departments will give common assessments and report scores weekly. Students who have not scored in the passing range will be tracked and given small-group remediation. Teams will meet twice a week for common planning. Lesson plans should reflect how you'll be targeting your ELLs in lessons and need to be submitted weekly to the office."

A low murmur of frustration and resentment quietly fills the room, as the principal continues on with his seemingly endless set of expectations based on the school improvement plan. It's not difficult to see that teachers are discouraged and overwhelmed as they file out of the room at the end of the meeting.

Scenario 2

The principal of School 2 doesn't want teachers in his school to become so consumed with their day-to-day challenges that their connection to the vision and school improvement plan weakens, so he brings his teachers together after the hubbub at the start of the year has died down.

"Our singular focus this year is to increase student achievement by developing ourselves professionally. We're just a few weeks into our new year and already have a lot on our plates each day. Is what we're spending our time on contributing to this 'one thing'?" he asks. "Do we have things that need to be reprioritized? This week in your team and department meetings, discuss how you're spending your most precious resource: time. Are you getting to the things that matter most? Are you developing yourself professionally? Are we growing as reflective practitioners? What can we do as a collective staff to support one another in a deeper way? I can't wait to hear about your conversations this week."

To follow up with the topic of the staff meeting and to model what they are asking of the staff, the principal decides to facilitate an optional book study and the coach offers to facilitate an optional lesson study/idea group around lesson planning. Through weekly e-mails of encouragement and thought-provoking questions, as well as visits to PLC team meetings, both capacity-builders continue to draw attention and set the stage for the understanding that no matter what an individual's instructional focus, there is power in the collective (and individual) ability to reflect frequently, accurately, and deeply.

In addition to this work, the principal sets tight/loose expectations that all teachers will work with their instructional coach (nonnegotiable, or *tight*) in whatever partnership or configuration best leads them to the accomplishment of their agreed-upon goals (flexible, or *loose*). Both principal and coach speak the language of reflection and encourage teachers to do the same, modeling such vocabulary and highlighting when hearing positive examples. By the end of the first quarter, the staff is feeling more empowered than ever before as they openly begin to discuss their professional growth with one another and the school leadership.

What's Really Going On?

In these scenarios, the leaders of School 1 erroneously believe that vaguely targeted "end results" provide the necessary expectations to make gains. At the same time, they also incorrectly reason that expectations need to be spelled out in detail and held to heavy scrutiny. The principal in School 1 adheres (whether indirectly or not) to the faulty belief that if we address teacher actions through expectations, we'll see positive results. Although this belief does hold some merit, it also falls vastly short.

School 2 is well on its way toward developing a strong culture of reflective practice. The leadership understands that with explicit expectations and communication synchronization, they can strengthen the inside workings of the collective school team. They're focused on capacity-building: lasting, enduring change that comes from the development of thinking habits that address commitment to the goal and mission, rather than compliance to supervisory directives.

We can alter someone's behavior, but if mindset does not accompany the shift, the change will be limited, at best. Expectations must address teacher *thinking* as much as they address teacher *doing*.

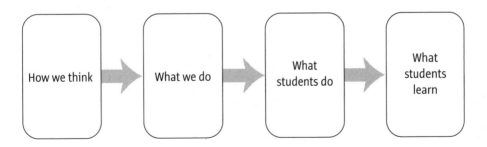

Wrapping Up

Thinking and doing aren't totally separate beasts. As capacity-builders, our aim is to address both simultaneously, rather than either one independently. Our communication and our expectations must be grounded in the thinking that *accompanies* the doing. As we've said before, shifting action doesn't always result in shifted thinking, but shifting thinking will *always* result in shifted action. It's teacher thinking that will drive student learning.

Fundamental 3:
Celebration and Calibration

Fundamental 3 Theory of Action: *If* we consistently celebrate our successes and calibrate our understanding and practices, *then* all our actions will coordinate to propel us powerfully toward a robust and resilient culture of reflective practice.

Success begets success. Chances are you've heard this before and probably nodded your head in general agreement. But have you ever stopped to deeply consider the science behind the cliché? These three small words have powerful ramifications when it comes to shifting the direction of an organization and realizing tangible results.

Scientifically speaking, we're referring to a concept called *psychological momentum*. Defined first by researchers Iso-Ahola and Mobily in 1980, psychological momentum is described as "an added or *gained* psychological power that changes a person's view of him/herself or of others, or others' views of him/her and themselves" (p. 392). Note the word *gained*. We see this phenomenon most prominently in sports. Players or teams, for reasons not fully understood, will suddenly go on a roll and experience an upswing of success, and often that big play (or series of big plays) will turn the tide of the game. Iso-Ahola (Iso-Ahola & Dotson, 2014) further explains, "One gains psychological advantage by his or her own successful performance and this advantage propels one toward additional successes" (p. 20).

To wit: On October 17, 2004, the Boston Red Sox, aching to reverse an 86-year-old trend of *not* winning baseball's World Series, sat one run behind with just three outs to go, facing elimination by their archrival New York Yankees. Down 3 games to 0 in the American League Championship Series, they needed to do the unthinkable: defeat the Yanks that night, then win the next three games—which no team in baseball history had ever done.

In a dynamic and mesmerizing manner, the Sox won Game 4 that night, thanks to a hit batter, a stolen base, and a single in the 9th inning, followed by David "Big Papi" Ortiz's 12th-inning home run. And the psychological momentum took hold.

Red Sox players and coaches shared their mantra: *Just win today. And watch out, because if we win today, we can win tomorrow.* Rather than focus on the enormity of the task ahead, they keyed in on the moment. And they relaxed. One game at a time made their challenge do-able. As Red Sox outfielder Manny Ramirez stated, "We found a way to make baseball easy" (*Boston Globe*, 2004, p. 11).

They won Game 5 on another Ortiz hit in the 14th inning. Then, venturing into the Yankees' lair in the Bronx, they won Game 6 and finally obliterated their enemies in the decisive Game 7 by a score of 10 to 3. By then, the confidence oozing out of the Red Sox clubhouse stood in stark contrast to the despair emanating from the Yankees' body language.

The World Series itself, not surprisingly, was simply a coronation, as the Red Sox extended their dominant winning streak to eight, sweeping the St. Louis Cardinals in four games and never trailing in the entire series. They were most definitely *on a roll*.

 Psychological momentum? It's real!

In *Good to Great*, author Jim Collins refers to this phenomenon as the "flywheel" effect (2001, p. 164). He explains that a flywheel is an incredibly heavy wheel that takes huge effort to push. Keep pushing and the flywheel builds momentum. Keep pushing and eventually it starts to help turn itself and generate its own energy, spinning faster and faster, driven by its own weight. Suddenly, what once took so much effort becomes effortless and self-sustaining. The flywheel is propelled by the "magic" of momentum.

"If you have a culture that understands how to celebrate its successes, people will remain motivated, achievements will be valued more completely, and deeper relationships will be forged within the group" says John Coleman (2012), founder of VIA Agency, on *Inc.*'s list of 500 of America's fastest-growing companies. By celebrating success, we reinforce the motivation that will carry us through the next achievement.

Waste of Time or Time Well Spent?

Despite good intentions, too often workplace celebrations result in eye rolling and sideline gossip. Well-meaning rewards are seen as political ploys or unattainable targets intended for top performers only. They end up contributing to pessimism rather than boosting morale. A Gallup poll published in 2016 found that almost 70 percent of workers across the United States feel disengaged and dissatisfied with their jobs, and their flagging employee motivation ends up costing U.S. businesses between $450 and $550 billion each year. Forty-one percent of employees indicated that they're unhappy with the frequency of the feedback and recognition they *do* receive (www.gallup.com/topic/employee_engagement.aspx). How does this happen?

Celebrations miss the mark when not directly calibrated to the expectations of the organization.

Celebrations become blunders when they are not directly connected with consistent and frequent calibration to the expectations of the organization. When it comes to recognizing and celebrating employees and their achievements, many managers take a random approach. If they were instead to align their recognition with business goals and organizational vision, they could drive performance, profitability, and productivity in new and successful ways. "World class managers understand this concept almost intuitively," agree Marcus Buckingham and Curt Coffman in an executive book summary of *First, Break All the Rules,* "and they see their role as focusing people toward performance" (1999b, p. 5).

Simply put, for celebrations to be effective, they must be aligned to the organization's vision and identified through frequent calibration to organizational expectations. In the business world, calibration is referred to as *performance management*: a systematic process by which an agency involves its employees, as individuals and members of a group, in improving organizational effectiveness in the accomplishment of agency mission and goals (see www.opm.gov for more information).

Defined by Merriam-Webster, *calibration* refers to the act of "standardizing by determining the deviation from a standard so as to ascertain the proper correction factors" or "measuring something in an exact and precise way."

We see calibration as keeping a finger on the pulse of an organization, if you will—the deliberate act of pausing, reflecting on current practices, identifying successes and trajectories, asking tough questions about what isn't going well, and determining new courses of action. Calibration is the realignment of certain priorities and the validation of others. It keeps all stakeholders focused and engaged on the work at hand. Essentially, calibration is an act of *institutional reflection*.

Calibration is a time of inquiry as well as a time of celebration. One cannot effectively exist without the other.

Rarely do we see or hear workplace celebrations connected to workplace calibration. They're frequently kept as separate components—we celebrate when things go well, and we calibrate when things go astray. And for many organizations, the celebrations do not often match the outcomes of calibration efforts.

Frederic Laloux, author of *Reinventing Organizations*, delineates the type of conversation that should occur between managers and their teams. He describes what the business world calls "appraisal discussions"—the moments when "contributions are celebrated and recognized, and where, without judgment, we inquire truthfully into what isn't going so well: places where our knowledge, experience, talent, or attitude fall short of what our roles require" (2014, p. 184). In other words, calibration is a time of inquiry as well as a time of celebration. Calibration and celebration are part of the same conversation, inexplicably woven. One cannot be brought to complete fruition without the other.

Great workplaces are great because their members are committed to engaging in authentic and transparent conversation about accomplishments, failures, learning, growth, and everything in between. These conversations are driven by the vision to succeed.

Rajeev Bhardwaj (2016), vice president for Sun Life Financial, one of the oldest and largest life insurance companies in the world, says, "An organization's success is the sum total of micro-successes that its employees experience each day" (https://www.entrepreneur.com/article/273004). Through frequent calibration and strategic celebration, we build momentum that propels us forward, toward exponential growth. Success begets success.

Celebration and Calibration Within a Culture of Reflective Practice

Celebrating success and engaging in continuous calibration to garner more success may be two of the most underused yet most powerful tools in your toolbox. In a culture of reflective practice, they are inextricably bound to the expectations you've established by following the guidance offered in Chapter 6. And as with Fundamentals 1 and 2, this fundamental must be deliberately and strategically developed in order to ensure alignment, with the question "How often will we engage in these practices?" at the top of the list.

The following two factors contribute to the successful development and implementation of Fundamental 3, contributing to a robust and successful culture of reflective practice:

a. Time is routinely set aside for small and big celebrations of teacher-capacity growth, progress toward goals, and other successes.

b. Staff review tools (instructional framework, research, data, site assessment and implementation plan, etc.) on a regular basis to calibrate understanding, expectations, vocabulary, and professional practices.

We invite you, the capacity-builders, to engage your school staff in dialogue and explore your understanding of these factors, each of which is described in greater detail throughout this chapter. More important than falling entirely in line with what *we* (the authors) mean when we use certain terms or why we've included something and omitted something else are your consensus and the process by which you build it. Feel free to add, delete, or modify the factors in this list to better meet your particular school's contextual needs. We ask only that you keep in mind the spirit and big ideas of this fundamental—minding the Theory of Action at all times!—and to think critically about your collective rationale for making any changes before doing so.

The Reflective Cycle can help us refine our thinking about how we celebrate our successes and calibrate our understanding and practices in a consistent, intentional manner. The questions in Figure 7.1 provide a macro-level (10,000-foot) perspective about this fundamental as a whole. As you continue to read about the factors that make up this fundamental, you will be able to drill deeper, develop a more detailed understanding, and generate a more specific (micro-level) approach to refine your thinking—and your practices.

To help you apply the Reflective Cycle to focus your thinking on each factor, we provide explanations that should help all capacity-builders (administrator, instructional coach, leadership team, and school staff) identify how to build awareness. For each factor, you'll also find a corresponding figure with some guiding questions to get you started. The rest is up to you and will be determined by your goals, context, and identified areas of emphasis.

FIGURE 7.1

The Reflective Cycle Within Fundamental 3: Celebration and Calibration

Building Awareness	How aware are we of the need to recognize and celebrate success as we engage in frequent calibration of our practices?
Working with Intentionality	How intentionally do we plan for engaging in the process of calibration? How intentionally do we link celebrations to our calibration?
Assessing Our Impact	How do we know to what extent the celebration and calibration of our expectations is having a positive impact on reflective practices in our school? How— and how frequently—do we check in?
Becoming Responsive	How do we adapt and adjust our celebration and calibration strategy as a result of our assessments and the shifting needs of the staff?

Factor 3a: Time is routinely set aside for small and big celebrations of teacher capacity growth, progress toward goals, and other successes. In *The Five Disciplines of PLC Leaders* (2011), author Timothy Kanold outlines four elements that make celebrations successful: identification, criteria, rewards, and storytelling. With all due respect, we'd like to reorder the list and add a new, equally essential element: timing.

1. **Effective timing.** Timing is everything. And it's simple. Before specifying, however, let's identify what it's *not*. It's not quarterly, biannually, or even end-of-year. And it's *not silent*. Effective timing is recognizing, rewarding, and celebrating successes as they occur. According to the published study *Timing in Reward and Decision Processes*, "The time of reward has several important influences on reward processing. The economic value of reward decreases with increasing delays. This temporal discounting may lead to the preference of sooner, smaller rewards over larger, later rewards" (Bermudez & Schultz, 2014). In essence, smaller rewards provided immediately create a bigger impact. Does this mean we shouldn't give monthly recognition at the staff meeting? Not at all. Can we send a daily or weekly email to highlight small successes in addition to monthly recognitions? Absolutely. What matters is that small and big victories are recognized often.

2. **Effective criteria.** Celebration is most effective when it's given in the context of a larger goal or schoolwide vision. Our valuation of this work is centered firmly around the development of deeper habits of reflective practice. In today's operating school cultures, we're taught to fear failure and hide our mistakes, yet in a culture of reflective practice, we celebrate learning, risk taking, growth of mindset, and yes (gasp!), even failure. It's natural to want to celebrate the positive outcome, to *toast the bottom line*, if you will, but the focus must also highlight the journey and

the hurdles that were overcome along the way. There's more to be gained from taking the opportunity to recognize the process than the end result alone. Doing so sends the message that it's OK to try, and if it doesn't work, we learn from it, adjust, and keep "failing forward" until we figure out what success looks like. Let's create criteria that place emphasis on exactly what we value. This should lead us right back to the expectations set in Fundamental 2.

3. **Effective identification.** Deciding who to honor can often pose the greatest challenge when it comes to celebrations. With an overall purpose to celebrate the development of stronger habits of thought and reflective practices, we can be more strategic in our identification process. This will lead us to folks on staff who aren't necessarily the typical high-flyers. It'll mean we celebrate a new teacher who's had a big "aha!" about classroom management or a veteran who is tirelessly trying to find the best instructional approach for a struggling learner. It may even be the identification of a team that has shifted collectively in their thinking about PLCs. Whatever the reason, with the right criteria in place and the purpose for celebration clear in our minds, identification will naturally follow.

4. **Effective recognition and rewards.** Author Scott Geller states, "When people discuss the difficulties in reaching a milestone, the accomplishment is meaningful. When managers listen to these discussions with sincere interest and appreciation, the incident becomes even more significant. When a tangible reward is distributed . . . a mechanism is established to support the memory of this experience and promote its value" (2016, p. 288). Recognition is an important psychological need, which means it is an absolutely critical piece in this work. However, there are times when adding an extrinsic reward will also serve a valuable purpose. Whether tangible or intangible, recognition

and rewards serve as communication tools to reinforce our culture of reflective practice.

5. **Effective storytelling.** People often get rewarded for great work, but the actual story of what they did—the struggles they overcame, the thought processes behind the achievement—isn't always shared. There's power in the story, as our brains respond differently to narrative than to other forms of communication. Stories create a sense of closeness, encouraging connection with others and fostering a sense of community. Not only do they move everyone forward toward the same goal, but we also learn more about one other and know who to go to for help. When celebrating the successes in your building, be sure to include the stories behind them and actively seek out ways to share across a variety of media—video, a story bank, social networking sites, newsletters, and websites. It's yet another way to recognize and reward each and every small win.

See Figure 7.2 for a set of guiding questions for capacity-builders related to the Reflective Cycle for Factor 3a.

Factor 3b: Staff review tools (instructional framework, research, data, site assessment and implementation plan, etc.) on a regular basis to calibrate understanding, expectations, vocabulary, and professional practices. Authentic calibration doesn't happen in isolation. At the same time, it doesn't have to involve all staff members sitting down together with the principal each week to pore over school expectations. Authentic calibration asks everyone to engage as individuals, in teams, and collectively as a whole staff in transparent dialogue about current realities. It is, as we said earlier, an act of *institutional reflection.*

In a culture of reflective practice, leaders understand the importance of and make time for schoolwide calibration to assess the "strength of the workplace," as Buckingham and Coffman have termed it (1999a, p. 29). Calibration does not just mean being responsive to problems that arise; it's an

FIGURE 7.2

Reflective Cycle for Factor 3a

Building Awareness	*Do we have a celebration system?*
	What do we celebrate?
	Does everyone on staff understand why we celebrate?
	How might we identify celebrations through our calibration process?
	How might we create celebration criteria?
	How will we introduce this to the staff?
Working with Intentionality	*What is our plan for this?*
Assessing Our Impact	*How will we assess the impact of our actions?*
Becoming Responsive	*How will we respond to the shifting needs of the staff?*

assessment that allows leaders to determine progress toward goals and that allows teachers to measure their alignment with school expectations. It occurs frequently, accurately, and deeply in order to keep all stakeholders engaged and focused on the clear and meaningful expectation of developing as reflective practitioners. Let's take a closer look at the particulars that make this process successful.

1. **Frequency.** Frequent check-ins are not *in addition to* the work of the school leaders. They *are* the work of the school leaders. There are many different ways to engage in the practice of calibration, but they all start and end with frequent contact with students, teachers, grade levels, departments, parents—in other words, all stakeholders. The more frequently (and we'll add *consistently*) leaders check in with those they lead, the greater the understanding they'll have about the realities of their school and the more effectively they'll be able to adjust and align their decisions to the changing needs of staff. Once frequent contact

with stakeholders has been established, the next step will be to determine when and how to foster calibration among staff on a frequent basis. This may occur in PLC, department, or team meetings, or it may happen at monthly staff meetings. It may be a three-question survey sent out every couple weeks or a question posed via e-mail each week that fosters team conversation and reflection. Calibration will evolve differently depending on each school and staff. What matters most is creating an environment for it to occur on a consistent and frequent basis.

2. **Accuracy.** There are three ways to ensure the accuracy of calibration efforts:

   a. *Keep it focused on the standard.* Because calibration is about measuring performance and outcomes against a standard, we must make sure that we keep our standard of *the continuous growth of professionals through the development of deep reflective habits* always before us. We can't take our eyes off the goal—it's what we're measuring ourselves against.

   b. *Engage others in transparent dialogue.* Jay Samit, author and public speaker, says, "Nothing helps calibrate reality [more] than the honest perceptions of those who work closest to you" (Carucci, 2016). With this in mind, calibration work must occur through dialogue with others.

   c. *Create a safe environment.* "It is absolutely critical to have both an authentic and transparent work environment," says Marc de Grandpre, 2016 Doug Hamilton Executive of the Year (Smith, 2013). "How can your company learn, grow and succeed if people are afraid to be themselves, voice their opinions and genuinely show that they care about . . . the team?"

3. **Depth.** In a culture of reflective practice, calibration is about *checking in* rather than *checking up*. The goal is not to hear the latest test scores, to scold folks for not yet meeting the expectations,

or to remind everyone about what you think is important; the purpose is to ask the right questions and engage in careful listening. To garner accurate results and drive deeper reflection, questions must be posed strategically. Here are a few examples:

a. What are the current priorities of the school? Are those priorities leading us forward?

b. From your point of view, how has thinking shifted across the school?

c. What's the most difficult part of staff transparency?

d. Do teachers feel safe to openly discuss their growth as professionals?

e. Do the expectations of the school support teacher growth?

f. Do you see your leadership team often enough? How have your leaders supported your development this year?

The explanations and examples just provided can shape the intentionality needed for successful calibration. See also Figure 7.3 for a set of guiding questions for capacity-builders related to the Reflective Cycle for Factor 3b.

FIGURE 7.3

Reflective Cycle for Factor 3b

Building Awareness	What does calibration look like in our building?
	Who is involved in the process?
	To what extent do we engage in deep conversation around the current realities?
	How accurate are our perceptions and understandings of school culture as it relates to a culture of reflective practice?
Working with Intentionality	What is our plan for this?
Assessing Our Impact	How will we assess the impact of our actions?
Becoming Responsive	How will we respond to the shifting needs of the staff?

Bringing Fundamental 3 to Life

In the following two scenarios, you'll read about some capacity-builders' efforts to implement Fundamental 3 within their schools. Though the characters are fictional, they're amalgams of real human beings, compiled from case studies within schools we have worked and consulted with over the past several years. After the scenarios, we'll offer some discussion to distill a few of our key learnings for this fundamental.

Scenario 1

It's the end of the second quarter, and the staff at School 1 file into the library for the monthly staff meeting. The principal shares that the leadership team has recently met and put together a new detention policy for the school. "After seeing the spike in detentions last quarter and hearing your complaints about behavior consequences, we've revised our policy and are excited to share what we've come up with," he states.

There are several audible sighs in the room and an under-the-breath "What now?" as the team steps up to share the new protocol for addressing behavior issues. Thirty minutes later the floor is turned back over to the principal, who is now joined by the instructional coach. "It's time for celebrations!" he shares. "Your coach has compiled all of the end-of-quarter data, and we have some classes that showed great achievement. Let's give these folks a big round of applause. I have a Starbucks gift card for each of them."

Someone snickers, and quiet snarking breaks out across the room. "Let me guess. I can name the winners now," someone sarcastically says. "Sure won't be me," another whispers. "Not with the group I have this year." Several names are called, and there's an awkward exchange of pleasantries and a few claps. The staff meeting ends as quickly as it started.

Scenario 2

It's time for the monthly faculty meeting at School 2, and the staff has been asked to bring devices today. As they file into the room, they're asked to log in to a site called *Padlet,* an online virtual bulletin board that allows people to express their thoughts on a common topic and read the responses of others. Today's reflective question is "Do teachers feel safe openly discussing their growth as professionals in our school? Please explain your answer."

Once everyone has arrived and the meeting officially starts, the principal asks everyone to move from the online discussion to table discussions, this time focused on the next question: "How can our school community better support your professional growth?" After another round of hearty discussion, the principal thanks the staff for their transparency, honesty, and ideas. She then announces that it's time to highlight some of the learning that has taken place over the past month. She asks the instructional coach to start the video that she and the coach created for this month's meeting. The video draws attention to three teachers in the building, telling a short story of how each has encountered struggle in the classroom and worked to refine their thinking in order to work through the struggle successfully. At the end of the video, the staff gives a round of applause. The principal then opens up the floor for others to share small stories of a recent success or a current struggle. Many open up, including a new teacher who shares that she loves hearing how fellow teachers think through problems because it's really helping her know where to place her focus during lessons. Others nod their heads in agreement.

As the meeting comes to a close, the principal shares her own story of learning through the refinement of her thinking as she encountered a struggle recently. She thanks the staff for supporting her growth as a leader and shares that she's excited to visit their team meetings this week to hear folks dissect their thinking in deeper ways. The meeting is called to a close.

What's Really Going On?

At first glance, we see two similar monthly meetings led by principals who engage the staff in slightly different ways. Both are attempting to incorporate the factors of Fundamental 3 into their faculty meetings, both have the best of intentions, and both show evidence of listening to staff and responding intentionally. Yet upon closer look, the manner in which each leader calibrates and celebrates is very distinct. The principal in School 1 is focused solely on actions, behaviors, and outcomes, whereas the principal in School 2 has a deliberate focus on capacity-building. The results are telling, but not surprising.

Altering someone's behavior might lead to compliance. Affecting someone's thinking will result in commitment.

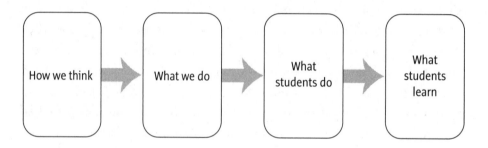

Wrapping Up

Aligning celebrations and calibrations to our work of growing reflective practitioners is an essential component of developing a culture of reflective practice. Both must be firmly grounded in what matters most: creating a culture where *cultivating strong habits of thought* is highly valued and drives the daily decisions that administrator, coach, and teachers make.

8

Fundamental 4: Goal Setting and Follow-Through

 Fundamental 4 Theory of Action: *If* we set meaningful goals—to address student achievement and our professional reflective capacity—and work purposefully and relentlessly to achieve them, *then* we will collectively bolster our establishment of a comprehensive and unified culture of reflective practice.

At the conclusion of the 2012 Summer Olympics in London, U.S. swimmer Michael Phelps had reached the breaking point. His accomplishments in the pool—23 gold medals over four Olympics experiences—paled by comparison to the sheer mental and physical exhaustion he felt.

Leading up to London, swimming had become a job, not fun. The joy he had once felt had turned to drudgery, and his priorities shifted. More interested in post-race parties than pre-race training, he had gained weight and endured public embarrassment due to drug and alcohol issues, yet he had still made his way to the Olympics. "Hate to say this," Phelps said in an interview for *Sports Illustrated*, "but in London I was going through the motions. . . . I wanted it to end" (Layden, 2016, p. 34).

And so it did. He retired. And in a bizarre and sobering twist for the world's most decorated Olympian in history, he hit rock bottom. Late in 2014, he was arrested for drunk driving and checked himself into rehab.

Then something clicked in Phelps. He rediscovered the joy and the drive. What had begun to be an issue of compliance—the long hours in the pool, the weight room, and the training centers—were once again something he committed himself to. He shoveled the dirt off his mission and passion and dove back into the pool, clean and focused.

And he set a goal: he would make the Olympic team and compete in Rio in 2016. And not just compete; he would dominate. He rededicated himself to the pursuit of excellence, quite aware that, at age 30, he would need to allocate more tenacity to his workouts, more ferocity to his swim schedule, and more relentlessness to his pursuits.

The power of his mind—committing to the clear, pledged goal and following through with whatever steps were necessary to achieve it—had more impact than what appeared to be freakishly long arms, webbed feet, and gills accounting for his swimming success. And the rest is history: five more golds and a silver. Phelps had become the greatest Olympian ever.

Connecting to Schools

In Kennewick, Washington, the school board and superintendent Dr. Paul Rosier weren't perfecting the butterfly stroke and chasing Olympic glory; instead, they had grown impatient with the low reading scores across the district. Not only was there a lack of proficiency; the scores seemed to have plateaued, and progress was stalling. Then came the day of reckoning. The board and the superintendent agreed to an audacious student achievement goal: 90 percent of the district's 3rd grade students would be reading at or above grade level within four years.

At the time, Kennewick's overall reading proficiency level sat at around 70 percent, with a span of 40 percentage points between the highest-achieving school and the lowest. As the 90 percent goal was unveiled, principals threatened revolt. "We all but mutinied," stated Washington Elementary School's principal, Dave Montague (Fielding, Kerr, & Rosier, 2004). Teachers cried foul. The community was in shock. Nevertheless, as the hubbub died down, all the stakeholders rolled up their sleeves, came together at the table, and started planning for how they were going to accomplish the goal.

> How would you respond to an audacious 90 percent achievement goal? How would your teachers? Your students? Your community?

The district asked the schools to set similarly audacious goals to feed the district's goal. Then principals recruited each individual teacher to set classroom goals that were equally lofty—so that if they met their goals, it would be simply a matter of gravitational math that the grades, departments, schools, and district would meet the 90 percent goal as well.

With the lofty goal firmly entrenched throughout the system, teachers began to follow through with their plans. They maximized every instructional moment. They analyzed students' skills relentlessly and provided interventions tirelessly. They collaborated as often as possible. They added instructional time to literacy instruction, demonstrating their level of commitment. And they aligned their practices with one another's—all part of the master plan to meet their goals.

For a couple years, schools knocked on the door of 90 percent, but there was no significant uptick in the district's statistics as a whole. Zealous teachers, principals, board members, and parents redoubled their efforts, analyzed their plans, and refined their approaches. And then it happened. Five years into the Era of Reading, three schools surpassed the 90 percent threshold. Over the following three years, 9 of the district's 13 elementary schools hit the 90 percent goal a total of 24 times, and the district's total 3rd grade achievement climbed to 88 percent. So the district upped the goal to 95 percent.

At Washington Elementary School, Year 7 brought a return of 99 percent, with just one student scoring below proficiency on the state reading exam. Amid the celebration, one teacher called for quiet and said, "Wait a minute. We're one student short. What's our plan to help him?" The party turned into an intervention-strategizing session.

This is what happens when teachers achieve a certain level of commitment to the vision. As you've read, we refer to this as being *mission-driven*. Teachers work interdependently to achieve their commonly agreed-upon goals, they partner to discuss methods and approaches, and they analyze performance to identify strengths and gaps with the intent to blanket students with opportunities to learn and grow. In the words of Principal Montague, "All kids can learn. We can teach them. No exceptions. No excuses" (Fielding et al., 2004, p. 28).

Goal Setting and Follow-Through Within a Culture of Reflective Practice

Goal setting and follow-through play integral roles in the development and achievement of any vision and any set of expectations. In a culture of reflective practice, each is carefully woven into the fabric of self-reflection—with the understanding that refinement of thinking leads to success of action. Goal setting includes a reflective component. Follow-through is centered on the development of thought. It's about crafting and perfecting a metacognitive fitness routine that strengthens our professional capacity and drives us to achieving the impossible.

 Refinement of thinking leads to success of action.

The following five factors contribute to the successful development and implementation of Fundamental 4, contributing to a robust and successful culture of reflective practice:

a. Administrator meets with each teacher at the beginning of the year to set SMART student achievement–based goals.

b. Staff take the Reflective Self-Assessment Tool to identify their current reflective stage on the Continuum of Self-Reflection.

c. Staff identify a personal—SMART-R—goal to grow as reflective practitioners, using the Reflective Cycle.

d. Staff work diligently toward their individual goals and strategic action steps in order to continuously grow as reflective practitioners.

e. Administrator intentionally follows up with staff on a regular basis to discuss progress toward goals and professional growth.

We invite you, the capacity-builders, to engage your school staff in dialogue and explore your understanding of these factors, each of which is described in greater detail throughout this chapter. More important than falling entirely in line with what *we* (the authors) mean when we use certain terms or why we've included something and omitted something else are your consensus and the process by which you build it. Feel free to add, delete, or modify the factors in this list to better meet your particular school's contextual needs. We ask only that you keep in mind the spirit and big ideas of this fundamental—minding the Theory of Action at all times!—and to think very critically about your collective rationale for making any changes before doing so.

The Reflective Cycle can help us refine our thinking about how our goals truly drive our focus, our actions, and our consistent follow-through. The questions in Figure 8.1 provide a macro-level (10,000-foot) perspective about this fundamental as a whole. As you continue to read about the factors that make up this fundamental, you will be able to drill deeper, develop a more detailed understanding, and generate a more specific (micro-level) approach to refine your thinking—and your practices.

FIGURE 8.1

The Reflective Cycle Within Fundamental 4: Goal Setting and Follow-Through

Building Awareness	What does goal setting and follow-through look like in our building? How aware are we of the process to set SMART-R goals and establish consistent follow-through with staff?
Working with Intentionality	How deliberately do we include reflection in the goal-setting process? Do we have a plan for ongoing follow-through?
Assessing Our Impact	How do we know if our goal-setting and follow-through process is having a positive impact on reflective practices in our school? How—and how frequently—do we check in?
Becoming Responsive	How do we adapt and adjust our goal-setting and follow-through process as a result of our assessments and the shifting needs of the staff?

To help you apply the Reflective Cycle to focus your thinking on each factor, we provide explanations that should help all capacity-builders (administrator, instructional coach, leadership team, and school staff) identify how to build awareness. For each factor, you'll also find a corresponding figure with some guiding questions to get you started. The rest is up to you and will be determined by your goals, context, and identified areas of emphasis.

Factor 4a: Administrator meets with each teacher at the beginning of the year to set SMART student achievement goals. Student learning is at the heart of all of our work and the very reason we push to develop ourselves as reflective practitioners. In a culture of reflective practice, this means kicking off our goal setting by establishing goals centered on student learning. To make them meaningful and outcome-based, we use the commonly known SMART goal format; however, we provide a preferred definition using the acronym SMART:

- *Strategically aligned.* Do the goals of individual teachers align with those of their teams? If teachers and teams meet their goals, their success should feed the achievement of the school-wide and districtwide goals. All our goals—and our work—should be that closely related. The more people we have rowing the same boat in the same direction, the more efficient and success-ful we'll all be.

- *Measureable.* Let's begin our definition by using a counter-example: if we can't measure our progress, we'll never know if we're on the right path or have met our goal. It's only reason-able to expect that we can measure the outcomes of our work to effectively monitor and gauge our levels of success.

- *Attainable, Aggressive, Audacious.* Many folks prefer to iden-tify an attainable, *achievable* level of expected performance. We consider this the lowest rung on the ladder that stands in front of us. With very little effort, we should be able to meet that expectation. Why not press harder, aim higher, and go for a more aggressive goal? Or let's take a lesson from the Kennewick School District, the home of that "audacious" 90 percent reading goal you just read about, and set the bar so high that we appear to be out of our minds (Fielding et al., 2004). It's just that sort of stretch goal that can redefine what we're capable of achieving!

- *Relevant.* The concept of relevance speaks to the idea that the goal and the content make sense to the teacher, the team, and the context of the school in question. Embedded in the SMART goal framework is an action plan, and the relevance of each action step within that plan should be clear, intentional, and likely to support the achievement of the goal.

- *Time-bound.* All stakeholders should be well aware of the param-eters of the goal's timeline: When will the final measurement occur? Along the way, what benchmark data will we collect to monitor progress, and when will these assessments take place? The answers to such questions are provided in advance to pro-vide clarity about the scope and sequence of the goal period.

See Figure 8.2 for a set of guiding questions for capacity-builders related to the Reflective Cycle for Factor 4a.

FIGURE 8.2

Reflective Cycle for Factor 4a

Building Awareness	Do all staff members understand the purpose for goal setting and hold the belief that it benefits their growth as reflective practitioners?
	Does each staff member understand the SMART acronym?
	Do we set SMART student learning outcomes at the beginning of our goal-setting process?
Working with Intentionality	What is our plan for this?
Assessing Our Impact	How will we assess the impact of our actions?
Becoming Responsive	How will we respond to the shifting needs of the staff?

 Student learning is at the heart of all of our work and the very reason we push to develop ourselves as reflective practitioners.

Factor 4b: Staff take the Reflective Self-Assessment Tool to identify their current reflective stage on the Continuum of Self-Reflection. The Reflective Self-Assessment Tool found in *Teach, Reflect, Learn: Building Your Capacity for Success in the Classroom* (Hall & Simeral, 2015) is downloadable at www.ascd.org/ASCD/pdf/books/HallSimeral2017.pdf (password: HallSimeral117006) and is intended to be used in conjunction with the goal-setting process. It serves an important purpose: to launch conversation around metacognitive habits and to assist in adding a corresponding reflective component to the teacher's SMART goal (see Factor 4c). It prompts us to articulate *why we do what we do*. The assessment helps

teachers gauge how (and how accurately, how deeply, and how often) they engage in self-reflection. The score, while certainly not static or definitive, offers information about self-reflective tendencies by identifying the stage on the Continuum of Self-Reflection at which teachers currently operate.

It's imperative to note that transparency is essential when taking the assessment. Encourage teachers to be as honest as possible, choosing the statements that most resonate with them first. There are no right or wrong answers, only choices that match patterns of thinking and information that informs next steps. The conversation generated by the assessment and the subsequently determined score will guide goal setting toward a specific capacity-building, reflection-centered goal. Although the assessment can be taken as many times as needed to frame goals and discussion, we encourage its use at least twice a year: during the initial goal-setting process and at the end-of-the-year evaluation meeting. See Figure 8.3 for a set of guiding questions for capacity-builders related to the Reflective Cycle for Factor 4b.

FIGURE 8.3

Reflective Cycle for Factor 4b

Building Awareness	How aware is the staff of the Reflective Cycle and the corresponding stages on the Continuum of Self-Reflection?
	How will we use the reflective self-assessment in our goal-setting process?
Working with Intentionality	What is our plan for this?
Assessing Our Impact	How will we assess the impact of our actions?
Becoming Responsive	How will we respond to the shifting needs of the staff?

Factor 4c: Staff identify a personal—SMART-R—goal to grow as reflective practitioners, using the Reflective Cycle. In a culture of reflective practice, we not only work "SMART"—we work "SMART-R," with the second *R* denoting *reflection*. SMART goals are augmented by the

integration of the school's, team's, and teacher's *reflective* focus, creating an even SMART-R goal. The beauty of this approach is that the reflective goal (attached to a teacher's capacity-building goal as noted in their stage within the Continuum of Self-Reflection) can be embedded into any content, unit, or instructional focus. We can grow as reflective practitioners *as we work toward our SMART student achievement goals.* That is SMART-R than what we were doing before, isn't it? Check out Figure 8.4 to see how

FIGURE 8.4

SMART-R Goals Showcased

Sample SMART Goal Statement	Corresponding SMART-R Action Step
During this 9-week course, 90 percent of my students will improve their ability to use scientific inquiry processes. Each student will improve by one or more levels on the district science assessment rubric in the areas of developing hypotheses, investigative design, and data analysis.	I will achieve this by working to develop a deeper awareness and understanding of engagement strategies that successfully draw students to participate in meaningful ways. *(Example at the Unaware Stage)*
By spring of this year, 75 percent of 11th graders will make a RIT gain of 6 points on the math MAP assessment.	I will achieve this by planning with greater intentionality for individual student needs each week. *(Example at the Conscious Stage)*
In this school year, 100 percent of my students will increase their ability to analyze primary and secondary source documents by at least one level on the rating rubric. Furthermore, 75 percent of students will score at "proficient" or above.	I will achieve this through developing my ability to accurately assess the impact of my lessons. *(Example at the Action Stage)*
By November, 80 percent of kindergarten students will be able to successfully identify a list of randomized numbers as measured by the kindergarten benchmark assessment.	I will achieve this through the development of my ability to respond quickly to the results of ongoing formative assessments throughout each lesson. *(Example at the Refinement Stage)*

a SMART goal can be bolstered by a SMART-R emphasis. In addition, see Figure 8.5 for a set of guiding questions for capacity-builders related to the Reflective Cycle for Factor 4c.

FIGURE 8.5

Reflective Cycle for Factor 4c

Building Awareness	Do all staff understand how the development of self-reflection affects student learning?
	To what extent do our goal-setting conversations include discussion about deepening our reflective habits?
	How can we embed a reflective component into our SMART goal process?
Working with Intentionality	What is our plan for this?
Assessing Our Impact	How will we assess the impact of our actions?
Becoming Responsive	How will we respond to the shifting needs of the staff?

Factor 4d: Staff work diligently toward their individual goals and strategic action steps in order to continuously grow as reflective practitioners. In a culture of reflective practice, all staff are committed to the process of taking action on a consistent and daily basis to grow as reflective practitioners. In *The Daffodil Principle* (Edwards, 2004), author Jaroldeen Edwards tells about the day her daughter, Carolyn, drove her to Lake Arrowhead to visit a daffodil garden:

> We turned a corner of the path, and I looked up and gasped. Before me lay the most glorious sight. It looked as though someone had taken a great vat of gold and poured it down over the mountain peak and slopes . . . There were five acres of flowers. Daffodils as far as the eye could see. (p. 2)

On the land was a house with a poster that read: "Answers to the Questions I Know You Are Asking." The first answer was "50,000 bulbs." The second answer was "One at a time, by one woman. Two hands, two feet, and [a] very little brain." The third answer was "Began in 1958."

This woman had adopted what Edwards would call "The Daffodil Principle," a lifelong commitment to a goal by taking one action every day. Extraordinary success is a result of ordinary actions performed with consistency and diligence; or, as public speaker Keith Cunningham is commonly credited as saying, "Ordinary things consistently done produce extraordinary results." To help capacity-builders create this kind of commitment, Figure 8.6 provides a set of guiding questions related to the Reflective Cycle for Factor 4d.

FIGURE 8.6

Reflective Cycle for Factor 4d

Building Awareness	How committed is the staff to the process of becoming reflective practitioners?
	What role does leadership currently play in the development of teacher commitment?
	How can we foster commitment to the process of reflective learning?
Working with Intentionality	What is our plan for this?
Assessing Our Impact	How will we assess the impact of our actions?
Becoming Responsive	How will we respond to the shifting needs of the staff?

Extraordinary success is a result of ordinary actions performed with consistency and diligence.

Factor 4e: Administrator intentionally follows up with staff on a regular basis to discuss progress toward goals and professional growth. From the administrator's point of view, conducting frequent rounds and walk-throughs is a terrific way to follow up on the goal-setting process; and certainly, a step into the classroom is a huge step in the right direction. However, just getting into classrooms on a regular basis won't accomplish this aim by itself, just as opening the hood of your car and looking inside won't make the car run more smoothly. Successful follow-through requires more than walk-throughs. It is face-to-face interactions, written notes, e-mailed messages, reflective questions, recognized successes, deliberate celebrations, strategic PLC support, differentiated coaching strategies, transformational feedback, and more. The two primary characteristics of this factor are its alignment to the culture of reflective practice and its continuousness—when follow-through becomes a constant part of the administrator-teacher relationship and develops into an accepted, repeated pattern of interaction. With continuous follow-through aligned to reflective growth goals, we ensure the success of all members on staff.

If the relationship is strong between administrator and teacher, the likelihood of professional growth increases, teacher-administrator trust increases, and the transparency, depth, and honesty with which they can engage in growth-oriented discussions increase. Follow-through is the means to build that strong relationship. See Figure 8.7 for a set of guiding questions for capacity-builders related to the Reflective Cycle for Factor 4e.

FIGURE 8.7

Reflective Cycle for Factor 4e

Building Awareness	*How strong are the relationships between teachers and administrators?*
	What does follow-through look like in our building?
	In what areas does the follow-through process need to be aligned and refined?
	How might we make our follow-through process more meaningful and use it to strengthen relationships between administrator and staff?
Working with Intentionality	*What is our plan for this?*
Assessing Our Impact	*How will we assess the impact of our actions?*
Becoming Responsive	*How will we respond to the shifting needs of the staff?*

Follow-through is the means to strengthening the administrator-teacher relationship.

Bringing Fundamental 4 to Life

In the following two scenarios, you'll read about some capacity-builders' efforts to implement Fundamental 4 within their schools. Though the characters are fictional, they're amalgams of real human beings, compiled from case studies within schools we have worked and consulted with over the past several years. After the scenarios, we'll offer some discussion to distill a few of our key learnings for this fundamental.

Scenario 1

The principal of School 1 invites Mrs. Hernandez into his office. "Welcome!" he says. "How's the beginning of the year going? Let's talk about your evaluation goal. Do you have something picked out? What domain and component would you like to focus on this year?"

Mrs. Hernandez says that she's decided to focus on student engagement strategies. She read a book over the summer and wanted to try some new ideas. Together they create a SMART goal and fill out the required district paperwork. The principal says that he's excited to see the new strategies implemented this year as he engages in walk-throughs and the required formal observations. The teacher returns to her classroom.

Throughout the months that follow, Mrs. Hernandez tries new engagement strategies with her students—some with more success and ease than others. The principal visits Mrs. Hernandez's classroom several times and leaves walk-through feedback. He completes the two required formal observations, and they meet back in his office at the end of the year to complete the final evaluation paperwork.

"Here's your evaluation for the year," he says. "Go ahead and read through the narrative, and let me know if you have any questions." Mrs.

Hernandez skims the document, thanks the principal, and signs the bottom. Both principal and teacher give a little sigh as they each return to their regular duties. One more item can be checked off the to-do list.

Scenario 2

The principal of School 2 smiles as Mr. Brooker steps into her office. It's the beginning of the year and time to set SMART student achievement–based goals with each teacher. "Welcome!" she says. "Are you ready to set some goals?"

Mr. Brooker nods and opens a folder of data on his laptop. "I looked over the past three weeks of formative assessment and DRA data with the help of my instructional coach, and we noted a couple of things: 60 percent of my students are below grade level in reading, and of those 60 percent, most are behind due to a lack of fluency. We also have determined that the boys are significantly less fluent than the girls overall. I'd like to set a SMART goal around increasing my students' reading levels by focusing on my instructional practices that address fluency."

"It's great to see you come into this meeting so informed!" affirms the principal. "Let's get started and align this goal to several other things. Have you taken the Reflective Self-Assessment?" asks the principal. "Yes," replies Mr. Brooker. "I scored in the Action stage."

"OK," says the principal. "Let's talk about how you're going to learn to *think* differently this year about fluency instruction in your classroom in order to meet your SMART goals and demonstrate highly effective performance on your evaluation."

Together, they create a SMART-R goal—one that weaves the Action-stage reflective goal (ability to accurately assess the impact of one's actions) into the student achievement objectives. They connect the goal to the evaluation and discuss all the ways they will work as a team to grow Mr. Brooker professionally this year. Mr. Brooker returns to his classroom with not only clear goals, but also a solid plan on how he'll grow and achieve them this year.

In the months that follow, the principal touches base regularly with Mr. Brooker. She pops into his room frequently, engages him in brief conversation about his goals, and sends an occasional e-mail with open-ended questions about student learning. Her walk-through feedback is targeted—prompting the teacher to think in new ways and consider alternate approaches that will provide more information about student thinking and learning. When Mr. Brooker starts to experience success, the principal asks him to share his new learning at the next staff meeting—particularly the ways that his thinking has shifted. With the principal and the instructional coach by his side as support, Mr. Brooker flourishes.

At the end-of-year evaluation conference, both the principal and Mr. Brooker celebrate his growth. It's been a challenging but productive year. Not only did he meet his SMART goal, with 100 percent of his students showing growth and 93 percent at grade level, but also he grew in his understanding and ability to assess student learning. In retaking his Reflective Self-Assessment, he now scores in the Refinement stage on the Continuum of Self-Reflection. His confidence has skyrocketed, and he's already excited about where he can grow and learn next.

What's Really Going On?

In these scenarios, the principal and teacher at School 1 followed the district-established protocol for goal setting and evaluation. Mrs. Hernandez, the teacher, chose her goal of engagement strategies based on a desire to implement new strategies that she had read about over the summer. The principal's follow-through consisted of intermittent walk-throughs that often did not address engagement strategies specifically. Formal observation steps were followed, and at the end of the year, Mrs. Hernandez could say that she had added a few new engagement strategies to her bag of tricks.

Mr. Brooker, the teacher in School 2, followed a similar yet distinguishably different goal-setting path. Using student data to drive his area of focus, he and the principal established a SMART-R goal—with the focus on refining Mr. Brooker's thinking around fluency instruction. The principal also engaged in a distinguishably different course of follow-through. All actions were aligned to the SMART-R goal, with heavy emphasis on Mr. Brooker's metacognitive growth as he engaged in new practices. At the end of the year, Mr. Brooker was a noticeably different teacher—able to articulate how his thinking shifted around student learning.

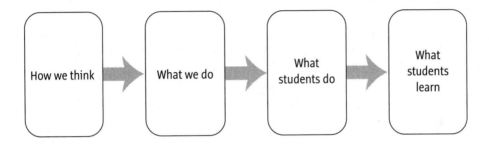

Wrapping Up

Setting goals is an exercise in which we all have experience. When the acronym "SMART" was introduced a couple of decades ago, we latched onto it pretty firmly. Now it's time to work "SMART-R" and add the emphasis on self-reflection into the work we're already engaged in. By doing that, and by following through relentlessly, persistently, and tirelessly, we can support our teachers in achieving incredible levels of success as they lead their students on a one-way journey to high levels of learning for all.

Part III: The Playbook

In Part III, we'll show you how all the moving parts come together to provide seamless, wraparound support for every teacher in the school. You'll see how capacity-builders join forces and circle the wagons around each individual staff member, virtually assuring significant reflective growth, powerful instructional development, and increased student learning.

Chapter 9 explores the last three fundamentals of a culture of reflective practice:

- Fundamental 5: Strategic PLC and Teacher-Leadership Support

- Fundamental 6: Transformational Feedback

- Fundamental 7: Differentiated Coaching

Then, in Chapters 10 through 13, we delve deep into the four stages on the Continuum of Self-Reflection—Unaware, Conscious, Action, and Refinement—and consider how capacity-builders might work with teachers to support their continual progress along the continuum.

Fundamentals 5, 6, and 7: Strategic Support, Feedback, and Coaching

As you've worked to establish a culture of reflective practice within your school, you've addressed Fundamentals 1 through 4 intentionally and consistently. And you'll recall that Fundamental 4 wraps up with a particularly necessary idea: follow-through. The playbook for capacity-builders is all about follow-through, which falls into three categories:

- Strategic PLC and Teacher-Leadership Support
- Transformational Feedback
- Differentiated Coaching

These three big ideas are, in fact, the approaches toward which the first four fundamentals were all leading. If the field is properly prepared and the players are ready to go, then we're ready to truly start the match! As we introduced them in Chapter 4, we call these categories Fundamentals 5, 6, and 7, and each consists of a number of factors that, when multiplied, create a robust and empowering product: a culture of reflective practice. Each is described in further detail in the following sections. (Each is also covered in Chapters 10 through 13, which include sections that explain how strategic PLC and teacher-leader support, transformational feedback, and differentiated coaching come into play for teachers in each of the four stages of self-reflection.)

Fundamental 5: Strategic PLC and Teacher-Leadership Support

In team sports such as football, basketball, crew, or cricket, it is the team that brings home the championship, not any one individual. This is the spirit that drives Fundamental 5. At the risk of mixing metaphors, the chain is only as strong as its weakest link. From a team's perspective, that means we must work to fortify and strengthen the reflective abilities, technical expertise, and overall impact of every member of the instructional staff. Together.

Fundamental 5 consists of five factors that tend to yield higher-performing teams and more effective individuals within the teams. Those five factors are listed here:

a. Administrator, coach, and teacher-leaders provide differentiated support for grade-level/department teams, using the Continuum of Self-Reflection.

b. Staff support one another in the collective pursuit of reflective practice and effective instruction.

c. Staff have formal and/or informal opportunities to provide peer-based feedback to one another.

d. Teacher-leaders assume a wide range of roles to shape the culture of their school, improve student learning, and influence practice among their peers.

e. Teacher-leaders engage in professional learning opportunities that support their professional growth.

To address these factors, capacity-builders refer to the Continuum of Self-Reflection (see Figure 3.2 on pp. 36–39), which provides guidance and options for supporting the reflective growth of teachers, matching their readiness and needs according to their self-reflective characteristics. In Figure 9.1,

FIGURE 9.1

Strategic PLC and Teacher-Leadership Support Along the Continuum of Self-Reflection

Unaware Stage	Conscious Stage	Action Stage	Refinement Stage
Capacity-Building Goal: *To build deeper awareness of students, content, and pedagogy*	Capacity-Building Goal: *To work with greater intentionality in addressing student needs, content, and pedagogical practices*	Capacity-Building Goal: *To build on experience and help strengthen expertise through accurate assessment of instructional impact*	Capacity-Building Goal: *To encourage long-term growth and continued reflection through responsiveness to ongoing assessments*
• Assign a specific task during team meetings. • Front-load the upcoming content/meeting with an article, video, or one-on-one discussion. • Debrief immediately following the meeting to support understanding and next steps. • Facilitate collegial idea sharing through professional learning protocols. • Strategically partner this teacher with a colleague (in particular, one in the Action stage) to build reflective capacity.	• Emphasize the use of data (pre and post) to clarify cause-and-effect relationships. • Analyze student work samples as a team. • Promote team lesson planning. • Facilitate collegial observations to see strategies at work in various settings. • Use protocols to guide discussion and promote engagement. • Strategically partner this teacher with a colleague (in particular, one in the Refinement stage) to grow reflective capacity.	• Provide opportunities for all teachers to share methods in team meetings. • Engage in healthy debate about the pros and cons of various pedagogical strategies. • Maintain a focus on data analysis during team meetings. • Incorporate professional learning (new and deeper instructional strategies) as a regular component of team meetings. • Strategically partner this teacher with colleagues (in particular, those in the Unaware stage) to build leadership capacity.	• Assign or encourage formal leadership roles within the team or department structure. • Encourage sharing and modeling of the thinking behind this teacher's decisions and actions in the classroom during team meetings. • Encourage leadership of a team action-research project. • Strategically partner this teacher with colleagues (in particular, those in the Conscious stage) to build their reflective capacity.

the approaches identified for capacity-builders to support their teachers using teammates, peers, and teacher-leaders are listed by stage along the Continuum of Self-Reflection (see Figure 3.2 on pp. 36–39).

As capacity-builders partner with teachers' teammates to provide this embedded, ongoing support, they focus on the link between each strategy they choose to implement and the capacity-building goal for the individual teacher they are working to support. Notice, also, the scaffolding that presents itself in greater depth and tapers as the teacher grows in reflective capacity. In a culture of reflective practice, the transparency, honesty, and deep desire to move the *entire organization* forward as a reflective entity drives the team, the partnerships, and the strategic support. It is truly a team effort.

 The Continuum of Self-Reflection is a multilayered tool that provides scaffolding for capacity-builders and their teachers.

Fundamental 6: Transformational Feedback

Fundamental 6 addresses the language we use when speaking with, supporting, and encouraging the reflective growth of individual teachers. We refer to this as *transformational* feedback because the prompts are designed to generate mental activity that opens the minds of our teachers to possibility, thereby transforming their thinking. It is this shift in thinking that will result in long-term growth and eventual professional expertise.

Fundamental 6 consists of five factors that are likely to result in the most effective feedback practices between professional adults, deepening the reflective growth of each and every individual on staff. Those five factors are listed here:

    a. Administrator provides regular feedback to staff to build their reflective tendencies and strengthen technical skill.

b. Coach provides regular feedback to staff to build their reflective tendencies and strengthen technical skill.

c. Clear look-fors, based on best practices, are established at the individual teacher, team/department, and schoolwide level.

d. Feedback matches individual staff members' needs as reflective practitioners, linked to current stage on the Continuum of Self-Reflection.

e. Feedback is growth-oriented, part of a continuous process, accurate, relevant to individual teacher goals, and timely (within 24 hours).

To address these factors, capacity-builders refer to the Continuum of Self-Reflection (see Figure 3.2 on pp. 36–39), which provides guidance and options for supporting the reflective growth of teachers, matching their readiness and needs according to their self-reflective characteristics. In Figure 9.2, the approaches identified for capacity-builders to support their teachers by engaging them in meaningful feedback interactions are listed by stage along the Continuum of Self-Reflection.

Feedback, as we know (Dean, Hubbell, Pitler, & Stone, 2012; Hattie, 2009), is a process, not a product. The prompts listed in Figure 9.2 are intended to launch a feedback discussion and get things started. Continuing with the sports metaphor, these might each be a throw-in, a kick-off, a pitch, or a serve. By beginning a conversation and starting a dialogue, we can engage our teachers in a feedback process that enriches their understanding, tightens their intentionality, gives them a way to assess their impact, and deepens their repertoire of responses, all while enhancing their reflective capabilities and increasing their impact upon student learning. Because the prompts are scaffolded to meet teachers' needs and readiness for reflective dialogue, the likelihood that the process continues is greater—and this is where the synapses begin to fire, the brains begin to storm, and the potential begins to expand.

FIGURE 9.2

Transformational Feedback Along the Continuum of Self-Reflection

Unaware Stage (Directive statements)	Conscious Stage (Leading prompts)	Action Stage (Open-ended prompts)	Refinement Stage (Challenging prompts)
Capacity-Building Goal: *To build deeper awareness of students, content, and pedagogy*	Capacity-Building Goal: *To work with greater intentionality in addressing student needs, content, and pedagogical practices*	Capacity-Building Goal: *To build on experience and help strengthen expertise through accurate assessment of instructional impact*	Capacity-Building Goal: *To encourage long-term growth and continued reflection through responsiveness to ongoing assessments*
• When you did this ___, the students did this ___. It worked because ___. Do that again! • I noticed you used ___ and it was effective because ___; use it whenever you want your students to ___. • When you did this ___, the students did this ___. Tomorrow try ___, and tell me what happens. • Your lesson was successful today because ___. • You (or your students) struggled today because ___. Next time that happens, try this: ___, and tell me what happens.	• Your goal is ___. How can I help you keep that focus and support your efforts? • I see you were using ___ today. Keep that focus! What worked well today? • Tell me about the purpose of today's activity. What is your evidence of success? • Today, your students were successful at ___. What did you do that directly led to their success? • I noticed ___ today. How might the outcomes change if you tried ___? Give it a shot and let me know how it goes.	• What was the purpose of today's activity? Was it successful? How do you know? • Which parts of today's lesson went well? Which parts didn't? Why? • What was the goal of today's lesson? How did you determine that goal? • Today I observed you ___. Did that contribute to your goal? How can you tell? • Why did you choose to ___ today? Was that strategy effective? How do you know? • What other strategy could you have used today to achieve your goals?	• Today your students did ___, and you immediately responded with ___. How did you plan to address that misconception? • In the middle of today's lesson, you abruptly changed course. What led to that decision? Was it a successful move? How do you know? • How do you know when students are learning in the middle of a lesson? What do you look for? • How do you identify specific learning styles of the students in your room?

Unaware Stage (Directive statements)	Conscious Stage (Leading prompts)	Action Stage (Open-ended prompts)	Refinement Stage (Challenging prompts)
• You appear frustrated with ___ and I noticed you ___ several times. Tomorrow, try to take note of how many times you ___. Then let's chat further. • I observed ___, which is not what you/we were going for in that lesson; try ___ to get the lesson back on track. This usually works because ___.	• Yesterday I observed your students ___; today, they are ___. How do you determine your daily lesson structure? • Tell me more about the planning that went into today's lesson. Why did you select the strategy you chose for this lesson? • How do you use what you know about your students to drive lesson planning each day? • When you did ___ today, I observed several students ___. How will you shift tomorrow's lesson to change the outcomes? • How does this lesson connect to prior and future student learning objectives? • What misconceptions might students have during tomorrow's lesson? How will you address that in your planning?	• How do you predetermine what your evidence of success will be for a lesson? • Do your anecdotal observations of student learning align with more formal assessment data? • If you could teach this lesson again, what would you do differently? Why? • Which students were successful achieving today's learning target? Which students struggled? Why was that so? • What does the student work from today's lesson tell you about ___ as a learner? • What can you tell me about ___ as a learner? How can you find out more?	• Explain the thinking that went into planning a lesson like this. How do you know which strategies to select? How do you decide which activities to choose? • To what extent are you collaborating with your colleagues to plan and deliver your lessons? How can you become more intentional in partnering with your teammates? • Your lesson today reminded me of a recent article I read in *Educational Leadership*. I'll put a copy in your box. I would love to hear your thoughts.

All capacity-builders share the responsibility to provide and exchange feedback with every teacher; this is not reserved for principals and other formal evaluators. In fact, when the various support systems (coach, administrator, teammates, and others) are working cohesively and intentionally to "circle the wagons" around a given teacher, the concerted attention to precise feedback practices can yield tremendous results. For these capacity-builders to truly transform a teacher's thinking, feedback must include all four descriptors in the acronym CART:

> *C = Consistent.* The feedback must be embedded into the teachers' and capacity-builders' regular practice. "Talking teaching" must become woven into the fabric of the school.

> *A = Accurate.* The providers of the feedback must know what they are talking about. Becoming well versed in the language of reflection is most important, followed by knowledge of high-leverage instructional practices, curricular expertise, and other metrics of instructional know-how.

> *R = Relevant.* Does the feedback's content match the teacher's goal, a clearly identified look-for, or a schoolwide instructional focus? If so, proceed. Feedback plucked from left field does little good and tends to exacerbate communication woes.

> *T = Timely.* The closer to the instructional event the feedback is provided, the more likely it is to yield positive results. Our rule of thumb is that it should be delivered within 24 hours.

With those guidelines in mind, capacity-builders can begin visiting classrooms, joining team meetings, connecting between classes and during planning periods, supporting their teachers in the complicated and nuanced art of ensuring high levels of learning for all students—all by engaging in transformational feedback practices. The possibilities are endless when we're "talking teaching" and we're indeed speaking the same language with our teachers!

Fundamental 7: Differentiated Coaching

Every team has a head coach; this goes without saying. Many teams also employ assistant coaches, often with specialized skills, experience, and approaches that support the varied and particular needs of the players. In the same spirit of job-embedded support, a culture of reflective practice employs instructional coaches to engage in frequent, embedded, differentiated coaching practices that support the reflective growth and technical development of its teachers.

The five factors of Fundamental 7 that constitute a robust instructional coaching approach and support teachers' ongoing professional growth are the following:

a. Administrator provides regular coaching support to staff to build their reflective tendencies and strengthen technical skill.

b. Coach provides regular coaching support to staff to build their reflective tendencies and strengthen technical skill.

c. Coaching strategies match individual staff members' needs as reflective practitioners using the Continuum of Self-Reflection.

d. Coaching strategies are growth-oriented, part of a continuous process, relevant to individual teacher goals, and provided in a timely manner.

e. Staff seek out coach for coaching support of their instructional goals.

To address these factors, capacity-builders refer to the Continuum of Self-Reflection, which provides guidance and options for supporting the reflective growth of teachers, matching their readiness and needs according to their self-reflective characteristics. In Figure 9.3, the approaches identified for capacity-builders to support their teachers by providing differentiated coaching strategies are listed by stage along the Continuum of Self-Reflection.

FIGURE 9.3

Differentiated Coaching Strategies Along the Continuum of Self-Reflection

Unaware Stage	Conscious Stage	Action Stage	Refinement Stage
Capacity-Building Goal: *To build deeper awareness of students, content, and pedagogy*	Capacity-Building Goal: *To work with greater intentionality in addressing student needs, content, and pedagogical practices*	Capacity-Building Goal: *To build on experience and help strengthen expertise through accurate assessment of instructional impact*	Capacity-Building Goal: *To encourage long-term growth and continued reflection through responsiveness to ongoing assessments*
• Make frequent contact, checking in often to talk about goals and progress toward them. • Build confidence through short-term goal setting. • Celebrate successes immediately. • Model a strategy or lesson. • Whisper-coach while co-observing another teacher's class. • Write lesson plans together. • Coteach a lesson. • Debrief a lesson together. • Record a lesson, provide clear look-fors, and debrief the video together. • Engage in side-by-side reflective journaling.	• Make daily contact, checking in often to talk about goals and progress toward them. • Build confidence through short-term goal setting. • Celebrate successes immediately. • Meet weekly for collaborative planning. • Engage through interactive journaling. • Invite participation in small-group discussions around a common problem of practice. • Model a strategy or lesson in the teacher's classroom. • Coplan, coteach, and debrief a lesson together. • Provide opportunities to observe in other classrooms—using clear look-fors. • Record a lesson, provide clear look-fors, and debrief the video together.	• Analyze data together. • Analyze student work samples together. • Collaboratively engage in diagnosis and action planning based on beliefs of how students learn. • Provide research from which to construct meaning. • Invite participation in small-group discussions around a common problem of practice. • Foster idea sharing through collegial observations. • Model new strategies in a gradual-release model. • Record lesson and discuss video analysis. • Model open-mindedness toward multiple approaches and perspectives. • Encourage participation in a professional book club. • Engage in interactive journaling.	• Analyze data and student work samples together. • Analyze schoolwide data together. • Stimulate discussions of personal vision and educational philosophy. • Serve as devil's advocate to challenge thinking. • Record lesson and discuss video analysis. • Facilitate idea sharing through collegial observations. • Encourage leadership of small-group discussions around a common problem of practice. • Encourage book club facilitation or leadership. • Arrange for student-teacher hosting opportunities. • Encourage conference participation and publication submission. • Engage in interactive journaling.

Coaching, as we noted in Chapter 4, is not a one-size-fits-all endeavor. Because each teacher reflects differently, has unique skills, and is working toward specific goals, the coaching support *must* be differentiated according to teachers' reflective readiness and their particular needs. Again, you'll note that the strategies listed are scaffolded to address the differences in reflective abilities. Each strategy tends to be more effective when applied alongside a teacher operating within a given stage on the Continuum of Self-Reflection. Just like with the transformational feedback prompts, these strategies are intended to launch the joint work between coach and teacher and are by no means an exhaustive list of coaching strategies. We encourage capacity-builders to work with teachers to identify their goals, readiness, and a specific plan that includes an array of coaching strategies.

Putting It All into Play

Well, there you have it. It's game time! In the next chapters, we'll provide you with a thorough view of how a culture of reflective practice wraps its protective and supportive arms around each individual teacher on staff—and nurtures each one's growth along the Continuum of Self-Reflection. We'll show you what each stage on the continuum (Unaware, Conscious, Action, and Refinement) looks like in real life, including a discussion of the stage itself; teacher vignettes; descriptions of a teacher's reflective tendencies; an explanation of the connection between the Continuum of Self-Reflection and the Reflective Cycle; a clarification of the complementary leadership roles to support teacher growth; and other details about the specific types of support provided.

10

Supporting Teachers in the Unaware Stage

We've all been there. Perhaps things are new—a new position, a different teaching assignment, an updated curriculum, unfamiliar resources, a change in clientele, new standards, modified evaluation tools—or maybe it's just that everything seems complicated, tricky, and confusing, and nothing's comfortable. Either way, we've got a job to do, so we buckle down and do it. Our directions are in front of us; all that's left is for us to follow them. Somehow, we make it through, with a goal to take it one day at a time, biting off only what we can chew. For one reason or another, in that particular place, we don't know what we don't know. And because we're unaware of our options, all we can do is . . . do.

As educators, we all experience what it means to be "unaware" when it comes to understanding students, grasping content we're required to teach, knowing the best pedagogical strategy to implement in a given lesson, or identifying an intervention strategy that will work for a child who is not making progress. The teachers we support are no different. During this time, in that spot, at that place, our teachers are operating in the Unaware stage (see Figure 10.1), a term we use to describe folks who have not yet learned about certain teaching strategies, aren't yet attuned to the finer details of their class and students, and do not yet reflect deeply about their particular responsibilities. As we build from this stage, teachers must

FIGURE 10.1

The Unaware Stage

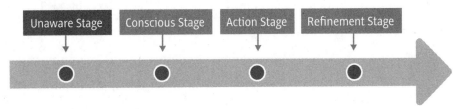

become aware of the instructional realities of their classrooms. Let's consider the term more closely.

Unaware: *having no knowledge of a situation or a fact*

There's not a human being on the planet who hasn't spent time in the Unaware stage on some version of the Continuum of Self-Reflection: going through the motions, unaware of better alternatives, and seeing no need to change. King and Kitchener (1994) describe this situation as "accepting without question the culture [we] live in . . . in a comfortable position and unaware that things could be different from how they are" (p. 48).

Simply put, the Unaware stage is best described as a state of mind. Not knowing what we don't know, we move forward with false confidence that we have sufficient knowledge or information to proceed; we may find ourselves lulled into complacency or, as is often the case with dramatic change, so overwhelmed that we resort to survival mode. Our lack of clarity causes us to make little effort to think about the driving forces behind our actions.

Sometimes, it's that very survival mode mentality that can jar a teacher out of the Unaware stage. Awareness is closely associated with attention—we must be aware of something to pay attention to it. And what do we pay attention to? According to John Medina (2008), professor of bioengineering at the University of Washington School of Medicine and author of *Brain Rules*, the two brain functions connected to attention are interest and emotion. For instance, stimuli that may prompt a teacher's attention might result in these thoughts: "I would sure like my students to use their vocabulary words more often in their writing" (interest) and "Egads! Our end-of-unit assessment scores show an unacceptable lack of understanding of these key concepts. I'm scared that they'll fail their next class if I can't help them learn it better" (emotion).

 We must be aware of something to pay attention to it.

Although many first-year teachers fall into this category, years of service do not necessarily reveal placement. The practice of reflective thought is the determining factor on the Continuum of Self-Reflection, and we can spend years "blissfully unaware" of more effective, or more efficient, ways to conduct our business. It's quite possible for experienced teachers to find themselves here after years of teaching. In fact, it's likely that *any teacher* might take a temporary step into this stage after shifting grade levels, changing content areas, or tackling brand-new responsibilities. Regardless of how a teacher arrives, what's most important is the understanding that with the right support from the right people, we can build our teachers' reflective capacity and help them proceed toward the Refinement stage on the Continuum of Self-Reflection.

It is essential to remember that the Continuum of Self-Reflection is not an evaluation tool; rather, it is a powerful instrument that serves two incredibly helpful purposes. First, it helps capacity-builders (and teachers themselves) identify their teachers' reflective tendencies. Second, it guides those capacity-builders (administrators and coaches) to the proper entry point and directs their capacity-building efforts. There is no value—no "better than" or "worse than"—assigned to any of the stages on the continuum; there are just terms that describe how teachers think about their work. The characteristics of thinking displayed by an individual teacher should be used without prejudice to help you, as a capacity-builder, determine the best course of action to support that teacher's growth as a reflective practitioner. The goal in using this tool is not to evaluate, label, or "fix" teachers; unyieldingly, the goal is to lead teachers to develop strong patterns of thought as we usher them down the path of self-reflection.

The First Step: Identification of Reflective Tendencies

Let's walk through several classrooms and take a closer look at teachers who are currently operating in the Unaware stage. As you read these vignettes, begin to assimilate the characteristics that describe thinking in the Unaware stage. This is the first step in identifying teachers' reflective tendencies. (The vignettes featuring Mr. Barnett and Mrs. Damon originally appeared in our earlier book *Teach, Reflect, Learn* [Hall & Simeral, 2015]. We present them here as examples to be considered from the viewpoint of the capacity-builders, including administrators and coaches.)

Vignettes, Part 1: Meet the Teachers

Visit 1: Mr. Barnett

It is unmistakable that Mr. Barnett is a popular teacher. Even though it's just a few months into his first year teaching 2nd grade, he has gained a favorable reputation as "the fun teacher." There isn't a bare spot on the wall, thanks to a peppering of student-created drawings between multiple Golden State Warriors posters.

At present, the students are transitioning from centers (which include computer games, a puzzle, a sight-word activity, letter writing, and the library nook) and gathering on the carpet for a read-aloud. The children are in no particular hurry, and Mr. Barnett engages in some playful banter with two girls near the drinking fountain.

After several minutes, the majority of the class is on the carpet and Mr. Barnett asks, "OK, so what book do we want to read today?" The students excitedly call out several titles. "Oh, so you want me to read *Finklehopper Frog* again?" He knew they would—they love the voices he makes.

When asked about his students' reading levels, Mr. Barnett smiles and shrugs. "I don't know the exact levels," he responds, "but they're all growing, I'm sure. I really enjoy this class, and I like teaching more than I thought I would. These kids are fantastic. At this point in their lives, it's my job to make sure they enjoy coming to school every day."

Visit 2: Mrs. Damon

Mrs. Damon, a 24-year veteran teacher, is seated at the front of the classroom. As she graphs an algebraic equation on a coordinate plane under the document camera, the image is projected on the screen. She is showing the third problem in a set of problems from the class textbook.

The students, seated in rows facing the screen, are generally on task. Mrs. Damon kindly reminds the class, "You should be copying these graphs on your own worksheets as I model them, so you'll be able to complete today's assignment."

A slight commotion catches Mrs. Damon's attention, and she looks up. Two students are turned around, talking with a classmate. This is a frequent occurrence, and Mrs. Damon raises an eyebrow.

"Boys," she says. "Attention up here, please." The boys turn forward momentarily but then resume their conversation when Mrs. Damon returns to the document camera.

Later, Mrs. Damon explains, "I worry about those boys. They don't seem to enjoy math or take school seriously at all. It's not really that hard for the kids to earn a good grade in my class—I always model the problems, and the textbook offers a very clear explanation. If they're failing my class, then they'll have a real eye-opener next year when they're in high school, that's for sure."

Visit 3: Mrs. Chan

Mrs. Chan has spent the past 10 years as a freshman English teacher. A strong, enthusiastic educator, she decided it was finally time for a change and volunteered to fill a need in the department and move to senior English. To Mrs. Chan's relief, last year's teacher left her unit plans behind. They've been invaluable as Mrs. Chan has looked to them to know when to teach what. It's the third month of school, and according to the plan, she's to introduce a complicated comparison unit with novels from various genres on Monday.

Last night as she read through the standards for the umpteenth time, she shared with her husband that she felt like a first-year teacher all over again—unsure of what to expect from seniors, not knowing the curriculum, and struggling to discern what her instruction should look like.

"I'm so thankful to have last year's lesson plans that I can follow and use. They give me direction and are saving me a lot of time."

When asked what steps she's taking to increase her effectiveness and have a greater impact on her students' learning, she sighed when responding. "Right now I'm just trying to stay afloat. If I can preview the plan before I have to teach it, I'll be in good shape. I'm already starting to line things up for next year."

As you read those profiles, what did you notice? At first glance, these class-rooms probably appeared very different—varying grade levels, subjects, and diverse teaching styles. But the trained capacity-building eye can spot impor-tant similarities between the thought processes of all three teachers. Each is focused on the act of teaching—lesson planning, assigning work, and keeping students busy—all for the sake of being a teacher. They have no awareness of how to get to know students as individual learners or to seek out better instructional strategies to help them learn. They lack awareness of how to understand content in a deeper way in order to facilitate learning. Student learning is simply not at the center of thought, nor is it connected to teacher actions. All three teachers are operating in the Unaware stage.

Reflective Tendencies of an Unaware-Stage Teacher

The way teachers think about their professional responsibilities speaks volumes, and teachers operating in the Unaware stage have some very particular patterns of thought for us to consider. Although our ability to accurately identify where on the Continuum of Self-Reflection a teacher reflects is primarily hinged upon a teacher's thinking processes, it's important to understand how those thoughts translate into actions. As we explain the following reflective tendencies of teachers in the Unaware stage, we will accompany the descriptions with examples of how those characteristics may appear in the classroom. According to Calderhead, Denicolo, and Day, "Teacher thinking is at once action," indicating the causative relationship between how we think and what we do in every moment of every day (2012, p. 58).

Teachers in this stage exhibit common characteristics when thinking about their role as teacher, their students as learners, and the pedagogi-cal strategies that positively affect student achievement. Compliance-oriented, they're propelled in their work by the acts of teaching. Lessons are taught, homework assigned, quizzes given—all with minimal connection to student learning. Often the hardest-working members on staff, they want to do a good job and often firmly believe that they are doing so. What follows are descriptions of the overarching reflective tendencies, as shown in Figure 10.2, of a teacher in the Unaware stage.

Demonstrates little or no awareness of instructional reality in the classroom. The "instructional reality" in a classroom is defined in terms of the dynamic interplay between students, content, and pedagogy. Instructional goals, both short-term and long-term, may escape our teachers' attention. Teachers in the Unaware stage may not see how the content or standards link with other courses or content, how they build upon and lead to other skills, or how they are relevant to students' lives beyond the immediate moment. Also unacknowledged are students' present levels of performance, prior knowledge, learning styles, interests, and academic trajectory. Without this awareness, teachers in the Unaware stage are not yet able to make intentional decisions about instructional strategies, approaches, and learning activities to meet those learning goals and student needs.

FIGURE 10.2

Teacher's Reflective Tendencies: Unaware Stage

- Demonstrates little or no awareness of instructional reality in the classroom.
- Engages in little or no self-initiated reflection.
- Defines problems or challenges inaccurately.
- Sees surface-level events and classroom elements.
- Collaborates infrequently with colleagues.
- Focuses on routine.
- Exhibits the best of intentions.
- Expresses confusion about own role in learning.
- Focuses on the job itself—the *act* of teaching.

Engages in little or no self-initiated reflection. Because the focus for a teacher in the Unaware stage is to survive the day, complete the lesson plan, and prepare for tomorrow's lesson, there is little (if any) self-directed thought to connecting the dots. Left to their own devices, teachers at this stage would continue down this day-to-day path, "blissfully unaware" of the alternatives that might help them—and their students—become much more successful.

Defines problems or challenges inaccurately. Mrs. Damon, as you'll recall from her vignette, believes that the structures she has established provide the opportunity for all students to learn. Her lack of a consistent management strategy and engaging lessons is affecting student behavior and their learning. In a "lead a horse to water and see what happens" sort of approach, she projects all the onus of learning onto her students. Ask her to define the problem and she points a finger at her students. It is not that she is trying to shirk responsibility by passing the blame; rather, she does not have a complete understanding of the problem or of the role she might play in addressing it.

Sees surface-level events and classroom elements. When students struggle in the classroom of an Unaware-stage teacher, they're met with broad generalizations. A report to parents might include the statement "Susie has a tough time with math," for instance, instead of a deeper, more thorough recognition that Susie struggles with one-to-one correspondence and multistep directions. Occasionally, a teacher may come up with a shortened spelling list or fewer problems on the homework assignment, but there is no acknowledgment of these students' underlying issues. Often, a teacher who recognizes that a student is struggling may assume it is because the student is not working hard enough and needs to be redirected to the task at hand. Because teachers in the Unaware stage don't pick up on variations in student readiness, skills, and strengths, they are unable to provide specific instruction that maximizes learning for all students in their classroom.

Collaborates infrequently with colleagues. The wisdom, experience, and expertise of professional colleagues often go untapped by teachers in the Unaware stage. Team meetings, collaboration sessions, and department- or grade-level meetings are typically viewed as opportunities to connect and socialize, to gather materials and prep for future lessons, or to exchange war stories. Because of the inability of Unaware-stage teachers to offer significant contributions or to ask pertinent, thought-provoking questions, their contributions to such gatherings are superficial and limited. Teachers operating in the Unaware stage rarely seek out their colleagues for instructional discussions, data analysis, or problem-solving strategies beyond what's indicated on the meeting schedule.

Focuses on routine. Teacher's editions always in hand, Unaware-stage teachers rely heavily on them to guide their day-to-day instruction. These teachers are more focused on finishing the daily lesson and accomplishing the tasks therein rather than monitoring and ensuring student learning. In fact, teachers in this stage tend to settle into a predictable, safe routine for proceeding through the day, the week, and the unit. Veteran teachers might be described as "set in their ways," whereas newer teachers may be grasping for anything that gets them closer to Day 180 without a significant negative incident.

Exhibits the best of intentions. Teachers in the Unaware stage may be among the most dedicated and caring professionals in the building. It is unlikely we will ever question their work ethic, though the old adage "Work smarter, not harder" comes to mind. Three months into the school year, Mrs. Chan, as you read in her vignette, is still trying to unpack the standards and is continuing to follow the previous teacher's lesson plans lock-step. Her volunteering to tackle the AP English class, which had once seemed gracious of her, now appears to have resulted in a monumental struggle. Undoubtedly, she will spend hours and hours planning and researching and preparing materials for activities she doesn't yet own. For a while at least, she will likely wind up with little to show for the time and energy she has spent.

Expresses confusion about own role in learning. Often the line between teaching and learning gets blurred, and the responsibility for ensuring learning remains a mystery to teachers in the Unaware stage. In the case of Mr. Barnett, the subject of another of our teacher vignettes, he was more focused on creating a positive environment for students to spend their day in—an admirable concept, to be sure—than in checking for understanding of student learning along the way. As you'll recall, he wasn't aware of what his students knew and didn't know to any degree of specificity. Rather than investigate strategies for creating opportunities for students to learn key concepts, he allowed—as unwitting as it may have been—his students to drift without specific differentiated attention.

Focuses on the job itself—the *act* of teaching. With little or no awareness of effective instructional strategies to use while teaching, teachers in the Unaware stage spend most of their class time lecturing and assigning work for the students to complete. We call this the "I'm teaching, you must be learning" assumption. In *The First Days of School*, Wong and Wong are clear in articulating quite the opposite: "Learning has nothing to do with what the teacher covers; learning has to do with what the student accomplishes" (1998, p. 210). Unaware-stage teachers think primarily in terms of "covering" subject matter, and in a very simplistic manner. The result is this: they do what teachers do.

Using the Reflective Cycle (Figure 10.3), we can take a closer look at the distinct thought patterns and reflective habits of teachers in the Unaware stage. This will provide us, as instructional leaders and capacity-builders, with valuable insights that enable us to accurately identify how our teachers are currently *thinking* about their professional responsibilities—which will allow us to support their continued growth as reflective practitioners.

At this point, it's probably pretty clear how far along the Reflective Cycle our teacher's thinking has developed, or at which quadrant our teacher's thinking is breaking down. Have you identified it? If you chose "Awareness of Instructional Reality" for a teacher operating in the Unaware stage, you're ready to proceed as a capacity-builder, and

FIGURE 10.3

Awareness in the Reflective Cycle

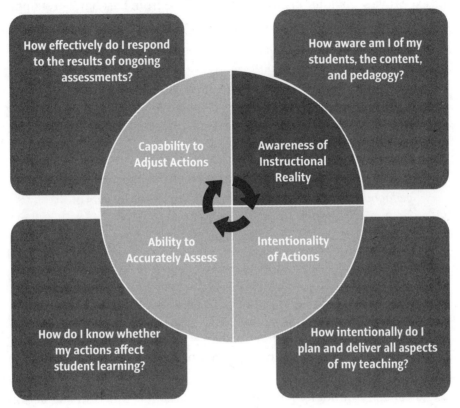

the question to ask is this: *How aware is the teacher of students, content, and pedagogy?*

The reflective focus for teachers in the Unaware stage sits right there, in this first quadrant of the Reflective Cycle diagram. To grow as a reflective practitioner and to progress along the Continuum of Self-Reflection toward the Conscious stage (or even leapfrogging directly to the Action stage), teachers in the Unaware stage must deliberately *observe* the goings-on in the classroom. When one observes with intentionality, one begins to truly *see* the students as learners and as human beings, *understand* their learning needs, *know* best-practice strategies, and *embrace* the realities of curriculum, assessment, structures, and procedures in the classroom. To be excessively obvious, heed the subtle advice from baseball's great philosopher, Yogi Berra: "You can observe a lot by just watching."

The Second Step: Supportive Practices

Each stage within the Continuum of Self-Reflection has a capacity-building goal to develop and support each individual teacher's reflective growth. Here is the overall goal for the Unaware-stage teacher:

> Our goal is *to build deeper awareness of students, content, and pedagogy* in order to shift the focal point from the acts of teaching to the thinking that drives those actions.

Teachers in the Unaware stage need to know their students as individual learners and as unique human beings. They must thoroughly understand their content in order to make deeper connections between concepts and to be able to identify possible misconceptions before they happen. To progress as reflective practitioners, Unaware-stage teachers must become aware of best-practice strategies that are proven to facilitate learning in effective and efficient ways.

As capacity-builders, it's crucial to understand that shifting action doesn't always result in shifted thinking, but shifting thinking will *always* result in shifted action. Our charge is to tackle the thinking that drives the doing. If we're to successfully cultivate a culture of reflective practice and facilitate long-term professional growth, we must ask teachers to *think* as often as we ask them to *do*. Their growth in thinking, then, will fuel a curiosity and a desire to learn more.

Leadership Roles

How do capacity-builders begin to address the specific needs of a teacher in the Unaware stage? To have the impact necessary for continued reflective growth, administrators and coaches simultaneously work independently (within their own roles) and collaboratively (as their roles are complementary to one another), as well as intentionally leveraging a teacher's peers within the PLC structure to provide additional support, as noted in the triad diagram in Figure 10.4. In the absence of an instructional coach, the administrator must be even more deliberate in the use of peer relationships to engage in this work. This strategic triangulation of support significantly increases the likelihood of success.

As described in Chapter 5, a couple of conditions must be established in order to proceed with our capacity-building efforts. First, the roles of administrator and coach must be defined, distinguished, and communicated clearly to one another. Second, the boundaries that encompass each role must be respected at all times. In the case of working with Unaware-stage teachers, these roles manifest themselves in unique and important ways as we work to guide the teachers toward their capacity-building goal.

 The administrator's role: *director.*

FIGURE 10.4

Triad Diagram for Unaware Stage

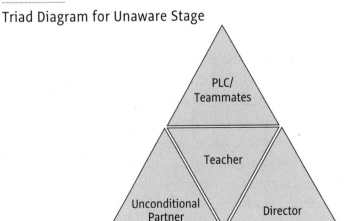

The administrator's role is that of *director*, providing the Unaware-stage teacher with specific, clear directions, with the intention of changing the teacher's *behavior* first, so the teacher's *thoughts* and *beliefs* will follow. Teachers in the Unaware stage are the only subgroup of a school's educators who receive this directive, unequivocal feedback. Because the teacher does not yet know (or has not yet learned, or has not been exposed to) some of the high-yield teaching strategies, efficient classroom routines, methods for learning about student needs, accurate assessment techniques, and other important teaching actions, it is the administrator's top priority to set a clear expectation. This direct tack will increase the frequency with which the teacher engages in sound instructional practices, thereby opening the door to reflective conversation.

It is important to note that the Unaware stage is *the one and only place* on the Continuum of Self-Reflection where a capacity-builder engages in *telling* rather than *asking*. In every other stage, the feedback and support consist of some variation of reflective prompt. Here we find the one exception to the rule: in this stage, we first look to shift behavior and follow it immediately with shifting thought.

 The coach's role: *unconditional partner.*

The coach's role is to work alongside the Unaware-stage teacher as an *unconditional partner* focused on the goal of helping to build awareness of the thinking behind one's actions.

In *The 7 Habits of Highly Effective Families*, Stephen Covey connects the term *unconditional* to what he calls the three Primary Laws of Love: "acceptance rather than rejection, understanding rather than judgment, and participation rather than manipulation" (1997, p. 61). The choice to be unconditional toward another human being does not lie in the other's behavior; rather, we choose to adopt and live by these laws simply on their merit alone. As we step into the role of unconditional partner, we choose to guide our work by these three principles.

Regardless of age or experience, teachers in the Unaware stage need to feel respected and valued as individuals. A coach starts by getting to know individuals' strengths, limitations, and specific needs—seeking to recognize and validate their potential. This happens best through active listening—asking questions and listening more; proactively searching for ways to build trust and rapport. Sharing personal life and learning experiences will create a collaborative environment as an unconditional partner. By putting deposits in what Covey describes as the "emotional bank account," a coach can build a high level of trust, and "communication is open and free" (1997, p. 46).

Working Complementarily

As we stated in Chapter 5, the coach and the administrator are partners in this work. Sharing a common goal of supporting a teacher's growth as a reflective practitioner, each assumes the role just outlined very intentionally, knowing the other will shoulder the complementary role.

For instance, you may be wondering this: if a teacher in the Unaware stage doesn't yet know about a highly effective instructional strategy and the administrator sets the expectation that this teacher employ that strategy, is that a realistic expectation? How is this teacher going to meet that charge?

The answer lies in the collaborative relationship between the parties. Knowing the expectation, the Unaware-stage teacher will seek out the instructional coach—the unconditional partner. With that teacher-coach relationship established and the communication lines open, this door is likewise open for the coach to provide differentiated support that meets the teacher's unique learning needs in that moment. This is how the roles complement one another. While the coach is working to establish the unconditional partnership, the administrator sets the bar, knowing that the teacher will access the coach to learn, practice, and implement the established best practice.

Strategic PLC and Teacher-Leadership Support

The administrator and the coach are not the only capacity-builders who share the immense responsibility of supporting teachers' growth as reflective practitioners. Because teaching is no longer done in isolation (those days are behind us, right?), educators' relationships with colleagues, peers, and other professionals within their grade level or department or professional learning community are vital in completing our triad (see Figure 10.4, p. 167). Within a culture of reflective practice, administrators set the expectation that teachers will work collaboratively to support each other in their pursuit of common goals, and then it's "all hands on deck" to engage in the practices that accomplish that objective.

Teachers in the Unaware stage often misunderstand the purpose of professional learning communities. The result? Collaboration is limited to a superficial level. To have meaningful conversations about student learning with colleagues, teachers need to be aware of their students, content, and pedagogy; and, very important, they must see collaborative time—and, in fact, every moment that they can seek others out for support—as an opportunity to deepen their practice, refine their skills, learn from one another, rely on one another, and share the trials and tribulations of education.

To nudge them beyond the specific, task-oriented jobs that teachers in this stage gravitate toward (such as making copies, creating posters, coordinating events, and serving as timekeepers), capacity-builders can strategically facilitate collaborative learning opportunities. The strategies in Figure 10.5 may strengthen an Unaware-stage teacher's ability to contribute, support, and learn within a professional learning community structure. Let's examine each one in greater detail.

Assign a specific task during team meetings. When participants are expected to fulfill certain duties, their attention tends to focus more directly—and the key here is to make sure the tasks are connected to

FIGURE 10.5

Strategic PLC and Teacher-Leadership Support: Unaware Stage

Capacity-Building Goal: To build deeper awareness of students, content, and pedagogy

- Assign a specific task during team meetings.
- Front-load the upcoming content/meeting with an article, a video, or a one-on-one discussion.
- Debrief immediately following the meeting to support understanding and next steps.
- Facilitate collegial idea sharing through professional learning protocols.
- Strategically partner this teacher with a colleague (in particular, one in the Action stage) to build reflective capacity.

students, content, or pedagogy. For instance, a team might ask an Unaware-stage teacher to take notes and provide a meeting summary for the administrator, thereby synthesizing the discussions. It might also be beneficial for the team leader (or department head) to review the notes with the teacher before submitting them to the office, just to clarify and ensure that the teacher is on the right page.

Front-load the upcoming content/meeting with an article, video, or one-on-one discussion. Research abounds on the value of "flipping" the learning experience and prepping students for new content before a discussion (e.g., Brame, 2013; Butzler, 2016; Straw, Quinlan, Harland, & Walker, 2015). Often we call this approach "building background knowledge." It might be as simple as providing a copy of the article the team will be reading in advance, logging onto a website to gain early exposure to an idea or a strategy, or engaging in a conversation about the upcoming session beforehand. This practice builds confidence, strengthens the relationships between team members, and provides essential awareness of key concepts.

Debrief immediately following the meeting to support understanding and next steps. What's better than an immediate check for understanding? Often, team meetings proceed right until the bell, resulting in a mad scramble back to everyone's classrooms. When a team leader, a department head, a trusted colleague, or an instructional coach makes time to sit down and discuss the content of the meeting, clarify any questions, and reiterate the expectations, it reinforces the learning and ensures that our Unaware-stage teacher is good to go with the team's plans for moving forward.

Facilitate collegial idea sharing through professional learning protocols. In many meeting structures, those with more experience—or more lung capacity—dominate the airwaves. Clear, predictable professional learning protocols, like those we repurposed in *The Principal Influence* (Hall et al., 2016) or *Protocols for Professional Learning* (Easton, 2009), offer a venue that ensures that all voices are heard and weighted equally. When everyone has to share, we all learn—and those formerly reluctant to share can work with a capacity-builder to prep for that sharing.

Strategically partner this teacher with a colleague (in particular, one in the Action stage) to build reflective capacity. Teachers operating in the Unaware stage need modeling from peers who are taking their knowledge and putting it in to practice. Action-stage teachers are perfect partners, because they're gung-ho and will push, pull, nudge, or otherwise drag their Unaware-stage colleagues along. This can be an extremely effective partnership, because it benefits both individuals and, therefore, the entire team.

Transformational Feedback

To effect a shift in teachers' *thinking,* capacity-builders must engage in a rigorous process of feedback. When the feedback indeed alters the way a teacher thinks, it becomes *transformational* feedback—and that's our ultimate goal. Administrators, coaches, department heads, and other capacity-builders can all engage in feedback-rich practices such as walk-throughs, rounds, and scheduled coaching sessions (Hall & Simeral, 2008) to obtain opportunities to "talk teaching" with their teachers. When selected intentionally to match their teachers' needs and readiness for reflective feedback, such conversations can help teachers deepen their thinking, expand their mental horizons, and grow as reflective practitioners, thus moving them forward along the Continuum of Self-Reflection.

See Figure 10.6 for a sampling of feedback stems in the form of directive statements that are designed to meet our Unaware-stage teachers' unique and distinct needs. Mind you, this list is but a taste of the ways you, as a capacity-builder, can *launch* a feedback dialogue or otherwise engage a teacher in reflective dialogue. We invite you to connect the dots

FIGURE 10.6

Transformational Feedback for Teachers in the Unaware Stage

Capacity-Building Goal: To build deeper awareness of students, content, and pedagogy

- When you did this ____, the students did this ____. It worked because ____. Do that again!

- I noticed you used ____, and it was effective because ____; use it whenever you want your students to ____.

- When you did this ____, the students did this ____. Tomorrow try ____, and tell me what happens.

- Your lesson was successful today because ____.

- You (or your students) struggled today because ____. Next time that happens, try this: ____, and tell me what happens.

- You appear frustrated with ____, and I noticed you ____ several times. Tomorrow, try to take note of how many times you ____. Then let's chat further.

- I observed ____, which is not what you/we were going for in that lesson; try ____ to get the lesson back on track. This usually works because ____.

between the prompts and the capacity-building goal, and we encourage you to enrich this list by adding your own prompts that match your style and your teachers' needs. Ultimately, beginning a conversation in this spirit should generate reflective thought and partnership. Where it goes from here is completely up to the parties involved.

As we mentioned earlier, teachers operating in the Unaware stage need transparent expectations, clear directions, and specific instructions. They'll believe it when they see it, and it's our role to help them see it. Engaging in teacher-talk with Unaware-stage teachers is not a time for waffling back and forth with ambiguous feedback. To meet this challenge, effective *directive* feedback has four distinct characteristics, as expressed in the following guidelines for delivery.

Draw attention to the goings-on of the classroom. Because teachers operating in the Unaware stage are, by definition, unaware of the details of their classrooms, it's the capacity-builders' responsibility to shed light on what's happening, to draw a connection between the teacher's actions and the students' response, and to identify when things go well (WOW! moments) and when things go awry (YIKES! moments).

Encourage repeated future use of an effective instructional approach. If the teacher engages in a behavior that works (and the practice isn't usually implemented), the capacity-builder should offer specific praise, which will acknowledge success, validate the practice, and provide motivation to repeat the action.

Compliment an attempted use of an effective instructional strategy (with a specific suggestion for improvement). If the teacher attempts an effective strategy that does not go exactly as planned, the capacity-builder should praise the attempt but be equally clear about the modification, which recognizes the effort and offers encouragement to strengthen the practice.

Discourage future use of an ineffective instructional approach. If the teacher uses a faulty strategy, the capacity-builder should provide specific feedback with clear expectations for future alternative actions.

Differentiated Coaching

With clear expectations provided to teachers, capacity-builders can roll up their sleeves and dive into the mucky underbrush of instructional coaching, wading and wrestling with the various approaches that will support teachers' growth as reflective practitioners—ultimately leading to significant levels of learning for all students.

A number of coaching strategies will help teachers operating in the Unaware stage to successfully achieve their capacity-building goal (to build greater awareness of students, content, and pedagogy). A sampling of such strategies, as outlined in the Continuum of Self-Reflection and shown in Figure 10.7, is described in further detail in the next paragraphs. Each of the strategies can be used in isolation or woven with another. Remember, what works splendidly with one teacher may not work as effectively with another, so be sure to *differentiate* your selection and application of these

FIGURE 10.7

Differentiated Coaching Strategies for Teachers in the Unaware Stage

Capacity-Building Goal: To build deeper awareness of students, content, and pedagogy

- Make frequent contact, checking in often to talk about goals and progress toward them.
- Build confidence through short-term goal setting.
- Celebrate successes immediately.
- Model a strategy or lesson.
- Whisper-coach while co-observing another teacher's class.
- Write lesson plans together.
- Coteach a lesson.
- Debrief a lesson together.
- Record a lesson, provide clear look-fors, and debrief the video together.
- Engage in side-by-side reflective journaling.

approaches. What's most important is that the strategy meets each teacher's unique needs and is explicitly connected back to the capacity-building goal, so we can see and monitor our impact more clearly.

Make frequent contact, checking in often to talk about goals and progress toward them. One of the first challenges facing a capacity-builder working with a teacher in the Unaware stage is the need to build a trusting relationship. To cultivate this rapport, frequent visits, casual conversations, and seemingly *inconsequential* actions (such as offering to help grade papers, update a bulletin board, or work one-on-one with a difficult student) can work wonders. These are excellent ways to show that you want to work alongside the teacher and aren't afraid to do the dirty work. In addition, this approach will create opportunities to model specific instructional strategies and ends up being a bridge to cross into the land of *consequential* coaching.

Build confidence through short-term goal setting. Most teachers set annual goals. For some reason that only agriculturalists understand, 10-month time frames are educators' default setting. For teachers operating in the Unaware stage, the finish line often seems like an unobtainable dream far in the distance. To help make this process manageable, the capacity-builder can facilitate a shorter-term, one-bite-at-a-time action plan. The ambition here is to build the teacher's awareness of this single instructional element and use it as the springboard for cultivating self-reflection and a more wide-ranging desire to learn. Once the short-term plan is established (think third period, then tomorrow, then five-day, then one-month time spans), stick with it. Proceed to the next step only when both of you are satisfied that the first step is actualized.

Celebrate successes immediately. When teachers in the Unaware stage complete a task successfully, obtain positive returns from an action, make an acute observation, or otherwise accomplish an intermediary step toward a goal, take advantage of that opportunity to celebrate the success. If it is indeed true that "success begets success"—and we believe it is—then acknowledging such accomplishments will help build awareness, pride, and motivation to continue to work toward the goal.

Model a strategy or lesson. Many teachers in the Unaware stage lack the depth of understanding that we often assume they possess. It's quite possible that despite "training" and experience, a teacher may not know how to use reciprocal teaching as an engaging, powerful instructional strategy. In fact, it's likely that a teacher operating in the Unaware stage knows nothing about such a strategy. As a capacity-builder, you can bring the words to life by modeling the approach right there in the teacher's classroom. By planning together and creating a context for the learning, modeling can be a very effective coaching tool that shows the teacher what an instructional strategy looks like when it's put into action.

Whisper-coach while co-observing in another teacher's classroom. Seeing a strategy put into action can go a long way toward increasing awareness and building knowledge. One structured way to provide additional modeling support is to observe a lesson in another class. After identifying a specific instructional strategy that you want to bring awareness to, strategically arrange for the teacher to observe in a classroom where another teacher is modeling this instructional approach. To add real-time learning, discreetly engage in a whispering dialogue with the teacher about what the host teacher is doing, how the strategy is being used, and ways that the teacher is meeting the specific needs of the students in the room with this particular strategy.

Write lesson plans together. A useful strategy for building awareness and leading a teacher toward intentionality is to plan together. By sitting down and crafting a lesson alongside the teacher, a capacity-builder can simultaneously begin to better understand how that teacher thinks, model what effective planning looks like, and ensure that the most important elements of instruction are intentionally included in the plans.

Coteach a lesson. When leaping out of an airplane, novice skydivers not only have a parachute strapped to their back; there's also an instructor there, helping to make sure things go smoothly as the joy-seeker learns. This can be a useful instructional coaching strategy as well—without the straps. When a teacher and a capacity-builder coteach a lesson, particularly one they have planned together, they can share the responsibilities, model and try out new strategies, and share immediate feedback in real time. Engaging in authentic dialogue about the nuances of the lesson and observations along the way can deepen the teacher's learning, as well as bring transparency of the teaching process to everyone in the room— including the students.

Debrief a lesson together. After a lesson, the post-teaching reflections can begin. Teachers in the Unaware stage, accustomed to receiving directive feedback, must eventually transition into receiving reflective prompts and addressing questions, and this is an excellent place to start. Capacity-builders can initiate thinking about the teacher's actions by bringing attention to the cause-and-effect relationships in that teacher's classroom. Start by asking a series of questions to help the teacher identify highlights (WOW! moments) and struggles (YIKES! moments) during the lesson. Initially the responses you receive may be general and vague, but they will provide a base from which you can build a castle of self-reflection over time. To truly encourage the development of self-reflective thinking, use the following questions as a guide:

- What worked well today? What didn't?

- Which students mastered today's learning objective? Which students didn't? What might account for the differences in learning?

- What was your goal during this lesson? What percentage of students must master the learning objective in order for you to view the lesson as a success?

- What did you learn about [select a student] as a learner today?

- What information did you collect today that you'll use to guide your planning for tomorrow?

Record a lesson, provide clear look-fors, and debrief the video together. Use of video is a strategy that is well acknowledged in education and other professions. With teachers in the Unaware stage, this strategy must be heavily scaffolded to achieve optimal levels of success. With a clear goal in mind, identify the elements you and the teacher will emphasize. Then, with those look-fors handy, watch the video and engage in focused dialogue together. For many teachers, the first effort at watching themselves on video will result in tangential observations about hair, posture, voice, and other distracting issues. For that reason, we suggest that teachers watch a first (practice) video of themselves individually, at home, with a glass of something reassuring in hand. Then destroy the video. Use the second (real) video for coaching and professional growth.

Engage in side-by-side reflective journaling. Writing down one's thoughts is perhaps the most powerful form of self-reflection. Writing, itself, is the great synthesizer of knowledge, learning, and understanding. Asking a teacher in the Unaware stage to record feelings and thoughts at the end of each day is a tangible way to begin the process of synthesis. If your teachers have a copy of our parallel teacher text, *Teach, Reflect, Learn* (Hall & Simeral, 2015), discuss their reflections and journal entries related to the many tasks and scores of reflective questions we offer to encourage reflective growth. Journaling simultaneously, and frequently examining the contents of each other's journals, can jump-start the dialogue and generate renewed synaptic energy. (And for bonus points, ask teachers to submit their reflections to one of our blog posts at http://bycfs.edublogs.org.)

The Unaware Stage in Real Life

Remember the three vignettes we presented earlier in this chapter? Those three teachers, though fictional, are amalgams of actual teachers with whom we've worked as administrators, coaches, teachers, or consultants over the years. We'd like to return to one of them now, to show you how that teacher's particular capacity-builders might come together to provide comprehensive support. In the scenario that follows, we'll provide some detail about their plan, share how the work unfolded, and identify their preliminary results as their teacher grew as a reflective practitioner. And even if the scenario stems from a different grade level than one you support directly, there are lessons to be gleaned from the interactions, the collaboration, and the focus on the *thinking* behind the doing. Remember, self-reflection is context-independent: our brains are the common denominator.

Vignette, Part 2: Mr. Barnett

Mr. Barnett's 2nd grade classroom was abuzz with excited children and much laughter and joy. Parent requests for current 1st graders to be placed in his class the following year were already beginning to arrive in the school office. Early assessment data raised some alerts, however, as the eager students and enthusiastic teacher had not yet connected in a way that had a positive impact on student learning.

The capacity-builders in Mr. Barnett's life—his principal, his instructional coach, and his grade-level team leader—saw potential and were determined to capitalize on their new teacher's strengths. In an early-year conversation, the principal and the instructional coach discussed Mr. Barnett's reflective tendencies and hypothesized that their first-year teacher was operating in the Unaware stage. When the principal sat down with Mr. Barnett and discussed his reflective self-assessment (available in *Teach, Reflect, Learn* [Hall & Simeral, 2015] or online at www.ascd.org/Publications/Books/Overview/Teach-Reflect-Learn.aspx), Mr. Barnett shared that he had scored himself in the Conscious stage. Believing there might be a little naïve exaggeration at play, the principal prepared to offer support from the Unaware stage, ready to shift to Conscious-stage strategies at any moment.

Mr. Barnett's principal clarified two points. The first was that their common goal was to support Mr. Barnett's growth as a teacher (both technical and reflective aspects), and the second was that, as a new teacher, he had a lot to learn, so his focus ought to be in the first quadrant of the Reflective Cycle: building awareness. The principal, the instructional coach, and Mr. Barnett agreed to work toward the capacity-building goal of building Mr. Barnett's awareness of his students and the direct impact he could have upon their learning.

Because the principal and the instructional coach had agreed on a course of action, the principal assumed the role of director, sitting down with Mr. Barnett and making the expectations very clear: the school had a strong focus on literacy skills, and it was essential that Mr. Barnett access local assessments to identify his students' reading levels, skills, gaps, strengths, and struggles so he could prepare lessons that met their individual and group needs. He suggested that Mr. Barnett seek out his instructional coach for support in learning how to use assessment results for these purposes.

The instructional coach, as an unconditional partner, had spent the first few months of the school year bopping in and out of Mr. Barnett's class, offering resources, helping to plan here and there, and getting to know him as a teacher and as a colleague. Now, as Mr. Barnett reached out for specific support with literacy assessments and ideas of differentiation, the relationship served its purpose: they could get on with the work. The coach selected two strategies for deepening Mr. Barnett's thinking. First, they spent time looking at the local literacy assessments and determining what the data meant and how they might be useful for him in planning differentiated lessons; and second, they began reflective journaling, with a particular focus on Mr. Barnett's keen ability to know his students and how that knowledge—and his strong relationships with them—might enable him to motivate students to read just-right books, challenge themselves, and better access the lessons.

The principal and the coach both provided frequent feedback through regular walk-throughs, offering nonevaluative praise (to support effective practice) and corrective statements (when Mr. Barnett "bungled things up," in his own words). They also made special efforts to sit down with him for 5 or 10 minutes during his planning time once or twice a week, just to "talk teaching," get his pulse, and offer support for anything with which he was struggling.

About midway through the year, the instructional coach noticed Mr. Barnett's metaphorical emergency hazard lights flashing. Mr. Barnett seemed stressed and worried, and he had called in sick on a Friday—highly unusual because of the fun classroom activities he usually planned for Fridays. On the following Monday, his coach visited his classroom first thing to connect and chat. It turned out that Mr. Barnett had reached his breaking point—the demands on his time, the constant assault of new information, the evaluation process, and the stress of always pushing forward were wearing him down. Astutely, his instructional coach scheduled a time when they could list the many demands and prioritize them, to ensure that he was handling the "big-deal" requirements first. Then, Mr. Barnett was very intentionally partnered with his grade-level team leader.

Recruiting the support of the 2nd grade team leader was the piece that had perhaps the greatest impact on Mr. Barnett. Knowing that Mr. Barnett was up to his eyeballs as a new teacher—everything to him was new, different, challenging, exhausting—the team leader agreed to spend a couple minutes before each team meeting, faculty meeting, and data session to preview the content or give Mr. Barnett an advance copy of the material. Then, after each meeting, the team leader made it a point to connect with Mr. Barnett to check in and make sure he was feeling confident and secure in his role. This not only supported the new teacher's attitude, technical skill, and reflective growth, it also helped to build a strong, collegial relationship within his team.

As his first year ended and he began the preparations for Year 2, Mr. Barnett was all smiles—and now it was because his students had experienced success. "We had 95 percent meet the grade-level benchmarks—one student out of 20 was close and making progress—and I didn't even know what those benchmarks were before my coach started helping me. And I was concerned that the kids would lose their love of school if I shifted my focus from fun to academics. It turns out they were highly motivated by success! The more they could read, the more they liked school. I'm looking forward to my next crop and starting teaching intentionally right away!"

The Unaware Stage at a Glance

In the journey toward expertise, the Unaware stage is the starting point. Before we learn something, try something new, grow as a professional, or develop our expertise, we must first realize what we don't know and pay attention to what it is we'd like to learn about. Teachers currently operating in the Unaware stage are primed for the expedition to parts unknown, and as capacity-builders, it's our responsibility to usher them forth—first helping to modify their behaviors and actions so their thoughts and beliefs will follow. And as our teachers are able to engage in more frequent, accurate, and deep reflections about their professional responsibilities, they become *conscious* of their students, content, and pedagogy. This growth in their reflective capacity ushers them along the Continuum of Self-Reflection toward the Conscious stage.

Supporting Teachers in
the Conscious Stage

Let's say you come to work one day and you're asked by your supervisor to complete all your tasks with your nondominant hand. If you're right-handed, that would mean that you'd have to write, use the computer mouse, cut with scissors, file papers, throw objects, pour coffee, and shake hands with your left hand. How do you suppose that would work for you? How would you respond to such a situation?

Research and our common experiences suggest that we'd somehow rebel against that directive. We might use our left hand while in the presence of the supervisor, but left alone, we'd work right-handed. Or maybe we'd skip some of the duties assigned to us, ask someone to do them for us, question the purpose of changing hands, or just dig in our heels and continue right-handed anyway. Perhaps, even, we'd try to work left-handed for a bit, but when it got too difficult, we'd revert back to our right-handed ways.

Without proper motivation, clarity, skills, and support, this rebellion would probably continue. Why? Maybe we couldn't understand why we were asked to change. Perhaps we didn't think the change was going to benefit us or our work. It could be that we didn't respect the person asking us to change. Or—most likely—we'd become so ingrained in operating a certain way that our default setting dominated our thinking. We had developed deep, powerful habits: "the choices all of us deliberately make at some point, and then stop thinking about but continue doing, often every day" (Duhigg, 2012, p. xvii).

The tasks themselves are rather pedestrian: writing, cutting, carrying, and so on. You know how to do all those things, you have a pretty clear vision of how they should look when done successfully, and you know why they're important. You may even have many years of successful use of a computer mouse in your repertoire of skills, and no one pours a cup of coffee as gracefully as you do. However, your knowledge and experience do you little good when you're forced to switch hands—because it's like starting all over again.

Although this scenario may seem far-fetched, it runs parallel to the reality our teachers face every day. In the field of education, as initiatives are unveiled during August back-to-school kickoffs every summer, as new curriculum and materials are dropped upon our teachers' desks, as assessment approaches with frighteningly new technology are introduced, and as the expectations of more, better, stronger, faster, bigger are levied upon educators at all levels, many of our colleagues find themselves in this educational purgatory: we *know* quite a bit, but the *doing* lags behind.

The knowing-doing gap, first introduced by Pfeffer and Sutton (2000), describes this phenomenon. There's ample research to describe best practices and the elements of teaching that will predictably lead to higher levels of student learning, so the *knowing* is rarely the issue. Applying that knowledge into our practice, then, is the challenge *du jour*.

Indeed, knowledge can take us only so far. The knowing-doing gap is an epidemic—across cultures, socioeconomic backgrounds, and every cross-section of our society. It can be found on global and corporate levels, and it may well include the districts in which we are employed, the schools in which we work, and the classrooms in which we teach. It's something that affects all of us as educators, no matter how many years of experience or how much expertise we have.

All teachers—all educators, really—have fallen victim to the knowing-doing gap. In fact, it's a predictable inevitability. As we learn something new and build our skills, our thinking moves us beyond the Unaware stage, and teachers begin operating in the Conscious stage (see Figure 11.1), a term we've coined to describe folks who may find themselves struggling to transfer their knowledge into solid, transformative action. In order to see the results we want, teachers must learn how to put what they know into practice, both intentionally and consistently. Let's consider the term more closely.

FIGURE 11.1

The Conscious Stage

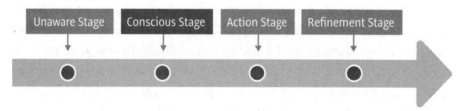

Conscious: *being aware of what is around you and having knowledge with the ability to think*

An educator might find herself operating in the Conscious stage for any of a dozen or more reasons, and it's not always because she is uncomfortable with a "new" or innovative approach or strategy. Because the research on increasing instructional effectiveness is so plentiful and accessible, it's often the rather "pedestrian" teacher moves that trip us up. Consider your own growth as a professional and your development as a reflective thinker. Do any of these sound familiar?

- Uncertainty about how to most effectively implement a strategy.

- Incomplete understanding of the approach or the reason for trying it.

- Confusion about how to fit everything onto the already overloaded plate.

- Distracted by competing demands for time and energy.
- Finding external explanations for lack of success and results.
- Preferring to continue with comfortable, reliable practices.
- Feeling threatened or worried about change.
- Lacking time to effectively plan and prepare for these strategies.
- Distrust of the source of the change, innovation, or expectation.

Perhaps the most influential factor that contributes to the Conscious-stage teacher's knowing-doing gap is the dominating presence of *habits*. Just as needing special motivation, clarity, skills, and support will enable right-handed filers to more efficiently begin to file left-handed, so will those influences alter the way teachers think about their behaviors in the classroom, empowering them to eschew their habitual actions and create new neural pathways to adapt their performance. For teachers operating in the Conscious stage, habits rule—and capacity-builders must help them *think* their way out in order to grow as reflective practitioners.

Capacity-builders must help teachers *think* their way out of their habits in order to grow as reflective practitioners.

It is essential to remember that the Continuum of Self-Reflection is not an evaluation tool; rather, it is a powerful instrument that serves two incredibly helpful purposes. First, it helps capacity-builders (and teachers themselves) identify their teachers' reflective tendencies. Second, it guides those capacity-builders (administrators and coaches) to the proper entry point and directs their capacity-building efforts. There is no value—no "better than" or "worse than"—assigned to any of the stages on the continuum; there are just terms that describe how teachers think about the work. The characteristics of thinking displayed by an individual teacher should be used without prejudice to help you, as a capacity-builder, to determine the best course of action to support that teacher's growth as a reflective practitioner. The goal in using this tool is not to evaluate, label, or "fix" teachers, unyieldingly; the goal is to lead teachers to develop strong patterns of thought as we usher them down the path of self-reflection.

The First Step: Identification of Reflective Tendencies

Let's walk through several classrooms and take a closer look at teachers who are currently operating in the Conscious stage. As you read these brief vignettes, begin to assimilate the characteristics that describe thinking in the Conscious stage. This is the first step in identifying our teachers' reflective tendencies. The vignettes featuring Ms. Esteban and Mr. Pickering originally appeared in our earlier book *Teach, Reflect, Learn* [Hall & Simeral, 2015]. We present them here as examples to be considered from the viewpoint of the capacity-builders, including administrators and coaches.)

Vignettes, Part 1: Meet the Teachers

Visit 1: Elementary, Ms. Esteban

At Friday's collaborative team meeting, the 3rd grade team decides to start Unit 2 on Monday. The weekend flies by, and Ms. Esteban doesn't have a chance to sketch out her lesson plans. She gets to school a few minutes early to figure out what she's going to do for the day. Glancing at the math text, she skims the lesson and decides she'll do what she always does—explain how to do the problem set, model, and have her students complete the practice problems in the book while she walks around to help them.

Math that day is painful—for both the students and Ms. Esteban. Everyone is frustrated and Ms. Esteban ends up deviating from the plan; she teaches a lesson on place value instead. She then assigns the practice problems for home-work. She knows that if she had spent more time preparing for the lesson, it probably would have been more successful, but she didn't have the time today.

That afternoon, Ms. Esteban runs into the school's instructional coach, who asks how the first lesson of the unit went.

"Horrible," states Ms. Esteban. "My kids are so low in math! They completely lack the basics. I had to explain place value to them today. Some acted like they had never even heard of the hundreds place. We'll continue slogging through the unit, but it's not going to be pretty. I can tell you right now, they're not going to do well on the end-of-unit test."

Visit 2: Middle School, Mr. Pickering

It's 30 minutes before the welcome bell rings, and Mr. Pickering, in his 12th year as an educator, is writing his social studies assignments on the board. As he outlines the directions, his mind jumps to the training that he received over the summer on student engagement. It was filled with great ideas, some of which he really wanted to try in his classroom.

This year, however, turned out to be much different than he expected. The very first day was filled with reprimands to students to put cell phones away and stop talking. He ended up giving an impromptu lecture on what it means to be respectful and assigning extra homework. It seemed to have little impact, as the weeks that followed were filled with more of the same. He knew it was going to be a long year.

Mr. Pickering shrugs to himself as he finishes up. This wasn't the year to offer the reward of "fun learning." He knew it would be a waste of his time. Plus, it took all of his after-hours energy just to keep abreast of the new standards and text-books the school had adopted. It was easier to stick with reading directly from the text and assigning the chapter questions when dealing with kids such as these. He'd just wait until next year, when things settled down, to try some new strategies.

Visit 3: High School, Mrs. Davis

In her eighth year of teaching, Mrs. Davis runs a tight ship. Her chemistry classes run like clockwork, and the precision with which she has established routines and expectations for her students is admirable—students know exactly how to file in, collect their entry task, and get to work on the day's lab without any prompting from their teacher.

When the school's leadership team announced that every classroom would share the responsibility of teaching vital literacy skills—in order to address their students' lagging scores and struggles with complex literacy concepts—Mrs. Davis shook her head. Why was she having to make up for what they weren't getting in English class? She had plenty to cover in chem, and she couldn't envision students reading novels about chemists when they could be learning by performing authentic chemistry experiments instead. It seemed an absurd twist.

Mrs. Davis attended staff professional development sessions on "literacy across the curriculum" but did not see the connections to her chemistry classes. Instead, she smiled along during the training and was happy to get back to her lab, where she could get on with the teaching of real science. If the students continued to struggle on the tests, maybe admin should rethink all that standardized testing, she thought. Or go talk to the English department.

These vignettes, while unique in many ways, contain a number of strong similarities. As capacity-builders, it's our responsibility to see beyond the teachers' actions in their classrooms, focusing our attention instead on the thinking that propels their doing. In the case of these three teachers, each has a particular way of conducting his or her professional business, and because of "outside" factors, the teaching and learning process hits a snag. Ms. Esteban's students got lost in some content they should have known, the behaviors in Mr. Pickering's room affect the students' learning, and the focus of Mrs. Davis's school frustrates her.

Looking closer, we can identify a common *thinking* pattern that contributes to a knowing-doing gap in all three: Mrs. Esteban's lack of planning caused tumult in her students' learning, Mr. Pickering waves an indifferent hand at the impact he can have on his learning environment, and Mrs. Davis actively dismisses what she perceives to be a misguided initiative. All three, it turns out, are focused on how their situations are affecting *them*, rather than vice versa. All three teachers are operating in the Conscious stage.

Reflective Tendencies of a Conscious-Stage Teacher

Teachers operating in the Conscious stage on the Continuum of Self-Reflection have several powerful characteristics that describe the manner in which they think about their professional responsibilities and their impact on student learning. As we've already mentioned, two powerful forces are *habit* and the *knowing-doing gap*. A third descriptor, highlighted in the three vignettes, is the teacher's interpretation of how the change (or the initiative, or the scenario, or the results) affects *them* as individuals. The Conscious stage is as much about efficacy as it is about change management. What follows are descriptions of the overarching reflective tendencies, as shown in Figure 11.2, of a teacher in the Conscious stage.

FIGURE 11.2

Teacher's Reflective Tendencies: Conscious Stage

- Demonstrates a consistent "knowing-doing" gap.
- Reflects when prompted by others.
- Offers external explanations for problems or challenges.
- Makes generalizations in observations about classroom reality.
- Collaborates inconsistently with colleagues.
- Tends to operate with strong habits and comfortable practices.
- Becomes easily distracted from goals.
- Disregards others' ideas.
- Focuses first on *self*.

Demonstrates a consistent "knowing-doing" gap. Pfeffer and Sutton (2000) define this tendency as "not the inertia of indifference or ignorance, but of knowing too much and doing too little" (p. 135). Today, in the information age, knowledge is plentiful and research on "best practices" or "high-yield strategies" fills our Twitter feed faster than we can scroll through it. For teachers in the Conscious stage, the combination of research, experience, and professional development is not sufficient to influence planning and teaching decisions. Although teachers thinking in this manner can talk the talk, for one reason or another they opt not to walk the walk.

Reflects when prompted by others. Self-reflection is a skill, not an inherited trait. As such, it can be developed, strengthened, and refined. At this point in their development, teachers in the Conscious stage tend to need prompting in order to engage in the skill of self-reflection. Left to their own devices, they won't engage in deep, accurate, and frequent reflections about their responsibilities, their plans, and their impact upon student learning. Rather, they will proceed along the well-beaten path they've laid and continue to engage in their habitual, comfortable practices.

Offers external explanations for problems or challenges. When things don't go as well as the teacher hoped, or if the students fared more poorly than expected, teachers in the Conscious stage often find a reason for the struggles. Perhaps the students didn't work hard enough, their behaviors in the classroom were too disruptive, the assembly interrupted the flow of the lesson, the curriculum pacing guide forced the class to progress too rapidly through the content, or some other external cause served as explanation. In the past, folks in leadership roles dismissed such concerns as "excuses," but our thinking has evolved. The term *explanations* offers us insight into the teacher's thinking and mindset, even if we don't agree with the cause-and-effect relationship it suggests.

Makes generalizations in observations about classroom reality. Teachers operating in the Conscious stage see their classroom with a big-picture point of view. Rather than dig into the finer details of a successful lesson, an upset parent, a struggling student, or a bombed quiz, teachers here tend to provide sweeping accounts, often using the dastardly pronoun *they.* For instance, one might hear a Conscious-stage teacher utter, "They just weren't into the lesson today," or "They can't sit still for more than seven minutes," casting the entire lot into the same bin—even though it may well have been one student, or one group of students, whose disinterest overwhelmed the teacher's perceptions.

Collaborates inconsistently with colleagues. Whether Conscious-stage teachers show it or not, they often recognize that they are not doing all that they can when it comes to delivering instruction in the classroom. A natural consequence is that they withdraw from the relationships that they feel will hold them accountable for their practices. Professional discussions are often limited to items that are most interesting or most directly affect them individually, and most collegial interactions are lighthearted and inconsequential to student learning. Teachers in this stage tend to avoid topics that require deep thought, vulnerability, and professional collaboration.

Tends to operate with strong habits and comfortable practices. We all have comfort zones, which are, by definition, comfortable.

Extending that thinking, anything outside of our comfort zones would be, well, *un*comfortable. In the Conscious stage, the comfort of the known and the tried-and-true trumps the disequilibrium of trying something different, venturing down a foreign path, or attempting a new approach—even when the research, the evidence, and the situation call for it. For any of myriad reasons, teachers operating in this stage are challenged by the act of plotting a course and strategically taking steps—comfortable, uncomfortable, or both—to progress toward their goals.

 Our advice? Embrace the disequilibrium.

Becomes easily distracted from goals. Many teachers operating in the Conscious stage have set goals to improve their teaching or to support gains in student learning. However, because of the influences of external factors and the reliance on habitual practices, these goals—often established with (or by) well-meaning administrators or colleagues—are often cast aside when the rigors and demands of the school year begin to mount. The challenge for Conscious-stage teachers is to pursue a focused path, follow through, and remain steadfast in their commitment to accomplishing goals that are truly meaningful and relevant to them.

Disregards others' ideas. As we've heard a thousand times, change is hard. When improvement is required, change becomes a necessity (we all can recite that famous quote from Albert Einstein, right?). For teachers in the Conscious stage, ownership of new efforts, alternate approaches, or universal initiatives is a critical piece of their motivation—if they don't own it, they likely won't buy into it. As a result, ideas proposed by others, in particular those in administrative roles, are often dismissed as *fads—something that we've tried and that didn't work*, or *great for another classroom or another school, but not mine*.

Focuses first on *self*. What do all these reflective characteristics have in common? A focus on self: How will this affect me? What does this mean for me? Decisions in a Conscious-stage teacher's classroom are based primarily on teacher preference, convenience, or comfort—their regard for the needs of their students takes a back seat to their own job satisfaction. It's important to note that teachers in the Conscious stage still care very deeply about the success and well-being of their students, and they are by no means sabotaging learning; rather, their motivation to select strategies, choose actions, and plan activities stems from within and what they *want* to do.

Using the Reflective Cycle (Figure 11.3), we can take a closer look at the distinct thought patterns and reflective habits of teachers in the Conscious

FIGURE 11.3

Intentionality in the Reflective Cycle

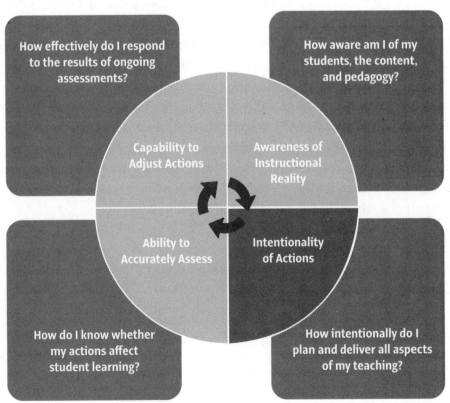

stage. This will provide us, as instructional leaders and capacity-builders, with valuable insights that enable us to accurately identify how our teachers are currently *thinking* about their professional responsibilities—which will allow us to support their continued growth as reflective practitioners.

At this point, it's probably pretty clear how far along the Reflective Cycle our teacher's thinking has developed, or at which quadrant our teacher's thinking is breaking down. Have you identified it? If you chose "Intentionality of Actions" for a teacher operating in the Conscious stage, you're ready to proceed as a capacity-builder, and the question to ask is this: *How intentional is the teacher's planning and instruction?*

Teachers operating in the Conscious stage have an awareness of instructional realities—they know their students to a certain extent and have knowledge of content and instructional practices. For them, the breakdown occurs in the second quadrant of the Reflective Cycle. To bridge the gap between what this teacher *knows* and what this teacher *does*, two forces must enter the equation: intentionality and consistency. Naturally, intentionality must come first, as our teachers' plans must reflect their knowledge of their students, the content and goals, and the instructional methods used to accomplish them. Then, when initial successes follow, those successful practices must be repeated, practiced, and consistently implemented—until they become the new norm, the new habit, the new modus operandi in the classroom. Excellence is not happenstance—it's a result of deliberate thought and intentional actions.

The Second Step: Supportive Practices

Each stage within the Continuum of Self-Reflection has a capacity-building goal to develop and support each individual teacher's reflective growth. Here is the overall goal for the Conscious-stage teacher:

> Our goal is *to work with greater intentionality in addressing student needs, content, and pedagogical practices* in order to

create new habits of mind and practice that lead to greater
results and increases in student learning.

Teachers in the Conscious stage have accumulated some experience, gathered some professional know-how, and are in the process of growing their expertise. Leading them to the promised land of consistent, deliberate, reliable, habitual action is perhaps the capacity-builder's most challenging—and therefore most rewarding—responsibility. The move from Conscious-stage thinking to Action-stage thinking will provide the most monumental change in a teacher's practice. It's a seismic shift in the geology of a teacher, a team, a school, or even an entire district. This is the epicenter of the conversion from compliance to commitment.

As capacity-builders, it's crucial for us to understand that shifting action doesn't always result in shifted thinking, but shifting thinking will *always* result in shifted action. Our charge is to tackle the thinking that drives the doing. If we're to successfully cultivate a culture of reflective practice and facilitate long-term professional growth, we must ask teachers to *think* as often as we ask them to *do*. Their growth in thinking, then, will fuel a curiosity and desire to learn more.

Leadership Roles

How do capacity-builders begin to address the specific needs of a teacher in the Conscious stage? To have the impact necessary for continued reflective growth, administrators and coaches simultaneously work independently (within their own roles) and collaboratively (as their roles are complementary to one another), as well as intentionally leveraging a teacher's peers within the PLC structure to provide additional support, as noted in the triad diagram in Figure 11.4. In the absence of an instructional coach, the administrator must be even more deliberate in the use of peer relationships to engage in this work. This strategic triangulation of support significantly increases the likelihood of success.

FIGURE 11.4

Triad Diagram for Conscious Stage

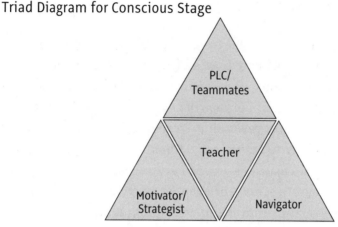

As described in Chapter 5, a couple of conditions must be established in order to proceed with our capacity-building efforts. First, the roles of administrator and coach must be defined, distinguished, and communicated clearly to one another. Second, the boundaries that encompass each role must be respected at all times. In the case of working with Conscious-stage teachers, these roles manifest themselves in unique and important ways as we work to guide the teachers toward their capacity-building goal.

 The administrator's role: *navigator*.

The administrator's role is that of *navigator*, steering the Conscious-stage teacher's thinking toward the agreed-upon goal and strategies that make up the teacher's action plan. In nautical or aeronautical terms, a navigator is responsible for charting the vessel's current location, its heading, and the most efficient course toward the ultimate destination. In the world of professional education, the administrator provides this essential assistance. Because teachers operating in the Conscious stage tend to be swayed from their goals due to outside influences (or their perception of them), are challenged by turning knowledge into action, and revert to comfortable habits, it's critical for them to have an administrator present to steer their thinking toward the proper bearings.

The navigator is a partner in the voyage, as even a school administrator realizes that teachers are captains of their own ships. Therefore, the administrator's functions include providing consistent reminders of the agreed-upon goal, redirecting conversations and actions back to the goal and action plan, and engaging in feedback that helps to focus and hone the teacher's thinking as it relates directly to the related actions. This role serves to limit the variability in what a Conscious-stage teacher might be *thinking about* and *acting upon* in the classroom—thereby charting a course that shrinks the disconnect between what the teacher knows and does.

 The coach's role: *motivator and strategist.*

The coach's role is to work alongside the Conscious-stage teacher as *motivator and strategist* focused on the goal of helping to increase the intentionality of the thinking behind the teacher's actions. Not surprisingly, teachers displaying characteristics of Conscious-stage thinking will need some additional motivation and strategizing in order to accomplish their goals. When their knowing-doing gap and reverting to habitual actions run up against the navigational influence of a supportive administrator, the coach's motivator/strategist role will help teachers channel back onto a course toward the agreed-upon goals and action plan. The motivation, which must necessarily stem from a strong professional relationship, will serve to boost the teachers' confidence, enhance their sense of efficacy, and strengthen their resolve.

The strategizing, meanwhile, takes the form of carefully articulated, intentional planning: What are the steps this teacher must take in order to meet the charge of the administrator and the needs of the students? This planning helps the teacher by lessening the anxiety about *how* to proceed, offers a thought partner to bounce ideas off, and provides unilateral support as the teacher tackles a challenge.

Working Complementarily

As expressed in Chapter 5, the coach and the administrator are partners in this work. Sharing a common goal of supporting a teacher's growth as a reflective practitioner, each assumes the role just outlined very intentionally, knowing the other will shoulder the complementary role.

This collaborative relationship is put to the test more urgently within the Conscious stage than at any other stop along the Continuum of Self-Reflection. Why? Because this stage can be, for lack of a better phrase, fraught with peril. The Conscious stage is where resistance holes up, where inaction takes hold, where arguments lurk, and where reluctance lingers. For each teacher operating in the Conscious stage, the knowing-doing gap exists for a very real, and very personal, reason. It's the capacity-builders' mission to explore that reason, identify the root causes, and help the teacher think through it in order to make progress.

As the administrator begins the process by helping the teacher identify goals and the beginning steps of an action plan, the coach continues to build the relationship and set the stage for continued support. Likely needing help in detailing the plan and preparing to implement it, the teacher will reach out to the coach for support—at which point the motivation and strategic planning come in. At each step along the way, the administrator will press and guide the Conscious-stage teacher's thinking toward the agreed-upon heading, and the coach will swoop in to provide timely support and unyielding partnership. With both roles complementing one another, our teacher will have no choice but to implement the plan, try the strategies, and reflect intentionally about the impact they're having on student learning outcomes.

Strategic PLC and Teacher-Leadership Support

The administrator and the coach are not the only capacity-builders who share the immense responsibility of supporting teachers' growth as reflective practitioners. Because teaching is no longer done in isolation (those days are behind us, right?), each educator's relationships with colleagues, peers, and other professionals within their grade-level or department or professional learning community are vital in completing our triad (see Figure 11.4, p. 198). Within a culture of reflective practice, administrators set the expectation that teachers will work collaboratively to support each other in their pursuit of common goals, and then it's "all hands on deck" to engage in the practices that accomplish that objective.

Teachers operating in the Conscious stage tend to be so focused on the impact everything around them is having on *them,* they miss the opportunity to truly have an impact on—or truly gain from—their colleagues. As a result, their contributions and participation in collaborative discussions are inconsistent and yield very little shift in their thinking. Teacher teams (grade-level teams, department teams, PLCs, or any other structure) can offer a tremendous amount of assistance and backing for their Conscious-stage colleagues, however, by engaging in practices that encourage intentionality and consistency in all their team actions. The strategies in Figure 11.5 may strengthen a Conscious-stage teacher's ability to contribute, support, and learn within a professional learning community structure. Let's examine each one in greater detail.

FIGURE 11.5

Strategic PLC and Teacher-Leadership Support: Conscious Stage

Capacity-Building Goal: To work with greater intentionality in addressing student needs, content, and pedagogical practices

- Emphasize the use of data (pre and post) to clarify cause-and-effect relationships.
- Analyze student work samples as a team.
- Promote team lesson planning.
- Facilitate collegial observations to see strategies at work in various settings.
- Use protocols to guide discussion and promote engagement.
- Strategically partner this teacher with a colleague (in particular, one in the Refinement Stage) to grow reflective capacity.

Emphasize the use of data (pre and post) to clarify cause-and-effect relationships. Although Conscious-stage teachers tend to make decisions based on personal preferences, hunches, or familiar practices, colleagues within a team can help focus their thinking—and their actions—by using data to inform their decision making. Using a protocol (see Hall et al., 2016; Easton, 2009; or www.nsrfharmony.org for great examples of professional protocols), teams can analyze data in a way that makes explicit the cause-and-effect relationship between teacher actions and student learning outcomes. These data can also serve as perhaps the most potent driver of future instructional decisions, student learning plans, intervention ideas, and professional learning needs.

Analyze student work samples as a team. The richness of a teacher's learning is enhanced by the dialogue with peers. When teacher teams get together and analyze student work samples, it's more than an exercise in determining scores from a rubric. These discussions often lead to greater investigations of educational philosophy, particular teaching maneuvers, adherence to plans, adaptations for individual students, and alternate strategies to accomplish similar goals. With proper parameters established in advance, these examinations lead to the creation and refinement of strategic plans to address student needs more directly.

Promote team lesson planning. What gets planned gets done—or so they say. (A decade ago that phrase changed to "What gets tested gets done," but that's another matter.) Not everything that goes into a lesson plan is implemented perfectly or universally, but the odds of it being carried out increase astronomically when all the teachers on the team agree to it and will revisit their results together afterward. The more opportunities that teams have to sit down and plan lessons, units, activities, and strategies together, the more effective their collective lessons will be—and the benefits for Conscious-stage teachers will be noticed straight away.

Facilitate collegial observations to see strategies at work in various settings. One stumbling block that Conscious-stage teachers encounter is the lack of understanding of what a particular instructional technique looks and sounds like in action. By opening colleagues' doors and by establishing an environment in which teachers can—and *want to*—visit each other's classrooms to observe lessons, practice approaches, provide and receive feedback, and share ideas, capacity-builders are effectively creating a *true* professional learning community, where interdependence and collaborative support reign. And for teachers in the Conscious stage, this strategy helps to provide the clarity, motivation, and intentionality they so desperately need.

Use protocols to guide discussion and promote engagement. Many teachers in the Conscious stage are hesitant to share their approaches or results with their colleagues. Others dominate the conversations or shift from one topic to another, essentially derailing team meetings and preventing the focus from remaining squarely on student needs and the instructional plans the team needs to make in order to meet them. With protocols for team discussions established, all members of the team have equal opportunity to submit ideas, to exchange thoughts, to question, and to provide input. This limits the dominators and coaxes the reticent so that all voices are heard and all minds are enriched.

Strategically partner this teacher with a colleague (in particular, one in the Refinement stage) to grow reflective capacity. Teachers in the Conscious stage must be paired intentionally in order to adequately deepen their thinking. The most beneficial partner is a colleague in the Refinement stage, because that person is likely to challenge the external explanations and forge a path forward anyway. Refinement-stage teachers are usually perfect partners because they can model effective reflection and problem-solving approaches for implementing strategies that the Conscious-stage teacher might otherwise bypass.

Transformational Feedback

To effect a shift in our teachers' *thinking,* capacity-builders must engage in a rigorous process of feedback. When the feedback indeed alters the way a teacher thinks, it becomes *transformational* feedback—and that's our ultimate goal. Administrators, coaches, department heads, and other capacity-builders can all engage in feedback-rich practices such as walk-throughs, rounds, and scheduled coaching sessions (Hall & Simeral, 2008) to obtain opportunities to "talk teaching" with their teachers. When selected intentionally to match their teachers' needs and readiness for reflective feedback, such conversations can help teachers deepen their thinking, expand their mental horizons, and grow as reflective practitioners—thus moving them forward along the Continuum of Self-Reflection.

See Figure 11.6 for a sampling of feedback stems in the form of "leading prompts" that are designed to meet our Conscious-stage teachers' unique and distinct needs. Mind you, this list is but a taste of the ways you, as a capacity-builder, can *launch* a feedback dialogue or otherwise engage a teacher in reflective dialogue. We invite you to connect the dots between the prompts and the capacity-building goal, and we encourage you to enrich this list by adding your own prompts that match your style and your teachers' needs. Ultimately, beginning a conversation in this spirit should generate reflective thought and partnership. Where it goes from here is completely up to the parties involved.

Working with a teacher in the Conscious stage tests you, as a capacity-builder, to be extremely clear, articulate, and intentional in your dialogue and feedback practices. Transparency around the *purpose* of the feedback process is also worth repeating—with great frequency and intentionality—to ensure that the Conscious-stage teacher understands why you're asking the questions you're asking and what the reflective goal is. Leading the teacher to more intentional, consistent application of practices that meet student needs is ultimately the goal. Effective feedback in this stage meets four criteria, as expressed in the following guidelines for delivery.

Confirm the teacher's focus on a previously agreed-upon goal or action plan. Connect the subheading with the characteristics of the sample prompts we've provided in Figure 11.6. How do the questions posed serve as "leading prompts"? You'll notice that each question, following a specific piece of observational (nonjudgmental) feedback, leaves the teacher with very little wiggle room to answer. This architecture is quite intentional, as it encourages teachers to tap into their existing knowledge, connect to their goals and action plans, and respond in a way that reestablishes their focus.

FIGURE 11.6

Transformational Feedback for Teachers in the Conscious Stage

Capacity-Building Goal: To work with greater intentionality in addressing student needs, content, and pedagogical practices

- Your goal is ___. How can I help you keep that focus and support your efforts?
- I see you were using ___ today. Keep that focus! What worked well today?
- Tell me about the purpose of today's activity. What is your evidence of success?
- Today, your students were successful at ___. What did you do that directly led to their success?
- I noticed ___ today. How might the outcomes change if you tried ___? Give it a shot and let me know how it goes.
- Yesterday I observed your students ___; today, they are ___. How do you determine your daily lesson structure?
- Tell me more about the planning that went into today's lesson. Why did you select the strategy you chose for this lesson?
- How do you use what you know about your students to drive lesson planning each day?
- When you did ___ today, I observed several students ___. How will you shift tomorrow's lesson to change the outcomes?
- How does this lesson connect to prior and future student learning objectives?
- What misconceptions might students have during tomorrow's lesson? How will you address that in your planning?

The more we say it, the more we tend to believe it; and the more we believe it, the more we're willing to act in accordance with it.

Encourage consistent application of effective instructional practices. Teachers in the Conscious stage need reassurance and compliments when things go well—and using Dweck's (2006) growth mindset, when they've made an *effort* to enact positive changes. Feedback that compliments such efforts and encourages replication of effective practices is likely to yield more consistent attempts from the teacher.

Redirect teaching behaviors toward the proper heading. Because the knowing-doing gap is real, when it rears its ugly head, capacity-builders must help illuminate the Conscious-stage teacher to that reality and reca-librate the focus back on the agreed-upon goals and action plan. By crafting questions that gently (or not so gently, depending on the situation) provide parameters for the teacher's responses, capacity-builders can ensure that the teacher's thinking—followed by actions—will be more in line with their common expectations.

Extend self-reflective efforts. Conscious-stage teachers haven't yet developed the skill of deep, accurate, and frequent self-reflection. That's OK, because we can teach it to them! By progressively including more open-ended reflective questions into the dialogue, "talking teaching" with a Conscious-stage teacher can rapidly progress into a veritable discussion, chock full of hypotheses, suggestions, wonderings, and inspirations.

Differentiated Coaching

With clarity around the goals and action plans, teachers and capacity-builders can roll up their sleeves and dive into the mucky underbrush of instructional coaching, wading and wrestling with the various approaches that will support teachers' growth as reflective practitioners—ultimately leading to significant levels of learning for all students.

A number of coaching strategies will help teachers operating in the Conscious stage to successfully achieve their capacity-building goal (to work with greater intentionality in addressing student needs, content, and pedagogical practices). A sampling of such strategies, as outlined in the Continuum of Self-Reflection and shown in Figure 11.7, is described in further detail in the next paragraphs. Each of the strategies can be used in isolation or woven with another. Remember, what works splendidly with one teacher may not work as effectively with another, so be sure to *differentiate* your selection and application of these approaches. What's most

FIGURE 11.7

Differentiated Coaching Strategies for Teachers in the Conscious Stage

---

Capacity-Building Goal: To work with greater intentionality in addressing student needs, content, and pedagogical practices

- Make daily contact, checking in often to talk about goals and progress toward them.
- Build confidence through short-term goal setting.
- Celebrate successes immediately.
- Meet weekly for collaborative planning.
- Engage through interactive journaling.
- Invite participation in small-group discussions around a common problem of practice.
- Model a strategy or lesson in the teacher's classroom.
- Coplan, coteach, and debrief a lesson together.
- Provide opportunities to observe in other classrooms—using clear look-fors.
- Record a lesson, provide clear look-fors, and debrief the video together.

---

important is that the strategy meets each teacher's unique needs and is explicitly connected back to the capacity-building goal—so we can see and monitor our impact more clearly.

Make daily contact, checking in often to talk about goals and progress toward them. When caught in the knowing-doing gap, accountability is something we often avoid at all costs, yet it is also exactly what is necessary to move forward. Teachers in the Conscious stage need frequent contact from capacity-builders, as their tendency is to shy away from relationships that will challenge their thinking. And by frequent, we mean *daily*. Consistency helps to solidify new habits, to keep teachers accountable to their goals, and to maintain and strengthen the relationships through regular reminders of the importance of this work. It is essential to emphasize that this strategy is about "checking *in*," not "checking *on*." "Checking in" is focused on our commitment to the goals, whereas "checking on" is more about compliance.

Build confidence through short-term goal setting. Research tells us that there are "powerful effects from the simple idea that a teacher's belief in his or her ability to positively impact student learning is critical to actual success or failure in a teacher's behavior" (Henson, 2001). Teacher confidence is crucial, particularly for those in the Conscious stage, and one of the best ways to build such confidence is the creation of short-term goals that lead to quick, small successes. By contrast, long-range goals may seem overwhelming and daunting, giving our Conscious-stage teacher reason to balk. Achieving short-term goals starts the process of garnering success.

Celebrate successes immediately. Success begets success, as we noted in Chapter 7. For teachers in this stage, every success must be recognized and celebrated immediately. This can happen in a variety of ways, from asking them to share their success at the next faculty meeting to third-party compliments (such as bragging about the success to a colleague within the teacher's earshot). We want to build confidence in personal ability and motivate intrinsically. Teachers in the Conscious stage often expect capacity-builders to point out what is wrong, because they know that they aren't working to their fullest potential. The act of identifying, focusing on, and celebrating successes, however small, builds both credibility and self-confidence.

Meet weekly for collaborative planning. Well-designed lesson plans lead to high-quality instruction and student learning, yet effective planning takes time and much cognitive effort. For the Conscious-stage teacher, the breakdown of thought occurs in the second quadrant of the Reflective Cycle: working with intentionality. Meeting each week to plan lessons can be a great support, providing a strategic way to guide thinking and to bridge the knowing-doing gap, as well as ensuring that you've got a standing meeting on the calendar with your Conscious-stage teacher.

Engage through interactive journaling. *Interactive journaling* is a term used to describe a structured writing process that guides individuals toward shifting their thinking. It can be a powerful strategy for a Conscious-stage teacher, in that it directs participants to respond to specific information through targeted content and questions. It is shared between coach and teacher, with the coach posing a leading question (see Figure 11.6, p. 205, for examples) or pasting a short piece of content on a page, and the teacher reflecting and subsequently responding or describing an experience that connects. Interactive journaling can be beneficial in a situation where the coach or teacher has limited time to meet together or the teacher needs extra time and space to process new information. Journaling should focus on building awareness of metacognitive habits in order to refine thinking. (And for bonus points, ask teachers to submit their reflections to one of our blog posts at http://bycfs.edublogs.org.)

Invite participation in small-group discussions around a common problem of practice. Another great, nonthreatening way to reach many Conscious-stage folks is to hold a 30-minute, idea-sharing discussion group around a common problem of practice, such as ways to engage reluctant students or incorporating more writing into math. Invite teacher-peers, including those the Conscious-stage teacher likes to spend time with. By strategically picking a topic that the teacher can speak confidently about, you can elicit participation and begin to refine that person's intentional thinking about the topic. This will eventually open doors for other conversations around areas in which the person is not so confident.

Model a strategy or lesson in the teacher's classroom. Many Conscious-stage teachers are stuck in their thinking because they are afraid to ask for help. Offering to model a lesson and asking for their feedback as they observe can serve a dual purpose: it allows them to learn without the pressure of failing and provides them an opportunity to see their students from a different vantage point. For this strategy to be fully effective, however, be sure to explicitly articulate your thinking as you taught the lesson when debriefing with the teacher afterward.

Coplan, coteach, and debrief a lesson together. With the purpose of creating a safe and successful environment for Conscious-stage teachers to become more intentional in their planning and decisions, coteaching can serve as an invaluable tool. By providing a successful learning experience for students and—very important—for the teacher as well, coach and teacher can connect the success back to the intentional planning and delivery of the lesson. When Conscious-stage teachers can see a direct correlation between intentionality and success and begin to embrace the cause-and-effect relationships at play in the classroom, we're well on our way to moving them into the Action stage.

Provide opportunities to observe in other classrooms—using clear look-fors. Often we need to see something fully in action before we're able to bring it to complete fruition. This strategy works well for Conscious-stage teachers who need the visual. The key to this strategy in a culture of reflective practice is that the Conscious-stage teacher should be looking for evidence of the other teacher's intentionality throughout the lesson. The look-fors should be directly linked to the Reflective Cycle: *As you observe this lesson, what is the teacher aware of when it comes to his students? His content? Pedagogical strategies? What evidence of working with intentionality do we observe? What might this teacher be thinking that led to the decision he just made?* Put the focus of the observation on *how* the model teacher *thinks.*

Record a lesson, provide clear look-fors, and debrief the video together. Just as our teachers in the Conscious stage can benefit from observing a coach teach a model lesson or a colleague teach a lesson, so can they grow from observing themselves in action in the classroom—with proper safeguards in place! Video can be intimidating, so effective coaches provide ample scaffolding. Practice-teaching in front of a camera and deleting the first few "takes," identifying a clear focus that relates to the teacher's goal and action plan as a look-for, watching the video together and directing all observations to the look-for, and following a tight protocol for debriefing can all help put the teacher at ease and ensure a positive experience. In the end, our plan is for our teachers to have an accurate picture of their own presentation and take a step toward increasing their effectiveness.

The Conscious Stage in Real Life

Remember the three vignettes we presented near the beginning of this chapter? Those three teachers, though fictional, are amalgams of actual teachers with whom we've worked as administrators, coaches, teachers, or consultants over the years. We'd like to return to one of them now, to show you how that teacher's particular capacity-builders might come together to provide comprehensive support. In the scenario that follows, we'll provide some detail about their plan, share how the work unfolded, and identify their preliminary results as their teacher grew as a reflective practitioner. And even if the scenario stems from a different grade level from one you support directly, there are lessons to be gleaned from the interactions, the collaboration, and the focus on the *thinking* behind the doing. Remember, self-reflection is context-independent: our brains are the common denominator.

Vignette, Part 2: Mrs. Davis

Mrs. Davis was exhausted. The demands of her position teaching several chemistry classes, in addition to monitoring a study hall and serving as an advisor to two after-school clubs, were wearing her down. And it was just a month into the school year.

On top of that, the administration was still pushing the "literacy across the curriculum" initiative. The teachers' association had gone to admin to discuss the legitimacy of this approach, but nothing changed as a result of that meeting, so evidently it was here to stay. Mrs. Davis sighed. Education is hard enough, she thought, without having to do other people's jobs too.

Earlier in the year, the assistant principal overseeing the science department had sat down with Mrs. Davis and the department chair (the school did not have instructional coaches) to discuss her goals for the year. In addition to her standard SMART goals for the end-of-unit chemistry assessments, they had pressed for the inclusion of some of the new literacy-based instructional strategies as part of her action plan. She didn't really know where to go with that, so she deferred to the department chair, who said they'd put that together as they learned more. That offer was a nice reprieve.

The department chair and the assistant principal had met earlier to discuss the science teachers, the department's goal, and the school's development as a culture of reflective practice. Both agreed that Mrs. Davis was currently operating in the Conscious stage, though they were eager to hear her perceptions. After discussing self-reflection in a couple of faculty meetings and reading an article together, they had given her the Reflective Self-Assessment (available in *Teach, Reflect, Learn* or online at www.ascd.org/ASCD/pdf/books/HallSimeral2017.pdf [password: HallSimeral117006]). Mrs. Davis had confidently scored herself in the Action stage, just above the Conscious stage, which opened the door for some great conversations.

When they met again to refine her action plan, neither the assistant principal nor the department chair revealed how they believed Mrs. Davis reflects; they just peppered her with questions about her thought processes as she planned lessons. Both agreed they wanted to spend as much time as possible "talking teaching" with her during the course of the year so they could get to know her processing better. Mrs. Davis was skeptical of the pressure this might add, but she was willing to go along with it.

As the conversation focused on her planning, her administrator asked her for some samples of her prior lesson plans. The plans Mrs. Davis produced were pretty generic: some background reading, labs with procedures and learning targets, assignments, and quizzes. The three of them agreed that her focus this year would be on intentionally planning lessons that met the target, met individual students' needs, and included components of "literacy across the curriculum."

After the meeting, the department chair and the assistant principal agreed that they would try strategies from the Conscious stage to support Mrs. Davis for the time being. The assistant principal would serve as navigator, steering conversations back to her agreed-upon goals: planning for meeting students' needs and incorporating literacy strategies in her chemistry classes. The department chair prepped for her role as motivator/ strategist to encourage Mrs. Davis to be intentional in her planning and to try out some new strategies.

Both capacity-builders made it a point to connect with Mrs. Davis on a daily basis. Knowing she needed daily contact in order to solidify new habits and to remain focused, they had split the days of the week: the assistant principal would take Mondays and Thursdays, and the department chair would take the other three. Their contact consisted of a variety of 5- to 15-minute walk-throughs, 1-minute rounds, quick-connects during her prep periods, informal "impromptu" visits in the hallways, formal coaching sessions, and even a handful of sticky notes in her faculty mailbox with inspirational messages and reminders of upcoming chats. They understood that they could not leave Mrs. Davis's growth to chance.

A couple of months later, Mrs. Davis confided to her department chair that the visits from her administrator were stressing her out. Even though the assistant principal had said the walk-throughs were nonevaluative, he was also her primary evaluator, so she was concerned. Her department chair agreed to meet with them together, and they agreed that he could reduce the number of his visits—though Mrs. Davis also indicated she'd like to work more with her department chair, because there was no evaluative concern there.

The science chair knew that her time was already being stretched, so she sought the support of her department. By structuring their team meetings to include a mix of data analysis and professional development on literacy strategies, she knew she could meet the team's needs and Mrs. Davis's needs simultaneously. By then building in time for the teachers to plan their lessons together and engage in a "triad protocol" (which she found online at www.ascd.org/publications/books/116026.aspx in Appendix B: Strategies for Reflective Growth) to refine and provide each other with feedback, she was able to build collaboration, ensure some mutual accountability, and strengthen the quality of the plans. She leveraged her team's interdependence to support Mrs. Davis's reflective growth.

Soon the department chair would open the team up for collegial observations and some exercises with video. In the meantime, she appreciated watching Mrs. Davis begin to work more intentionally, plan more deliberately, and engage in collaborative dialogue that helped her process her actions and, ultimately, affect student learning in a positive way.

The Conscious Stage at a Glance

The Conscious stage in the Continuum of Self-Reflection is a common spot for teachers to land. Left to our own devices, we might all end up in the Conscious stage in many parts of our lives, both personal and professional. With proper support, however, we can help usher our teachers into deeper, more accurate, and more frequent reflective behaviors. The two keys that signify growth from the Conscious stage are *intentionality* and *consistency*—both of which symbolize a significant transformation: from compliance to commitment. When we plan to implement a strategy on purpose, it shows we're committed to affecting the outcomes. When we continue to use that strategy on a regular basis, it demonstrates our commitment to becoming an expert and positively affecting student learning. In this regard, our teachers who do so are taking action—which, predictably, leads them into the Action stage on the Continuum of Self-Reflection.

Supporting Teachers in the Action Stage

One of the most well-known Renaissance figures was the Italian artist/ inventor/scientist Leonardo da Vinci. You may recognize his paintings *Mona Lisa* and *The Last Supper*, as well as his anatomical exploration of *Vitruvian Man* and his investigations of the viability of helicopters, parachutes, and loads of other ideas that were hundreds of years ahead of their time.

Like many others during the Renaissance period (14th–17th centuries), Leonardo was dissatisfied with the status quo and had a yearning to learn more, to know more, to innovate more, and to influence the world in a profound and powerful way. Through many apprenticeships and commissions, he collected information and gathered skills, to be sure. His mind, however, was the key to unlocking the questions of the day.

Relentless in his pursuit of facts, relationships, possibilities, and the beauty of life, Leonardo was once quoted as saying, "It had long since come to my attention that people of accomplishment rarely sat back and let things happen to them. They went out and happened to things." As he did so often in so many fields, Leonardo provided an expressively descriptive summary of the Action stage on the Continuum of Self-Reflection—nearly 500 years before we truly "invented" it!

In the classroom, teachers who are dissatisfied with the status quo (this might mean they're not satisfied with current student achievement rates or other measures of educational outcomes, not just structures or policy or other input factors) and have made the decision that they're going to do something about it are reflecting in the Action stage. *Action stage* is a term we use to describe teachers who are proficient in the science of teaching and need to connect it with the art of making necessary alterations. Data are everywhere, and Action-stage teachers have moved beyond *acknowledging* the problem; rather, they are committed to *addressing* the problem.

For teachers who have moved beyond the Conscious stage, the Action stage is where the wheels are rolling and the rubber meets the road (see Figure 12.1). Here, our teachers are inspired, motivated, and working hard to achieve. They are making the effort to do what's best for their kids on a consistent basis. Occasionally they'll realize a missed opportunity or a lost chance at learning, and it may challenge their self-confidence or bring about frustration. Action-stage teachers are open and ready to do what needs to be done in order to meet the specific needs of their classroom, and often, Leonardo-like, will seek out ways to grow knowledge on their own.

A telling characteristic of the Action stage is that the teachers have the agreed-upon goal squarely in front of them at all times: increasing student learning for every child under their care and direction. With such a clear target in focus, they are compelled to do *something* in an attempt to achieve it. John F. Kennedy once clarified our options by stating, "There are risks and costs to action. But they are far less than the long-range risks of comfortable inaction."

FIGURE 12.1

The Action Stage

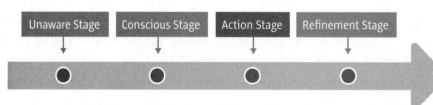

Teachers in the Action stage refuse to stand by while their students waft or fail, while assessments and demographics take control of the narrative, and while education is something that happens to them and their students. They *act*. They *do*. They begin to *take charge* of the outcomes, realizing that they, as teachers, truly are the primary determinant of student success. This commitment is genuine; they begin to build on their "effort optimism"—the sense that if they work hard enough and smart enough, then their students will be able to reach and exceed the lofty goals they set for them. In short, Action-stage teachers are "in it to win it." Let's consider the term more closely.

> **Action: *the fact or process of doing something, typically to achieve an aim***

It's pretty easy to become confused by the term *action* and think of this stage along the Continuum of Self-Reflection as engaging in the *actions* of teaching. What separates an Action-stage teacher from a teacher in the earlier stages is the *thinking* that drives these actions. Teachers operating in the Action stage aren't simply punching the clock and following directives; rather, they're taking deliberate, intentional steps to address an urgent, identified need in order to meet a clear, agreed-upon goal. In their minds, they—as teachers, educators, leaders—are the variable that must change in order to alter the outcomes in a positive way. They are, for all intents and purposes, mission-driven.

Teachers operating in the Action stage are truly mission-driven.

It is essential to remember that the Continuum of Self-Reflection is not an evaluation tool; rather, it is a powerful instrument that serves two incredibly helpful purposes. First, it helps capacity-builders (and teachers themselves) identify their teachers' reflective tendencies. Second, it guides those capacity-builders (administrators and coaches) to the proper entry point and directs their capacity-building efforts. There is no value—no "better than" or "worse than"—assigned to any of the stages on the continuum; there are just terms that describe how one thinks about the work. The characteristics of thinking displayed by an individual teacher should be used without prejudice to help you, as a capacity-builder, determine the best course of action to support that teacher's growth as a reflective practitioner. The goal in using this tool is not to evaluate, label, or "fix" teachers; unyieldingly, the goal is to lead teachers to develop strong patterns of thought as we usher them down the path of self-reflection.

The First Step: Identification of Reflective Tendencies

Let's walk through several classrooms and take a closer look at teachers who are currently operating in the Action stage. As you read these brief vignettes, begin to assimilate the characteristics that describe thinking in the Action stage. This is the first step in identifying our teachers' reflective tendencies. (The vignettes featuring Mr. Cano and Miss Nakano originally appeared in our earlier book *Teach, Reflect, Learn* [Hall & Simeral, 2015]. We present them here as examples to be considered from the viewpoint of the capacity-builders, including administrators and coaches.)

Vignettes, Part 1: Meet the Teachers

Visit 1: Elementary, Mr. Cano

Mr. Cano was frustrated. Although his mornings usually flowed fairly smoothly, his afternoons were a struggle. It was the third week of school, and his 1st graders seemed to fall apart every day after lunch. He'd tried to structure his math block just like reading—with center rotations so he could differentiate the necessary instruction and keep students engaged in meaningful tasks—but it didn't work. He tried to reinforce students with positive rewards, such as gummy bears for students who stayed on task. He also tried pulling the class back together between rotations for quick check-ins. His efforts had little effect. James continued to bother the other kids in his group, and Javier refused to do any work at all. It was a constant up and down for Mr. Cano as he sought to keep everyone engaged while attempting to teach a group at the back table.

Over lunch, he decided what he'd try next. The following day, he'd swap reading for math, running math centers in the morning and reading in the afternoon. It made sense. His class was perfect during reading and had the centers dialed in. Perhaps moving them to the afternoon would work better. He would try anything at this point to find a successful solution.

Visit 2: Middle School, Mrs. Woods

When the principal had asked for volunteers to learn about blended-learning techniques, online options, and "flipping" the classroom, Mrs. Woods had leapt out of her seat. With student engagement rates tumbling at the same rate new iPhone apps are released, she knew there had to be a way to infuse technology in a way that captured students' interests. After all, 8th grade American history wasn't as exciting to all her kids as it was to her.

Now, two months into the school year, she had incorporated a couple of the ideas she'd learned and was busy trying to train her class to use their technology devices to learn and to get ahead. Some of her students were flying; others struggled with the concept of self-paced and self-directed learning, falling a couple of modules behind their classmates already.

Where was the initiative and drive she had imagined they'd all show? Mrs. Woods was painstakingly searching the Internet for captivating videos that supported the learning targets, and she was weaving activities and structures into her lesson plans that she believed would enthrall her students.

Sitting at her desk one afternoon, Mrs. Woods scrolled through the online program that monitored the completion rates of her students. She grimaced at the success rates next to their names. Was this any better than the traditional educational experience she had been providing before all this flipping and blending? Certainly it was, right? What was she missing? Blinking her eyes and shaking her head, she turned off the computer. Tomorrow she would visit her instructional coach, and they'd brainstorm together. There's got to be a way to make this work for her kids, she thought.

Visit 3: High School, Miss Nakano

Miss Nakano sighed as she glanced at the day's classwork piled on her desk. Emma was really struggling with the math concepts she was introducing this week. Today she'd partnered Emma with Joanna, whom she knew could provide solid, in-class tutoring support, and she'd given the class extra time to work through the assignment. She'd also modified the homework for the week. It didn't seem to be working, and she didn't know what else to do. Maybe she'd seek out Mrs. Hannigan, the department head, and ask her advice.

As luck would have it, Mrs. Hannigan was still in her classroom grading papers. Miss Nakano quickly explained the situation with Emma, ending with an emphatic, "I just don't know what else to do for her! Can you give me any advice?" Mrs. Hannigan thought for a moment and then posed the following thoughts for Miss Nakano to consider: "You've told me what Emma can't do. Now explain what she can do. In your observations, what basic math concepts does she show evidence of grasping? What strategies do you observe her using as she attempts to solve harder problems? Where in the problem does she get stuck, and what does that tell you about her understanding or lack thereof?"

It was a sleepless night for Miss Nakano as she tossed and turned in realization that she couldn't answer those questions without further observation of Emma. She'd spent so much time helping her work through problems but hadn't known to look for those specific things. She was excited to return to Emma with fresh eyes and further evaluate her specific needs so she could respond appropriately.

In these vignettes, each of the three teachers has unique challenges, assignments, and professional contexts. Mr. Cano knows his students need to be more engaged in their math lessons, so he's willing to restructure his schedule to present math instruction at a more productive time of day; Mrs. Woods has committed to using technology and now realizes that the whole point of that tool is to meet the students' needs, and not vice versa; Miss Nakano desperately wants to help a particular student, Emma, and has sought help from a colleague. Despite the surface-level differences, the thinking processes of these teachers have some pretty strong similarities: they've identified a need and they're committed to addressing it. They're driven to take action to further their students' success.

These responses to their students' needs are not plucked randomly from the tree of education strategies; rather, they're intentionally selected and carefully thought out. Does this mean they'll be successful every time? Heavens, no! If only it were that easy. Education is a game of strategic trial and error, simply because of the unique nature of working with developing human brains. However, with deliberate thought, quality research and rationale, and a clearly identified outcome awaiting, these teachers' approaches will experience a higher-than-average likelihood of success. Each of these three teachers is operating in the Action stage.

Reflective Tendencies of an Action-Stage Teacher

Teachers operating in the Action stage believe that their actions influence the learning outcomes in the classroom. Because of this belief, they understand that student success—or lack of success—is something they can affect. It's their responsibility to ensure that their students are learning and progressing, and if the students are not, something's got to change. Either through research, collaboration, innovation, or a combination of these, teachers in the Action stage will put their minds to the test and seek a solution to the challenges they face. What follows are descriptions of the overarching reflective characteristics, as shown in Figure 12.2, of a teacher in the Action stage

FIGURE 12.2

Teacher's Reflective Tendencies: Action Stage

- Commits to taking steps to affect student learning outcomes.
- Engages in reflection before and after teaching.
- Evaluates problems or challenges objectively.
- Notices trends and themes in student performance and classroom elements.
- Collaborates on a limited basis with colleagues.
- Seeks to incorporate research-based concepts and strategies.
- Gravitates toward a particular structure or strategy.
- Struggles to identify solutions to long-term problems.
- Craves feedback from trusted partners.
- Focuses on the *science* of teaching.

Commits to taking steps to affect student learning outcomes. We expect by now we've made this point: teachers in the Action stage are subscribers to the philosophy espoused by the ancient Chinese philosopher Laozi, who is credited as the source of the saying "If you do not change direction, you may end up where you are heading." Because the current heading does not sit well with Action-stage teachers, they are committed to changing direction.

Engages in reflection before and after teaching. The growth in a teacher's reflective habits is evident in the frequency of that reflection. At the Action stage, teachers do not wait for someone else to provide the impetus to reflect; rather, they consider the conditions within which they operate on their own volition. Because they are driven to alter the outcomes, their thoughts lead them to the options they have available before taking action and the results of their actions afterward. The compelling questions they ask themselves include "What can I do to address this need?" and "To what extent did that lesson meet the goal I had identified?"

Evaluates problems or challenges objectively. Open-mindedness is a common characteristic of teachers operating in the Action stage. Willing to weigh multiple variables and examine a situation from multiple angles, teachers in the Action stage dissect quiz results, review student work samples, and analyze student performance data in their classrooms before determining a course of action. Much like the scientific method with which we're all pretty familiar, Action-stage teachers develop a hypothesis that then guides their decision-making process.

Notices trends and themes in student performance and classroom elements. While analyzing student data and other factors that may be influencing student achievement, teachers in the Action stage also attend to big-picture happenings. Are more students struggling with the current topic than a previous one? Are there particular concepts that the students have grasped more thoroughly than others? Why might that be so?

Collaborates on a limited basis with colleagues. Teachers in the Action stage put a lot of energy (both mental and physical) into improving the student learning outcomes in their classrooms. When it comes to working with colleagues within their grade-level, department, or PLC structures, their oomph has been significantly sapped. Adding to this challenge is the intensity with which Action-stage teachers pursue solutions to the problems they encounter within their own classrooms—the problems of their colleagues are often perceived as a peripheral issue. Action-stage teachers may try to recruit teammates to help them in their ventures, though they infrequently offer themselves up to others.

Seeks to incorporate research-based concepts and strategies. The gold standard of effective teaching is to use proven best practices in the classroom. For teachers operating in the Action stage, the thorough research base of *high-yield, high-reliability, high-promise,* or *deck-stacked-in-your-favor* teaching strategies provides the one-stop shop for making decisions on instructional maneuvers that are most likely to return positive learning gains. In the Action-stage teacher's thinking, if the research experts back a certain strategy, it must be worth implementing—and implementing with fidelity. This is no time to go willy-nilly into a classroom and try to reinvent the wheel.

Gravitates toward a particular structure or strategy. Action-stage teachers are instructional predators. They prey on failure, illiteracy, and student struggles. And much like the universally feared *Dendroaspis polylepis* (you know it as the black mamba), they set their sights and latch on with abandon. Sometimes this tendency causes teachers to be hyper-focused on a particular strategy at the expense of missing all the others that might be as (or more) useful in a particular situation. Usually, this is the result of an Action-stage teacher learning about a research-based approach and making the determination that *this* strategy is *the* strategy. Although this laserlike focus will be useful in mastering the strategy itself, it may detract from the diversification of the teacher's tool kit.

Struggles to identify solutions to long-term problems. Rectifying the issues related to today's lesson is the Action-stage teacher's forte. Addressing the lingering struggles, widespread failure, and long-term problems provides quite a challenge. This is especially true if the teacher has identified a learning gap, researched a solution, and then planned and delivered a particular intervention—and it didn't yield the intended results. Action-stage teachers can get frustrated in this scenario and will need support and guidance as they seek tools to add to their repertoire.

Craves feedback from trusted partners. Teachers operating in the Action stage want to know "Am I doing this right?" Prone to selecting research-based strategies and honing their attention on one at a time, they are desperate for feedback, validation, suggestions, and modifications from colleagues. They will go to their administrator, instructional coach, department chair, mentor, and any other teammate who can add value and ask, "Will you come visit my class and tell me what you think?" They open their doors for the express purpose of deepening their own understanding and improving their practice.

Focuses on the *science* of teaching. Researchers, investigators, analysts . . . the truth is, teachers operating in the Action stage are scientists. Thoughtful, deliberate, and intentional, their instructional decisions are made based on the best information available at the moment: student achievement data, error analyses, work samples, research, prior experience, and well-churned hypotheses. Like our Renaissance man Leonardo, Action-stage teachers tend to crave learning, wanting to know more and to maximize their pedagogical skills so they can truly affect student learning outcomes in a consistent, positive way.

Referring to the Reflective Cycle (Figure 12.3), we can take a closer look at the distinct thought patterns and reflective habits of teachers in the Action stage. This will provide us, as instructional leaders and capacity-builders, with valuable insights that enable us to accurately identify how our teachers are currently *thinking* about their professional responsibilities, which will allow us to support their continued growth as reflective practitioners.

At this point, it's probably pretty clear how far along the Reflective Cycle our teacher's thinking has developed, or at which quadrant our teacher's

FIGURE 12.3

Assessment in the Reflective Cycle

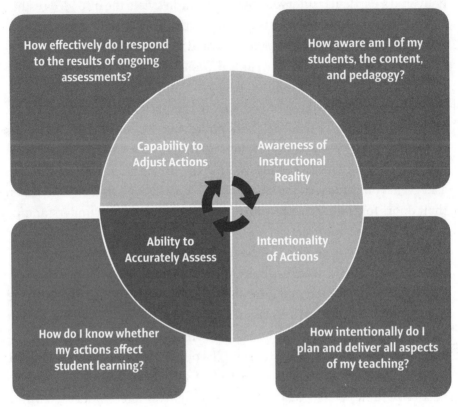

thinking is breaking down. Have you identified it? If you chose "Ability to Accurately Assess" for a teacher operating in the Action stage, you're ready to proceed as a capacity-builder, and the question to ask is this: *How does the teacher know whether his or her actions affect student learning?*

Teachers whose thinking has progressed to the Action stage most likely have a solid awareness of their students, content, and pedagogical strategies. In fact, they're probably pretty well versed in teaching methods. And because they're committed to having a positive impact on their students, they have begun to plan their lesson elements intentionally and are consistent in their application. This turns their focus to the assessment realm. *Is it working? For which students is it working? To what extent? When doesn't it work? Why not?* To answer these questions and deepen their reflective habits, teachers in the Action stage must focus their mental energies at a finer grain size, beneath the surface, to the underlying causes for individual student struggles with individual learning targets. They must begin to *consider student thinking as they assess*—not just the *right and wrong*, but the *why* that accompanies it. This undertaking will unveil a whole host of new opportunities for Action-stage teachers to adapt and adjust in the moment, rather than after the lesson, quiz, or activity.

The Second Step: Supportive Practices

Each stage within the Continuum of Self-Reflection has a capacity-building goal to develop and support each individual teacher's reflective growth. Here is the overall goal for the Action-stage teacher:

> Our goal is *to build on experience and help strengthen expertise through accurate assessment of instructional impact,* in order to determine which strategies are most effective to meet specific students' needs.

Because our teachers in the Action stage are "in it to win it" and are committed to changing the outcomes for their students, the critical element of motivation is already in place. Capacity-builders can then focus their attention on the next steps, supporting their Action-stage teachers' plans and assessment strategies to monitor the impact of their actions. Ultimately, if we as capacity-builders can be there to support our teachers as they begin to expand their horizons, adopt multiple approaches, and identify the strategies that are most effective in specific situations, we will be successful in continuing their growth as reflective practitioners.

As capacity-builders, it's crucial to understand that shifting action doesn't always result in shifted thinking, but shifting thinking will *always* result in shifted action. Our charge is to tackle the thinking that drives the doing. If we're to successfully cultivate a culture of reflective practice and facilitate long-term professional growth, we must ask teachers to *think* as often as we ask them to *do*. Their growth in thinking, then, will fuel a curiosity and desire to learn more.

Leadership Roles

How do capacity-builders begin to address the specific needs of a teacher in the Action stage? To have the impact necessary for continued reflective growth, administrators and coaches simultaneously work independently (within their own roles) and collaboratively (as their roles are complementary to one another), as well as intentionally leveraging a teacher's peers within the PLC structure to provide additional support, as noted in the triad diagram, Figure 12.4. In the absence of an instructional coach, the administrator must be even more deliberate in the use of peer relationships to engage in this work. This strategic triangulation of support significantly increases the likelihood of success.

As described in Chapter 5, a couple of conditions must be established in order to proceed with our capacity-building efforts. First, the roles of

FIGURE 12.4

Triad Diagram for Action Stage

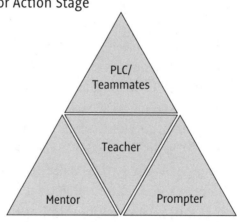

administrator and coach must be defined, distinguished, and communicated clearly to one another. Second, the boundaries that encompass each
role must be respected at all times. In the case of working with Action-stage
teachers, these roles manifest themselves in unique and important ways as
we work to guide the teachers toward their capacity-building goal.

 The administrator's role: *prompter.*

The administrator's role is that of *prompter*, spurring the Action-stage
teacher's thinking toward new and different approaches, expanding the
teacher's repertoire of skills and options in the classroom. In the role of
prompter, the administrator does exactly what you might think: asks questions. Lots of questions. Not only that, but when the Action-stage teacher
asks questions of the administrator, the response is yet another question,
and the more open-ended the better. All of this questioning is geared to
generating reflective thought in the teacher.

Although administrators acting in this role may have ideas and suggestions, or even believe that they *know* the answer to a particular issue
the teacher is facing, providing a solution to the teacher actually short-
sheets the teacher's thinking and sets back any reflective progress. Instead,
administrators truly *prompt* the teacher to think more carefully, to consider options more thoroughly, to analyze the situation more deeply, and
to ponder the possible outcomes more comprehensively. This sort of
meticulous approach is helpful for the teacher but can be a challenge for
administrators, who sometimes feel pressure to prove their own level of
expertise or hesitate to see teachers struggle with difficult circumstances.
For a capacity-builder, however, this approach—biting one's tongue and
asking yet another reflective question—will yield amazing benefits. The
struggle is real, and it is through the struggle that we grow.

 The coach's role: *mentor.*

The coach's role, meanwhile, is to work alongside the Action-stage teacher as a *mentor*, focused on the goal of deepening the thinking behind the teacher's actions. With teachers who are ready to spread their wings yet also desperately crave feedback and reassurance, the instructional coach's role of mentor is complex and nuanced. Action-stage thinkers tend to want the feedback and ideas of experts, so their expectation is that the coach is indeed that: someone who has experience, know-how, and a track record of success. This doesn't mean that to be successful in supporting a biology teacher, for example, a coach must have been an award-winning biology teacher; but many teachers in this stage seek out viable sources of expertise. It is essential that coaches model open-mindedness, critical reasoning, and discernment skills to help teachers deepen their thinking.

Coaches must be careful to not impose their own will or approaches onto their teachers, however. Rarely do Action-stage teachers appreciate unsolicited tales of "Well, this is how I would do it" when working with new and different scenarios. Instead, providing partnership and support for ideas, reflective thought, brainstorming, and experimentation can be much more powerful. Ultimately, this is where the gradual-release model shifts balance—in the Action stage, the teacher begins to take the bulk of the workload, while the coach is there to serve as a thinking partner, a research ally, a feedback provider, and a confidant as the teacher begins to soar.

Working Complementarily

As we stated in Chapter 5, the coach and the administrator are partners in this work. Sharing a common goal of supporting a teacher's growth as a reflective practitioner, each assumes the role just outlined very intentionally, knowing the other will shoulder the complementary role.

Action-stage teachers need prompters as much as they need mentors. The prompter is there to provide the right questions to deepen the teacher's thinking, and the mentor is there as a sounding board and a trusted partner for an exchange of ideas. Because the capacity-builders in this equation already have agreed upon two key pieces of information—the teacher's stage on the Continuum of Self-Reflection and the teacher's professional goal—the work can commence in earnest.

Savvy administrators engage in robust dialogue with Action-stage teachers, including a peppering of questions—all open-ended and related to the teacher's goal. An important point is that the administrator, in the role of prompter, informs the teacher that his or her responses to the questions are not the most important thing; rather, it's the administrator's expectation that the teacher will take the questions and ponder them, ruminate over them, examine them, consider them, scrutinize them, and eventually seek a partner with whom to kick them around. That partner will be the instructional coach, who will not know the questions in advance but will be prepared to engage in dialogue and debate about the merits of different courses of action, leading the teacher to perhaps try something new, analyze the data, and determine the pros and cons of various strategies. Together, the two capacity-builders will generate reflective growth.

Strategic PLC and Teacher-Leadership Support

The administrator and the coach are not the only capacity-builders who share the immense responsibility of supporting teachers' growth as reflective practitioners. Because teaching is no longer done in isolation (those days are behind us, right?), educators' relationships with colleagues, peers, and other professionals within their grade level or department or professional learning community are vital in completing our triad (see Figure 12.4, p. 228). Within a culture of reflective practice, administrators set the expectation that teachers will work collaboratively to support each other in their pursuit of common goals, and then it's "all hands on deck" to engage in the practices that accomplish that objective.

In the Action stage, teachers are gung-ho and expect their colleagues to follow suit. Not surprisingly, not all teachers display the same gusto in working toward an agreed-upon goal. Although this may frustrate Action-stage teachers, it will not deter them. They may decide to proceed without the active support and participation of their teammates, which is a thought process we'd like to amend. Because teammates can be vital sources of information, knowledge, expertise, and various approaches, the elements of collaboration, idea sharing, and dialogue are critical to the long-term growth of teachers operating in the Action stage. Not only that, but teacher-teams are great sources of data—the currency of change and the evidence of effectiveness for various teaching approaches. The strategies in Figure 12.5 may strengthen an Action-stage teacher's ability to contribute, support, and learn within a professional learning community structure. Let's examine each one in greater detail.

Provide opportunities for all teachers to share methods in team meetings. For those of you who haven't had the opportunity to visit multiple classrooms throughout a school, this may come as a surprise: not all teachers teach the same way. Even when presenting information from the same sources and using a lesson plan created together in a team meeting by several teachers who have the same teaching assignment, each teacher puts a personal twist and flavor to it. This is healthy, and we applaud that

FIGURE 12.5

Strategic PLC and Teacher-Leadership Support: Action Stage

Capacity-Building Goal: To build on experience and help strengthen expertise through accurate assessment of instructional impact

- Provide opportunities for all teachers to share methods in team meetings.
- Engage in healthy debate about the pros and cons of various pedagogical strategies.
- Maintain a focus on data analysis during team meetings.
- Incorporate professional learning (new and deeper instructional strategies) as a regular component of team meetings.
- Strategically partner this teacher with colleagues (in particular, those in the Unaware stage) to build leadership capacity.

characteristic. So, at team meetings, teachers—all teachers—really must share their efforts. *How did you teach a certain lesson or lesson segment? How was it introduced? What questions did you ask? How did the students respond?* When we all share, we get an immediate boost in the number of possible options we can include in our lessons.

Engage in healthy debate about the pros and cons of various pedagogical strategies. One of our goals for Action-stage teachers is to expand their repertoire of skills. Because they tend to gravitate toward one "right" strategy and a desire to teach it the "right" way, it's important for capacity-builders to create an environment where multiple strategies are suggested and debated in an open forum. The more strategies discussed, and the more evidence of effectiveness presented and analyzed by the team, the better the options all the teachers on the team have, including Action-stage teachers.

Maintain a focus on data analysis during team meetings. When teams use data—actual evidence—during their grade-level, department, and PLC meetings, the entire team becomes better informed about the effectiveness of certain structures and strategies. With evidence, teams can move from *cardiac assessment* (I love this strategy!) to *formative assessment* (Here are the data that we collected from this lesson—what do they tell us?). The former is a firework. The latter is a work afire.

Incorporate professional learning (new and deeper instructional strategies) as a regular component of team meetings. Team meetings are terrific opportunities to learn together. Common professional development experiences ensure that all teachers are calling plays from the same playbook and have more or less the same key knowledge; the common experiences give them a common language with which to interact. For an Action-stage teacher, continuing learning offers more strategies from which to choose when attempting to meet students' learning needs.

Strategically partner this teacher with colleagues (in particular, those in the Unaware stage) to build leadership capacity. This may come as a bit of a surprise, but a teacher in the Unaware stage can be a valuable partner to a teacher in the Action stage. The Unaware-stage teacher needs a role model, someone who is walking the walk and truly getting after it, and the Action-stage teacher needs a partner with whom to try a strategy, collect some data, and discuss the outcomes. Although the dialogue may not be enriching, the experience is mutually beneficial and serves as a de facto leadership role for the Action-stage teacher.

Transformational Feedback

To effect a shift in our teachers' *thinking,* capacity-builders must engage in a rigorous process of feedback. When the feedback indeed alters the way a teacher thinks, it becomes *transformational* feedback—and that's our ultimate goal. Administrators, coaches, department heads, and other capacity-builders can all engage in feedback-rich practices such as walk-throughs, rounds, and scheduled coaching sessions (Hall & Simeral, 2008) to obtain opportunities to "talk teaching" with their teachers. When selected intentionally to match their teachers' needs and readiness for reflective feedback, such conversations can help teachers deepen their thinking, expand their mental horizons, and grow as reflective practitioners, thus moving them forward along the Continuum of Self-Reflection.

See Figure 12.6 for a sampling of feedback stems in the form of open prompts that are designed to meet our Action-stage teachers' unique and distinct needs. Mind you, this list is but a taste of the ways you, as a capacity-builder, can *launch* a feedback dialogue or otherwise engage a teacher in reflective dialogue. We invite you to connect the dots between the prompts and the capacity-building goal, and we encourage you to enrich this list by adding your own prompts that match your style and your teachers' needs. Ultimately, beginning a conversation in this spirit should generate reflective thought and partnership. Where it goes from here is completely up to the parties involved.

Capacity-builders wanting to speak the "correct" language with Action-stage teachers needn't take a crash course on the Rosetta Stone. Instead,

FIGURE 12.6

Transformational Feedback for Teachers in the Action Stage

Capacity-Building Goal: To build on experience and help strengthen expertise through accurate assessment of instructional impact

- What was the purpose of today's activity? Was it successful? How do you know?
- Which parts of today's lesson went well? Which parts didn't? Why?
- What was the goal of today's lesson? How did you determine that goal?
- Today I observed you ___. Did that contribute to your goal? How can you tell?
- Why did you choose to ___ today? Was that strategy effective? How do you know?
- What other strategy could you have used today to achieve your goals?
- How do you predetermine what your evidence of success will be for a lesson?
- Do your anecdotal observations of student learning align with more formal assessment data?
- If you could teach this lesson again, what would you do differently? Why?
- Which students were successful achieving today's learning target? Which students struggled? Why was that so?
- What does the student work from today's lesson tell you about ___ as a learner?
- What can you tell me about ___ as a learner? How can you find out more?

---

one piece of advice from us ought to do the trick: be sure it ends with a question mark.

Could it really be that simple? Probably not, but that's the gist. If you look at Figure 12.6, you might find the prompts familiar. They include the now-standard reflection questions that well-meaning administrators were trained to ask during post-observation conferences with teachers. They're open-ended and posed with one end in mind: to generate reflective thought.

Capacity-builders must take care to not ask a *leading* prompt masquerading as an *open* prompt. If we have a specific idea of how the teacher *should* respond or what answers the teacher *should* provide, capacity-builders must heed this advice, too: nobody likes being should upon. Think about it.

Effective, thought-provoking feedback for teachers operating in the Action stage has four elements, as expressed in the following guidelines for delivery.

Identify the impact of particular instructional strategies. *What was your goal? Did you meet it? How do you know?* We can safely assume that teachers in the Action stage have intentionally selected a strategy in order to meet a specific learning goal in the classroom. Now it's time to invite them to share their findings and to explore the effectiveness of the strategy.

Consider alternative approaches or points of view. *What other way could you have done that? What might you do differently if you were to teach this lesson again tomorrow?* Broadening our Action-stage teachers' horizons will help them see there are indeed multiple paths that can lead to the same destination. If their response is, "Well, I don't know," it's incumbent upon the capacity-builder to respond with "How might you research additional strategies?"

Dig deeper to determine the causes of student performance. *Which students struggled with this assignment? Why?* Sometimes it's helpful to select a specific student and really examine the root causes for poor performance. By looking at that student's strengths and gaps, the Action-stage teacher can get a fuller picture of the student as a learner—and this understanding can help immensely in crafting an instructional plan to support further learning.

Propose continued professional learning. *What else are you interested in? How can I help you learn about it?* Teachers operating in the Action stage are committed to the product and the process, and they crave knowledge. Much like Leonardo, they will be willing to seek out new information, diverse approaches, and additional strategies in order to change the outcomes for their students. Capacity-builders can help by offering support and opportunities to learn.

Differentiated Coaching

With our teachers eager to change the outcomes, capacity-builders can roll up their sleeves and dive into the mucky underbrush of instructional coaching, wading and wrestling with the various approaches that will support our teachers' growth as reflective practitioners—ultimately leading to significant levels of learning for all students.

A number of coaching strategies will help teachers operating in the Action stage to successfully achieve their capacity-building goal (to build on experience and help strengthen expertise through accurate assessment of instructional impact). A sampling of such strategies, as outlined in the Continuum of Self-Reflection and shown in Figure 12.7, is described in

FIGURE 12.7

Differentiated Coaching Strategies for Teachers in the Action Stage

Capacity-Building Goal: To build on experience and help strengthen expertise through accurate assessment of instructional impact

- Analyze data together.
- Analyze student work samples together.
- Collaboratively engage in diagnosis and action planning based on beliefs of how students learn.
- Provide research from which to construct meaning.
- Invite participation in small-group discussions around a common problem of practice.
- Foster idea sharing through collegial observations.
- Model new strategies in a gradual-release model.
- Record lesson and discuss video analysis.
- Model open-mindedness toward multiple approaches and perspectives.
- Encourage participation in a professional book club.
- Engage in interactive journaling.

further detail in the next paragraphs. Each of the strategies can be used in isolation or woven with another. Remember, what works splendidly with one teacher may not work as effectively with another, so be sure to *differentiate* your selection and application of these approaches. What's most important is that the strategy meets each teacher's unique needs and is explicitly connected back to the capacity-building goal, so we can see and monitor our impact more clearly.

Analyze data together. Data analysis and interpretation is not an easy task and is often more effective when done by working in tandem with a colleague or a coach, or both. Essentially, teachers start with a look at the fundamentals: *What type of assessment am I using? What exactly is the assessment measuring?* From here, they begin to move from data to action, forming conclusions, identifying potential root causes, and developing plans of action. *What areas of student performance are at/above/below expectations? How do these data confirm what we already know? What "aha" do the data bring to light? Do we notice any patterns or trends?* When we build Action-stage teachers' knowledge in this area, they have the information to focus instructional decisions and develop thinking.

Analyze student work samples together. For the Action-stage teacher, one of the greater breakdowns in thinking occurs in the ability to assess instructional impact. Pulling out student work samples and engaging in dialogue about how the work samples show evidence of student thinking can be one of the most powerful coaching strategies you can use. Together, ask: *What does this student know? What gaps in learning exist? What patterns of student thinking can we identify?* By identifying how students' thinking influences their successes or struggles in the classroom, teachers and their capacity-building partners can better plan for instructional interventions at an individual level.

Collaboratively engage in diagnosis and action planning based on beliefs of how students learn. Beliefs are similar to attitudes and knowledge. They tend to be unexamined by teachers because many are implicit, unarticulated, or unconscious; yet, they are a strong part of teachers' identities and have a direct impact on student learning. Using guided questions to unearth thinking (for example, by asking, "To what extent do you agree with the following statements ... ?"), guide the teacher toward engaging in actions that validate or challenge such beliefs.

Here are some examples of belief statements in a questionnaire provided by the Organisation for Economic Co-operation and Development (n.d.):

- Effective/good teachers demonstrate the correct way to solve a problem.

- It is better when the teacher—not the student—decides what activities are to be done.

- My role as a teacher is to facilitate students' own inquiry.

- Students learn best by finding solutions to problems on their own.

- A quiet classroom is generally needed for effective learning.

It's essential to recognize, understand, and articulate our beliefs and then explicitly connect them to our daily instructional decisions.

Provide research from which to construct meaning. Our Action-stage teachers are hungry for knowledge, as well as validation that they're on the right track. At the same time, they aren't always able to identify *why* something works. By providing resources that explain the rationale behind a specific pedagogical strategy or instructional approach, we can support meaning making and develop deeper reflection.

Invite participation in small-group discussions around a common problem of practice. We want to encourage the Action-stage teacher to build relationships with others. This strategy, also a great strategy for Conscious-stage folks, can serve teachers in the Action stage quite well. Hold a 30-minute idea-sharing discussion group around a common problem of practice, such as ways to engage reluctant students or incorporating more writing into math. Invite teacher-peers, including those the Action-stage teacher likes to spend time with. In advance, prep the Action-stage teacher with questions with which to engage the others in the group, such as "When might this idea be the better choice that leads to student learning?" Follow up afterward with support connecting the newly gained ideas to the knowledge the teacher has about students in his or her classroom. We want to keep focus on the *how*. *How* do we know the decisions we're making are working or not?

Foster idea sharing through collegial observations. Often we need to see something fully in action before we're able to bring it to complete fruition. This strategy works well for Action-stage teachers who need the visual. The key to using this strategy within a culture of reflective practice is that the Action-stage teacher should be looking for evidence of the other teacher's ability to accurately assess. The look-fors should be directly linked to the Reflective Cycle: *As you observe this lesson, what is the teacher looking for as she teaches? What type of evidence of learning does this teacher note? How does she know when a lesson is successful? How does she know what to do when a student is struggling? What might this teacher be thinking that led to the decision she just made?* Even though we cannot expect teachers to climb into each other's minds to fully grasp another person's thinking, put the focus of the observation on how the model teacher thinks.

Model new strategies in a gradual-release model. Modeling a lesson and asking for teacher feedback during the observation can serve a dual purpose: it allows teachers to learn without the pressure of failing and provides them an opportunity to see their students from a different vantage point. For this strategy to be fully effective, however, be sure to explicitly articulate your thinking as you taught the lesson when debriefing with the teacher afterward. Keep the focus on accurately assessing instructional impact.

Record a lesson and discuss video analysis. Action-stage teachers can grow tremendously from observing themselves in action in the classroom, and though the temptation is to release them to conduct a self-analysis with their own video, they still need subtle scaffolding to maximize the benefit. With a clear focus that relates to the teacher's goal or a problem of practice, identify the look-fors that will guide the video analysis. This will help Action-stage teachers focus, even though they may benefit from a second or third run-through to look for additional classroom elements. The debriefing ought to begin with the first look-for, though it is perfectly acceptable to encourage teachers to reflect on their teaching with open-ended questions and eyes wide open. In the end, our plan is for our teachers to have an accurate picture of their own presentation and take a step toward increasing their understanding of their impact.

Model open-mindedness toward multiple approaches and perspectives. Action-stage folks can often become set in "one right way" of doing things, getting stuck in their focus on the science of pedagogy. It's essential that capacity-builders model trying new strategies and making mistakes for the purpose of learning and challenging the status quo. Failure is necessary to learning. We want to challenge these teachers to shift their perspective from being driven by pedagogy to being driven by student learning.

Encourage participation in a professional book club. Creating a culture of sharing and professional dialogue is an essential element for school success. Teachers who read, discuss, and implement current educational research are typically motivated and engaged. The key to book clubs for teachers in the Action stage is to make sure the emphasis is not just on the new ideas developed through research; importance must be placed on the subsequent conversation: *When might this be a good strategy to use? How might you be able to weave this into the work you're already doing? How does this add value to your teaching repertoire? How will you know if it's successful? If it's not, how will you determine next steps?*

Engage in interactive journaling. Writing down one's thoughts is perhaps the most powerful form of self-reflection. Writing, itself, is the great synthesizer of knowledge, learning, and understanding. Ask teachers in the Action stage to note evidence of student learning as they teach, as well as evidence of struggles students are having. Then collect the journals and respond with thoughts and questions to drive deeper thinking. If your teachers have a copy of our parallel teacher text, *Teach, Reflect, Learn: Building Your Capacity for Success in the Classroom* (Hall & Simeral, 2015), discuss their reflections and journal entries related to the many tasks and scores of reflective questions we offer to encourage reflective growth. (And for bonus points, ask them to submit their reflections to one of our blog posts at http://bycfs.edublogs.org.)

The Action Stage in Real Life

Remember the three vignettes we presented earlier in this chapter? Those three teachers, though fictional, are amalgams of actual teachers with whom we've worked as administrators, coaches, teachers, or consultants over the years. We'd like to return to one of them now, to show you how that teacher's particular capacity-builders might come together to provide comprehensive support. In the vignette that follows, we'll provide some detail about their plan, share how the work unfolded, and identify their preliminary results as their teacher grew as a reflective practitioner. And even if the vignette stems from a different grade level than one you support directly, there are lessons to be gleaned from the interactions, the collaboration, and the focus on the *thinking* behind the doing. Remember, self-reflection is context-independent: our brains are the common denominator.

Vignette, Part 2: Mrs. Woods

Blended learning. Online platforms. Flipped classrooms. All night long, Mrs. Woods tossed and turned, unable to sleep, as these concepts fluttered before her droopy eyelids. In the morning, she went directly to her instructional coach's office. "Help!" she exclaimed.

Her instructional coach looked up. "I'm glad you're here," she said. "How can I help you?"

Mrs. Woods bared her soul, expressing her initial excitement at the innovative ideas for increasing student engagement though the infusion of technology and then slumping into a comfy chair while sharing her disappointment that they didn't seem to make any difference. "It's just more work for me," she sighed. "But I believe it's the way of the future. What should I do?"

Her instructional coach, as a trained capacity-builder, asked her a couple of questions about what she'd tried so far and what results she'd collected. Then, after a dramatic pause, the coach asked, "In the end, what is it you're really trying to accomplish? How will you know if you're successful?"

The light bulb flickered in Mrs. Woods's head. Her goal wasn't to have the district's best blended-learning program; it was to use blended learning as a way to support deeper student learning for each and every one of her kids. Was she guilty of giving the educational pendulum an unnecessary shove? Had she gotten confused about technology as the end as opposed to being a means to an end? Could she truly blend the educational experience for her students, based on what each student needed?

"OK," said Mrs. Woods excitedly. "We're going to need to look more closely at my student data." Together, teacher and coach planned to analyze the data together and look up ways to infuse minilessons and whole-class discussions with the online content and self-directed learning experiences Mrs. Woods had begun to include in her classroom.

Later that day, the instructional coach met with the school principal, and they discussed the teachers' goals and their work plans to support them. When Mrs. Woods's name came up, the instructional coach shared the morning's epiphany. Both capacity-builders had previously agreed that Mrs. Woods was likely operating in the Action stage, and the self-assessment she had completed (found in *Teach, Reflect, Learn* [Hall & Simeral, 2015] and online at www.ascd.org/ASCD/pdf/books/HallSimeral2017.pdf [password: Hall Simeral117006]) had confirmed their thinking. Their game plan was set.

The principal crossed paths with Mrs. Woods in the copy room during her prep period and casually posed a couple of reflective questions, really pressing her for an open-minded analysis of her student learning outcomes. For most of the questions, Mrs. Woods provided an answer right away. Then the principal asked, "What can you tell me about Elise as a learner?" The teacher paused. Elise was a quiet young lady, played soccer for the school team and could ride a unicycle, but Mrs. Woods didn't have a firm grasp on her preferred learning styles or what contributed to her being successful in the classroom. "Thank you!" burst out Mrs. Woods, as she ran down the hallway to her classroom.

When Mrs. Woods and her instructional coach met again later that week, there were still unanswered questions. "How will you know if your blended-learning experience is having a positive effect on learning?" asked her coach. Scratching her head momentarily, Mrs. Woods conjured up strategies from her former science classes. "I'll need a control group," she said. Fortunately for her, there were two other teachers with 8th grade American history assignments in the building. Her coach took the initiative to put this conversation on the agenda at the next department meeting.

Before that meeting, the instructional coach met one on one with each of the other teachers in the social studies department, helping them to refine their goals—and planting the seeds about their colleague's blended-learning plans and need for some additional data. The teachers were receptive—and even a little envious—of Mrs. Woods's ventures into the land of useful technology in the classroom.

Over the next several months, Mrs. Woods and her teammates gathered data, discussed the differences (and similarities) in how they were presenting their lessons, and shared ideas with one another. Thrilled to have partners who would listen, Mrs. Woods offered many of her blended-learning strategies as tools for her teammates to learn. As the unofficial team-meeting facilitator, the instructional coach noticed that Mrs. Woods was dominating the discourse, and she created a series of protocols to ensure that all voices were being heard—and that ideas were being passed back and forth, not just forth.

The principal, meanwhile, continued to pop into Mrs. Woods's class to observe lesson segments and to "talk teaching." Often, the conversations seemed to include a series of interested, open-ended questions from the principal and a thoughtful response from Mrs. Woods. When she didn't have a response, she would simply nod and say, "Great question," and write it down to consider later. They had a clear understanding of the role of principal—not to be the person with all the right answers, but rather to be the person who asks the right questions and to build Mrs. Woods's reflective capacity. Higher levels of student learning were right around the corner.

The Action Stage at a Glance

The shift from compliance to commitment is enormous in its significance to a school, to a team, and to an individual teacher. It also can be very subtle in practice. On the surface, an observer might not be able to tell the difference between a teacher who is using a particular instructional strategy because the situation calls for it or just because the principal wants to see it. Because those lines get blurred, it's important to dig deeper to unravel the *thinking* behind the teacher's actions.

In the Action stage, that enormously significant shift is evident. Teachers have begun to *own* the outcomes in their classrooms: student learning, behavior management, ease of transitions, use of resources, everything. And this level of commitment leads to the investigation and pursuit of practices that lead to the accomplishment of their goals. Teachers operating in the Action stage refuse to sit back and let life happen to them and their students. Instead, they go out and happen to life!

Supporting Teachers in the Refinement Stage

Ever watched an artist at work? Marveled at the smooth strokes of the brush on the palette, mixing colors with ease and then calling images to life on the canvas, as if it were a matter of just touching the surface to reveal the beautiful painting beneath? Sculptors are the same: carving and chiseling and smoothing edges that seem predetermined—a sort of ethereal experience like the one that prompted Michelangelo to say, "I saw an angel in the stone and carved to set it free."

Excellence—in any arena—is usually quite enjoyable to observe. Musicians, surgeons, auto mechanics, skateboarders, baristas, chefs, gymnasts, glassblowers—you name it. Peyton Manning on the football field, as we described in Chapter 3. Now, you might have found yourself screaming at your television set, "Just hike the darn ball!" while he called all those audibles, but you also must have admired the cunning and preparation of Manning and his ability to analyze his situation and (eventually) make the right decision.

This level of expertise and performance is not accidental, nor is it solely a result of otherworldly physical gifts. In fact, because of the work ethic, commitment, preparation, and powerful self-reflection of the players involved, the artistic outcomes are quite predictable.

A high level of teaching performance is very much an art form. The way great teachers move about their classrooms, interact with students, interject or hold back at just the right moments, anticipate students' responses and actions, see the goings-on with the eyes in the back of their heads, and can describe everything that's going on in the room at every single moment with precise detail and aplomb is graceful, fluid, seemingly effortless. Sometimes we just sit back and watch with admiration.

When teachers' minds have grown and evolved to this point—when they have an acute awareness of the reality of their classroom, take deliberate steps to intentionally progress toward their goal, assess the impact of their actions consistently, and adapt and adjust on the fly—they have touched upon the Refinement stage (see Figure 13.1). We use the term *refinement* to describe teachers who think critically throughout their day, continuously reflect on their practice, and dial in to the learning that is taking place in each moment of every day. These teachers are highly motivated, knowledgeable about best-practice strategies, and adept at turning the science of teaching into a beautiful art. Let's consider the term more closely.

Refinement: *improvement or clarification of something by making small changes*

FIGURE 13.1

The Refinement Stage

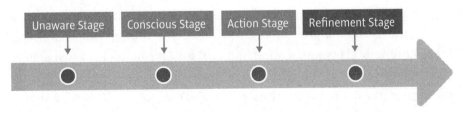

Teachers operating in the Refinement stage are highly attuned to the minute details of individual student learning. Whatever data are collected—test-item analyses, quiz results, written or oral responses, and even looking over a student's shoulder as he works—the Refinement-stage teacher processes it quickly and efficiently to make a decision about what support to provide. More often than not, these interventions are immediate and effective, not put off until the next unit, next week, or even tomorrow.

> With Refinement-stage thinking, excellent teaching performance is predictable. Remember, the more reflective we are, the more effective we are.

And how do Refinement-stage teachers make these decisions with such speed and confidence? Their intuitive judgment is developed by experience, training, knowledge, and repetition. Their brains collect information and commit it to memory that can be drawn upon later. "Eventually," says science journalist Amanda Rose Martinez, "through constant practice, you get to the point where . . . these processes get pushed down into the subconscious. They don't need to be consciously worked out anymore. They become a subroutine" (Martinez, 2010, para. 14). Here is another way of looking at it: Refinement-stage teachers are so dialed in, they can think—and think deeply—without even thinking about it.

If this sounds confusing, have lunch with an artist. The good news is this: reflection is a skill we can teach, learn, and grow in ourselves and others.

It is essential to remember that the Continuum of Self-Reflection is not an evaluation tool; rather, it is a powerful instrument that serves two incredibly helpful purposes. First, it helps capacity-builders (and teachers themselves) identify their teachers' reflective tendencies. Second, it guides those capacity-builders (administrators and coaches) to the proper entry point and directs their capacity-building efforts. There is no value—no "better than" or "worse than"—assigned to any of the stages on the continuum; there are just terms that describe how one thinks about the work. The characteristics of thinking displayed by an individual teacher should be used without prejudice to help you, as a capacity-builder, determine the best course of action to support that teacher's growth as a reflective practitioner. The goal in using this tool is not to evaluate, label, or "fix" teachers; unyieldingly, the goal is to lead teachers to develop strong patterns of thought as we usher them down the path of self-reflection.

The First Step: Identification of Reflective Tendencies

Let's walk through several classrooms and take a closer look at teachers who are currently operating in the Refinement stage. As you read these vignettes, begin to assimilate the characteristics that describe thinking in the Refinement stage. This is the first step in identifying our teachers' reflective tendencies. (The vignettes featuring Mr. Torres and Mrs. Phung originally appeared in our earlier book *Teach, Reflect, Learn* [Hall & Simeral, 2015]. We present them here as examples to be considered from the viewpoint of the capacity-builders, including administrators and coaches.)

Vignettes, Part 1: Meet the Teachers

Visit 1: Elementary School, Mrs. Phung

It's writing time in Mrs. Phung's 2nd grade classroom, and everyone pulls out their personal journals. Mrs. Phung projects hers (decorated with pictures of her family) and proceeds to think aloud as she writes about her weekend trip to the lake. Today she wants to introduce her students to the concept of writing with more details (part of the narrative writing lesson she's going to be doing later that afternoon), so she makes sure to model explicit descriptions of the sights and smells she experienced. After a few minutes, she looks up in mock surprise. "Oh my goodness! I forgot that you haven't started writing yet! I was so caught up in thinking about this beautiful place and was so excited to paint the picture using descriptive words. Please, please, go ahead and begin writing. Don't let me keep you waiting!"

With that, she takes her journal and moves to Christopher's desk. "Christopher, do you mind if I sit next to you today to write?" Christopher shakes his head and goes back to staring at his blank page. After a few moments of writing more in her journal, Mrs. Phung quietly leans over, "Are you struggling to think of a topic today?" Christopher nods his head. "Do you remember last week when I was struggling to come up with an idea? Do you remember what I did?"

Francine calls out from her desk next to Chris, "You wrote a list of your favorite things."

Mrs. Phung smiles and says, "Maybe you can think of a list to write."

"My favorite thing is Pokémon." Christopher says.

"I don't know much about Pokémon," Mrs. Phung shares. "Perhaps you can list the different characters and describe them for me so I have a better idea." Christopher's eyes light up as he picks up his pencil to write.

Mrs. Phung then scoots over to another table to intentionally use proximity to keep students on task. She checks in with Andrea, a struggling writer who has what appears to be a jumbled mix of letters on her page. Andrea is able to read what she wrote, and Mrs. Phung immediately asks her to be the first to share during rug time. Fifteen minutes later, she pulls the class together. As various students share their work, Mrs. Phung asks pointed questions to draw out how students decided what to write and the thinking that went into picking choice detail words.

Later Mrs. Phung explains, "I use a 15-minute writing time each morning to identify specific minilessons that will drive my formal writing instruction later in the day. Journaling provides a window into student thinking and helps me get to know my students in a deeper way."

Visit 2: Middle School, Mr. Torres

"I want you to watch a very brief video of a man stacking coins in fast motion," Mr. Torres tells his Algebra II class. "As you watch, please write down the first question that comes to your mind. [Three minutes later.] Great! I'm curious what questions are out there, so throw some out to me." He proceeds to write the questions on the board. "Now, talk in your groups, share your question with the others, and decide, as a team, which question from your group you find the most interesting." Mr. Torres then listens to the conversations of each of the prearranged teams of four.

"Now," he continues, after making a few handwritten notes about student comments, "your team is charged with two more tasks. As a group, guess a correct answer to your question and determine what an incorrect answer would look like." He continues to walk around the room, listening in on conversations and taking anecdotal notes. At this point, Mr. Torres highlights a question he previously heard—one that specifically addresses the standards he has built this unit around.

"Now, I'd like you to consider this question. As a team, decide what elements are important and what strategies could be used to solve the problem. Each of you has a different colored marker. Explain your thinking on the chart paper in front of you. Everyone must show participation in some way. Andrew,

Marcus, Coral, and Annalise, please meet me at the back of the room."

While the class is working on the posters, Mr. Torres quickly gathers four students who need concrete examples to build conceptual understanding and has them begin stacking pennies on the back table. He then sees that one table group is arguing over a strategy. He pops over, listens to the heated discussion, and poses a few clarifying questions to guide their thinking down the right path. He then returns to the students in the back of the room to provide some explicit small-group instruction.

After the lesson is over, Mr. Torres explains, "I believe in inquiry-based learning. With math, that's the only way to engage students who have preconceived notions about themselves as mathematicians. Tomorrow, I'll formalize and consolidate the math expressed today, reconcile conflicting ideas, and finally ask students to provide a title that would summarize the entire lesson. Then I offer my own. It's not always perfect, but I learn so much about my students' thinking through this approach and am better able to specifically address misconceptions that arise right on the spot."

Visit 3: High School, Miss Spark

It's the first day of school, and Miss Spark is ready for her three periods of English I, two periods of English II, two periods of creative writing, one period of AP English, and one release period where she can provide support to her colleagues throughout the building in "literacy across the curriculum" strategies. Some people might be overwhelmed by such a schedule, but Miss Spark is ready.

When asked if her confidence stems from the fact that she taught all those same courses last year and so probably has a stockpile of leftover activities and materials ready to use, she laughs. "No, no," she says. "I throw everything away at the end of the year and start fresh. I want to make sure my kids get the very best from me, not my lazy leftovers."

As the students file into her classroom and find a seat, Miss Spark greets them warmly and shares a little bit about herself, then tells them this: "There are really only two things we need to know this year. One: Who are you? And two: What are our goals for this class?" The rest of the first day is a discussion in which students take turns sharing what they're comfortable sharing, providing an introductory writing sample, and ingesting the big ideas of the course.

"OK, I'm ready," says Miss Spark at the end of the day. "I was surprised by some of my students' writing abilities—on both ends of the spectrum. I can see we're going to have to dig into some sentence-structure conversations, which will be helpful to everyone, especially the couple of students I'm going to invite to be peer tutors and expert editors."

While she's talking, Miss Spark has moved to the considerable collection of books on her classroom bookshelf. She starts picking titles off the ledges individually, flipping through pages and either putting books back or placing them on the table beside her. "I can't wait for tomorrow," she says excitedly. "We're going to learn to write with style, verve, emotion, wonder . . . ." Her voice trails off as she immerses herself in her planning.

All three of the artists—whoops, *teachers*—just described have skills and knowledge about instructional pedagogy, to be sure. Undoubtedly, they are committed to their profession, to excellence in the classroom, and to supporting high levels of student learning. For all students. Every day. With every learning target. Without exceptions.

Beyond those similarities, you might have noticed that all three are constantly thinking about their responsibilities as a teacher. Not a moment goes by without their attention focused squarely on how they might modify a lesson, a question, an activity, or an entire course in order to better meet their students' needs. In the Refinement-stage teacher's classroom, learning is not the variable; it is the expected and anticipated outcome. The process by which learning occurs for each student might vary significantly, and therein lies the art.

Reflective Tendencies of a Refinement-Stage Teacher

For teachers operating in the Refinement stage, it's all about adapting and adjusting to the changing needs of the students in front of them. They've got a deep awareness of their instructional reality, they act with great intentionality, they assess to what degree things are working, and they spring into action the moment they see a need. In the Refinement stage, such responsiveness is part of their standard operating procedure—to see a need and leave it unaddressed would be considered a form of educational malpractice. What follows are descriptions of the overarching reflective characteristics, as shown in Figure 13.2, of a teacher in the Refinement stage.

Accepts responsibility for the success of each student and for ongoing personal growth. Because learning is the expected, constant outcome, teaching and learning activities become the variables. And the Refinement-stage teacher takes ownership of designing and implementing those approaches. To provide options and meet all the diverse needs of the students in their classroom, teachers in the Refinement stage know that they must truly engage in lifelong learning—filling their toolkits and equipping themselves with the strategies necessary to ensure high levels of learning by *every* student.

FIGURE 13.2

Teacher's Reflective Tendencies: Refinement Stage

- Accepts responsibility for the success of each student and for ongoing personal growth.
- Reflects before, during, and after taking action.
- Modifies lessons and plans to meet students' varied needs.
- Dissects lessons and learning to reveal options for improvement.
- Pursues opportunities to work and learn with colleagues.
- Maintains a vast repertoire of instructional strategies.
- Recognizes that there are multiple "right" courses of action.
- Thinks globally, beyond the classroom.
- Focuses on the *art* of teaching.

Reflects before, during, and after taking action. When do teachers in the Refinement stage reflect? Short answer: always. Longer answer: reflection that occurs before teaching—when considering the learning target, students' current knowledge, and the multiple pathways to learning—might as well be called "preflection"; and teachers in the Refinement stage make a practice of thinking before acting. When the lesson is over, these teachers consider the strengths and weaknesses in light of the data regarding the lesson's effectiveness. What sets the Refinement-stage teachers apart, however, is their ability to pay attention and reflect on the state of affairs right there in the heat of the battle. Why wait? The moment a student struggles, a response (to act or to let the struggle play out) can be implemented.

Modifies lessons and plans to meet students' varied needs. Not all students learn in the same way, at the same rate, or from the same starting point. These are facts. Teachers in the Refinement stage act on this knowledge and create subtle (or dramatic) modifications to lessons, activities, and plans to meet their students' different needs. This doesn't mean that the teachers teach 27 lessons in order to support the learning of 27 unique learners—though the teachers will ensure that all 27 students have access to the learning and have a way that works for them to demonstrate their mastery.

Dissects lessons and learning to reveal options for improvement. Remember dissecting a frog in science class? We did this to better understand the inner workings and relationships of organs and systems we can't always see from the outside. Refinement-stage teachers consider each lesson to be very much like a science lab frog, and they don't always wait for the lesson to be over before they begin to slice it open and peer inside. In this way, they can see what worked, why it worked, and how it might be modified for future (greater) successes.

Pursues opportunities to work and learn with colleagues. Teachers in the Refinement stage understand that they alone will never know it all; thus, they'll need their colleagues to diversify their thinking, broaden their horizons, and deepen their well of strategies. So they seek out their teammates, other teachers, and even their online professional learning network to engage in dialogue, earnest debate, and an exchange of ideas.

Maintains a vast repertoire of instructional strategies. Since "one size fits all" really fits none, teachers who touch upon the Refinement stage must be avid collectors of teaching approaches. Filling their toolkits with all sorts of pedagogical strategies ensures that when a student (or a group of students) is struggling, there's *something* available to the teacher that will help to address the particular struggle. And that toolkit is like the magician's sleeve: it seems to have no limit to what it can contain.

Recognizes that there are multiple "right" courses of action. The only constant in the Refinement-stage teacher's classroom is that the students will learn. Period. With that clear and compelling destination in hand, teachers operating in this stage may choose any of a number of different strategies that might lead to that end. There is no "right" or "wrong" in this classroom—only "effective" or "ineffective," and often there are many paths leading to the same goal.

Thinks globally, beyond the classroom. In the perfect world, which is the world we're creating, greatness is shared openly, borrowed freely, and disseminated widely. Teachers operating in the Refinement stage agree with this school of thought, and they consider the implications of their practice upon their fellow teachers, educators beyond their schoolhouse walls, and the profession of education as a whole. How can we all benefit? If it's in the best interest of kids, it's worth sharing with others.

Focuses on the *art* of teaching. Need we say more? Refinement-stage teachers see angels in their classrooms and teach to set them free.

Using the Reflective Cycle (Figure 13.3), we can take a closer look at the distinct thought patterns and reflective habits of teachers in the Refinement

FIGURE 13.3

Capability to Adjust Actions in the Reflective Cycle

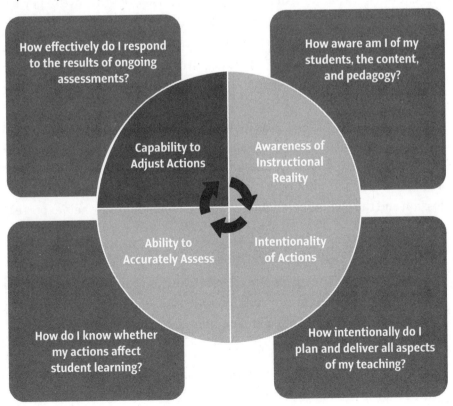

stage. This will provide us, as instructional leaders and capacity-builders, with valuable insights that enable us to accurately identify how our teachers are currently *thinking* about their professional responsibilities, which will allow us to support their continued growth as reflective practitioners.

At this point, it's probably pretty clear how far along the Reflective Cycle our teachers' thinking has developed, or at which quadrant our teachers should focus their reflective attention. Have you identified it? If you chose "Capability to Adjust Actions" for a teacher operating in the Refinement stage, you're ready to proceed as a capacity-builder, and the question to ask is this: *How effectively does the teacher respond to the results of ongoing assessments?*

As we have mentioned, teachers who have progressed to the Refinement stage (even if it's just to visit the stage momentarily, not to move in permanently) are aware of their instructional reality and take steps intentionally to meet their goals, assess their impact, and modify their actions in order to better meet student needs. Their reflective focus then shifts to the effectiveness of their adaptations—are the adaptations truly helpful in deepening student learning? For this, they must continue to proceed through the Reflective Cycle, *trusting their intuition* and staying alert for signs of success and struggle along the way. In addition, for us as capacity-builders, we must begin to find ways to extend the scope of our Refinement-stage teachers outside their classroom (and the school) environment, assisting the profession and the legions of students who could benefit from their expertise.

The Second Step: Supportive Practices

Each stage within the Continuum of Self-Reflection has a capacity-building goal to develop and support each individual teacher's reflective growth. Here is the overall goal for the Refinement-stage teacher:

> Our goal is *to encourage long-term growth and continued reflection through responsiveness to ongoing assessments* to maximize the impact on each and every student.

The Refinement stage is not the finish line. Any teacher who has checked into the Hotel Refinement understands there is always room for growth, always opportunities to learn, and always space for improvement. Operating in the Refinement stage, with the mind constantly whirring and analyzing and running through hypotheses and scenarios, is just plain exhausting! Mentally and emotionally draining, Refinement-stage thinking is more likely to be an exercise that teachers engage in sporadically or occasionally than a permanent state of mind. That said, as capacity-builders, we must help all our teachers—including those operating in the Refinement stage—to continue to grow, learn, stretch, dabble, analyze, and evaluate their work in order to continue to improve their practice.

As capacity-builders, it's crucial for us to understand that shifting action doesn't always result in shifted thinking, but shifting thinking will *always* result in shifted action. Our charge is to tackle the thinking that drives the doing. If we're to successfully cultivate a culture of reflective practice and facilitate long-term professional growth, we must ask teachers to *think* as often as we ask them to *do*. Their growth in thinking, then, will fuel a curiosity and desire to learn more.

Leadership Roles

How do capacity-builders begin to address the specific needs of a teacher in the Refinement stage? To have the impact necessary for continued reflective growth, administrators and coaches simultaneously work independently (within their own roles) and collaboratively (as their roles are complementary to one another), as well as intentionally leveraging a teacher's peers within the PLC structure to provide additional support, as noted in the triad diagram in Figure 13.4. In the absence of an instructional coach, the administrator must be even more deliberate in the use of peer relationships to engage in this work. This strategic triangulation of support significantly increases the likelihood of success.

As described in Chapter 5, a couple of conditions must be established in order to proceed with our capacity-building efforts. First, the roles

FIGURE 13.4

Triad Diagram for Refinement Stage

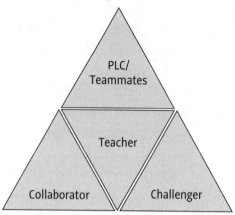

of administrator and coach must be defined, distinguished, and communicated clearly to one another. Second, the boundaries that encompass each role must be respected at all times. In the case of working with Refinement-stage teachers, these roles manifest themselves in unique and important ways as we work to guide the teachers toward their capacity-building goal.

 The administrator's role: *challenger.*

The administrator's role is that of *challenger*, providing the Refinement-stage teacher with opportunities for growth, leadership, and contributions beyond the classroom. Great teachers are often left alone, not unlike a retired horse put out to pasture, because well-meaning administrators have grander issues on which to focus their time and energy. When a teacher is struggling, it's obvious that the administrator must tend to that teacher, providing support and encouragement and strategic professional interventions; it's difficult to give the same credence to helping teachers who appear strong, successful, and effective in their responsibilities. But that's exactly what administrators must do—they must provide their Refinement-stage teachers with challenges.

Challenging teachers to excel beyond their role is not always an easy task. Some Refinement-stage teachers abhor the idea of public speaking, writing, or in any way detracting from the very duties that they must attend to in order to remain effective. However, it is our belief that greatness carries with it an obligation to the profession, in whatever manner it is communicated, to be widely shared and used. It is administrators' responsibility to provide the opportunities and the structure and support that allow for that leadership to occur—from sharing strategies in a team meeting to mentoring a colleague to writing an article for publication in a nationally recognized education journal.

 The coach's role: *collaborator.*

The coach's role is to work alongside the Refinement-stage teacher as a *collaborator* focused on the goal of refining and expanding the finer details of the thinking behind the actions.

We mentioned earlier that Refinement-stage teachers need colleagues to enrich their professional experience, and who better to serve in this role than an instructional coach? As a collaborator, the coach is there, sleeves rolled up and boots pulled on, prepared to support the teacher's investigations, questions, and grand schemes.

Teachers in the Refinement stage are highly motivated, highly reflective individuals. For them, there is promise in every class period, potential in every student, and new learning around every bend. Challenges and opportunities for growth empower these teachers along their path. In a poetic sense, the journey is their destination. Instructional coaches join this journey to provide a sounding board, a research partner, a devil's advocate, a guinea pig, a debate foe, or whatever particular role the teacher needs at any given point in time. Sometimes Refinement-stage teachers need to be reined in, and at other times they need to be set free. Their coach plays a vital role in ensuring that happens.

Working Complementarily

As expressed in Chapter 5, the coach and administrator are partners in this work. Sharing a common goal of supporting a teacher's growth as a reflective practitioner, each assumes the role just outlined very intentionally, knowing the other will shoulder the complementary role.

With teachers in the Refinement stage, the capacity-building approaches of administrators and instructional coaches really aren't that different. Because the teachers' reflective tendencies are so well developed, both capacity-building roles put little emphasis on *deepening* self-reflective practices. Instead, the focus is on *maintaining* those thoughtful habits while influencing peers and ensuring that every student's educational needs are being met. For instance, if a teacher such as Miss Spark (from our high school vignette on p. 252) has multiple courses on her class schedule, both coach and administrator can check in to ensure that she's addressing her students' needs and moving them toward the proper learning outcomes, and offer any support and assistance she requires.

Meanwhile, with that special 9th period assignment of serving in a teacher-leadership role in the building, Miss Spark might work closely with the administrator or the coach—or both—to plan collegial observations, deepen strategic partnerships, facilitate cross-content dialogue, or otherwise build a culture of professional learning throughout the campus. As the administrator suggests opportunities for formal leadership, the teacher might naturally seek out the coach to serve as the collaborator in this venture. As a team, the two capacity-builders link arms with their Refinement-stage teachers in a joint effort to build systemic reflective growth. Truly, these are the architects of a culture of reflective practice.

Strategic PLC and Teacher-Leadership Support

The administrator and the coach are not the only capacity-builders who share the immense responsibility of supporting teachers' growth as reflective practitioners. Because teaching is no longer done in isolation (those days are behind us, right?), each educator's relationships with colleagues, peers, and other professionals within their grade-level or department or professional learning community are vital in completing our triad (see Figure 13.4, p. 260). Within a culture of reflective practice, administrators set the expectation that teachers will work collaboratively to support each other in their pursuit of common goals, and then it's "all hands on deck" to engage in the practices that accomplish that objective.

Because engaging in Refinement-stage thinking tends to demonstrate to others that a teacher possesses deeply reflective habits and highly effective instructional practices, often the Refinement-stage teacher is assigned leadership responsibilities, even if the teacher may not have "natural" leadership abilities or even a hint of leadership inclinations. That said, those in this stage on the Continuum of Self-Reflection frequently seek out colleagues for partnership, reflective dialogue, and instructional collaboration. These can be outstanding opportunities for leadership to flourish. The strategies in Figure 13.5 may strengthen a Refinement-stage teacher's ability to contribute, support, and learn within a professional learning community structure. Let's examine each one in greater detail.

Assign or encourage formal leadership roles within the team or department structure. Capacity-builders can help jump-start a Refinement-stage teacher's foray into leadership by providing a designated role for the teacher to assume: department chair, team leader, leadership team representative, model classroom, or some other assignment that nudges the teacher into the world of teacher-leadership. Sometimes starting small—say, within the teacher's own department or grade-level peer group—is a safe way to get the effort started.

Encourage sharing and modeling of the thinking behind this teacher's decisions and actions in the classroom during team meetings.

FIGURE 13.5

Strategic PLC and Teacher-Leadership Support: Refinement Stage

Capacity-Building Goal: To encourage long-term growth and continued reflection through responsiveness to ongoing assessments

- Assign or encourage formal leadership roles within the team or department structure.
- Encourage sharing and modeling of the thinking behind this teacher's decisions and actions in the classroom during team meetings.
- Encourage leadership of a team action-research project.
- Strategically partner this teacher with colleagues (in particular, those in the Conscious stage) to build their reflective capacity.

Most teachers within a department or grade level understand which teachers on their team are highly reflective—and highly effective. By structuring the team's dialogue to include intentional think-alouds or accounts of *how* a teacher processed a situation to arrive at a conclusion, capacity-builders can support the entire team's reflective growth. This modeling becomes less about *what* the teacher did and more about the *thinking* that drove the action, and that's where true capacity lies.

Encourage leadership of a team action-research project. Often, teachers operating in the Refinement stage have come across a situation or a learning snag that has caused them to stumble. To solve this new mystery, they are interested in trying something new. But what? And how will they tell the difference in outcomes without other teachers attempting other strategies to solve the same problem? In an action-research protocol, that's exactly what happens. If the Refinement-stage teacher acquires the skills to lead such an expedition, that gain can also deepen the entire team's learning.

Strategically partner this teacher with colleagues (in particular, those in the Conscious stage) to build their reflective capacity. When arriving at a stumbling block, teachers in the Conscious stage, as you'll recall, tend to fixate on the external factors that interfere with success. Teachers in the Refinement stage, on the other hand, acknowledge those factors and accept them as challenges. By sharing their mindset and gently leading their Conscious-stage colleagues to investigate their options, Refinement-stage teachers can support their colleagues' reflective growth along with their own. Capacity-builders can position these two to partner intentionally.

Transformational Feedback

What feedback could we possibly give to teachers who are deeply reflective and highly effective in their classroom? How could we possibly add value to their practice? The answers to those questions may or may not surprise you: with Refinement-stage teachers, we must provide challenge.

See Figure 13.6 for a sampling of feedback stems in the form of challenging prompts that are designed to meet our Refinement-stage teachers'

FIGURE 13.6

Transformational Feedback for Teachers in the Refinement Stage

Capacity-Building Goal: To encourage long-term growth and continued reflection through responsiveness to ongoing assessments

- Today your students did __ and you immediately responded with __. How did you plan to address that misconception?
- In the middle of today's lesson, you abruptly changed course. What led to that decision? Was it a successful move? How do you know?
- How do you know when students are learning in the middle of a lesson? What do you look for?
- How do you identify the specific learning styles of the students in your room?
- Explain the thinking that went into planning a lesson like this. How do you know which strategies to select? How do you decide which activities to choose?
- To what extent are you collaborating with your colleagues to plan and deliver your lessons? How can you become more intentional in partnering with your teammates?
- Your lesson today reminded me of a recent article I read in *Educational Leadership*. I'll put a copy in your box. I would love to hear your thoughts.

unique and distinct needs. Mind you, this list is but a taste of the ways you, as a capacity-builder, can *launch* a feedback dialogue or otherwise engage a teacher in reflective dialogue. We invite you to connect the dots between the prompts and the capacity-building goal, and we encourage you to enrich this list by adding your own prompts that match your style and your teachers' needs. Ultimately, beginning a conversation in this spirit should generate reflective thought and partnership. Where it goes from here is completely up to the parties involved.

Capacity-builders aren't there to give teachers the answers or to *tell* them what to do better; rather, the mission involves helping the teachers to *think* more regularly, accurately, and profoundly about their professional practices. And even our Refinement-stage teachers can strengthen their reflective muscles. So we challenge them. Not in a confrontational way, but in a "let's get serious about this continuous improvement" kind of way. We provide feedback that tests their beliefs, perceptions, biases, knowledge, creativity, and professional practice.

And because Refinement-stage teachers are predisposed to critical thought, they need tough probes and questions that force them out of their comfort zone to consider new paths, extend their thinking, examine their beliefs and values, and debate their positions. These actions will shuttle Refinement-stage teachers into deep, reflective dialogue with themselves and their colleagues, as well as send them to extensive professional resources for guidance. To accomplish that lofty task, the feedback process that capacity-builders engage in with teachers in the Refinement stage tends to meet four criteria, as expressed in the following guidelines for delivery.

Drive personal reflection. As we discussed earlier, it's quite possible that our Refinement-stage teachers have assimilated their reflective practices so deeply that they no longer recognize their own thought processes. With this in mind, it's important for capacity-builders to prompt the teachers to become even more self-aware. Cognizance—in this stage just as much as in any other stage—will lead to deeper reflections that affect student learning outcomes.

Introduce new ideas. *What else could you do? What options haven't you considered yet?* By asking these questions, capacity-builders peel the curtains back from a world of additional strategies that Refinement-stage teachers can't wait to explore. With a considerable array of teaching strategies at their disposal, Refinement-stage teachers may fall into the habit of simply using what they've got. They can sometimes benefit from a nudge to stretch their boundaries by learning more, seeking more, investigating more, trying more, and using more.

Serve as devil's advocate. Sometimes, those operating in the Refinement stage seek solutions to problems that don't yet, and may not ever, exist. This situation may sound familiar: a teacher arrives at school first thing in the morning, all excited because she had a vision of a classroom setup much different than her own, and is now going through the process of dismantling her room and rearranging everything. As a devil's advocate, we interrupt the *actions* of restructuring to concentrate on the *thinking* that prompted it. *Was it completely thought out? What haven't you considered yet? What if you make this change, realize you've made a horrible mistake, and have to replace it all tomorrow?* Sometimes it's best to provide that challenge *before* the teacher enacts widespread changes.

Encourage involvement in leadership. Teachers who excel in certain aspects of teaching have an obligation to share it with fellow teachers. As capacity-builders, we can provide the feedback, suggestions, and avenues to help our Refinement-stage teachers spread their professional wings and strengthen the profession. Any time Refinement-stage teachers can affect others outside their own classroom, we're all lifted to a higher level.

Differentiated Coaching

With our teachers well versed in reflection practices, capacity-builders can roll up their sleeves and dive into the mucky underbrush of instructional coaching, wading and wrestling with the various approaches that will support our teachers' growth as reflective practitioners—ultimately leading to significant levels of learning for all students.

A number of coaching strategies will help teachers operating in the Refinement stage to successfully achieve their capacity-building goal (to encourage long-term growth and continued reflection through responsiveness to ongoing assessments). A sampling of such strategies, as outlined in the Continuum of Self-Reflection and shown in Figure 13.7, is described in further detail in the next paragraphs. Each of the strategies can be used in isolation or woven with another. Remember, what works splendidly with one teacher may not work as effectively with another, so be sure to *differentiate* your selection and application of these approaches. What's most important is that the strategy meets each teacher's unique needs and is

FIGURE 13.7

Differentiated Coaching Strategies for Teachers in the Refinement Stage

Capacity-Building Goal: To encourage long-term growth and continued reflection through responsiveness to ongoing assessments

- Analyze data and student work samples together.
- Analyze schoolwide data together.
- Stimulate discussions of personal vision and educational philosophy.
- Serve as devil's advocate to challenge thinking.
- Record a lesson and discuss video analysis.
- Facilitate idea sharing through collegial observations.
- Encourage leadership of small-group discussions around a common problem of practice.
- Encourage book club facilitation or leadership.
- Arrange for student-teacher hosting opportunities.
- Encourage conference participation and publication submission.
- Engage in interactive journaling.

explicitly connected back to the capacity-building goal—so we can see and monitor our impact more clearly.

Analyze data and student work samples together. To make this strategy highly effective, bring an Action-stage teacher and a Refinement-stage teacher together to analyze student work samples and engage in dialogue about evidence of student thinking. Doing so provides a good practice opportunity for Refinement-stage teachers to slow down their thinking and learn to articulate clearly. At the same time, Action-stage teachers need to hear the thinking of Refinement-stage colleagues. Take samples from high-level, medium-level, and struggling students and dissect the evidence of learning. *What does this student know? What learning gaps exist? What patterns of student thinking can we identify? What are the next steps?* Through this facilitated dialogue, both Action- and Refinement-stage teachers can grow professionally.

Analyze schoolwide data together. Often we find Refinement-stage teachers behind closed doors making an amazing difference in their classrooms with little connection to the rest of the school. One way we can challenge them to move beyond the walls of their own rooms and develop a more global perspective is through the analysis of schoolwide data. Elicit the teacher's help in clarifying the vision for the use of data in the school, developing hypotheses about factors that affect student learning, and identifying content areas and skills that need to be reinforced across grade levels and subject areas. Asking teachers to analyze schoolwide data together can be a powerful strategy to both recognize their expertise and experience and challenge them to develop a more global perspective.

Stimulate discussions of personal vision and educational philosophy. For many Refinement-stage teachers, excellence in the classroom comes naturally. Personal vision and educational philosophy aren't something they often stop to think about—in particular, how their vision and philosophy have shifted as their experience and expertise have grown. Prompting discussion around this topic can serve several purposes. First, it strengthens the teachers' understanding of their own mindset; second, it provides them practice articulating their beliefs (often a challenge for those whose strong teaching comes "naturally"); and finally, it can encourage them to be more vocal with peers in sharing how their personal vision and educational philosophy connect directly to the instructional decisions they make each day, or expressing how their educational philosophy has shifted over time.

Serve as devil's advocate to challenge thinking. Having a devil's advocate that is responsible for raising tough questions in a constructive way is critical for success, particularly with Refinement-stage teachers. Making this strategy work successfully, however, can be tricky. The devil (his advocate, that is) is in the details. We've found there are three keys to success:

1. Together with the teacher, commit to an explicit process. Start with a particular strategy or idea that the teacher wants to refine or tackle. Determine together that you will play the role of devil's advocate throughout the process. Plan tough questions in advance rather than hope that they will spontaneously emerge.

2. Frame the purpose of your role clearly—this definition is essential. This exercise can't be about killing an idea or identifying all of its flaws. It's not a game of "gotcha." The purpose is to reduce uncertainty and drive deeper understanding by challenging thinking before, during, and after the action.

3. The devil's advocate role needs to function constructively throughout the process, rather than be an inquisition at the end. The coach doesn't wait for the teacher to try something before asking challenging questions to probe thinking.

Record a lesson and discuss video analysis. Teachers in the Refinement stage can also grow from observing themselves in action in the classroom. Videotaping can be an extremely valuable assessment tool, allowing the teacher to view and listen to the class from a learner's perspective and gain valuable insights into their own teaching style and approach. The key to making this strategy successful for Refinement-stage teachers, however, is to hone in on their thinking. As they watch themselves, direct them to describe their thinking throughout the lesson. This provides them with practice in articulating reflective thought and can be followed up with encouragement to share this thinking aloud with colleagues in PLCs.

Facilitate idea sharing through collegial observations. Ample research supports peer observation as a successful form of professional development as well as a powerful component in the reflection process, yet teachers rarely have the opportunity to visit other classrooms. Once the environment is established in which this is desirable, capacity-builders can accelerate the process by setting up a time to cover a teacher's class so the teacher can visit another classroom. If possible, strategically partner a Refinement-stage teacher with one in the Conscious stage. Encourage dialogue around the *when, where, why,* and *how* of new ideas, fostering critical thinking.

Encourage leadership of small-group discussions around a common problem of practice. Another way to challenge Refinement-stage teachers' thinking is to develop their teacher-leadership skills. Supporting them to lead a small-group discussion around common problems of practice with their peers can do just that. Prompt the use of the Reflective Cycle to unpack common challenges, and encourage them to think aloud as they describe problems they currently face. Provide questions that they can use to guide conversation around thinking more accurately and deeply about subjects.

Encourage book club facilitation or leadership. To successfully facilitate a book club, one must be thoroughly familiar with the content presented, as well as skilled in the art of discussion. This requirement can present new challenges to teachers who are new to the role of teacher-leader. An alternate approach is to initiate a group-led book club. Teachers can approach their colleagues or post an invitation in the staff lounge to participate in a group-led discussion. One person can be the organizer, with the entire group sharing responsibility for leading the conversation each week. Regardless of the approach, encouraging facilitation or leadership in a small way can be an excellent way to challenge the Refinement-stage teacher.

Arrange for student-teacher hosting opportunities. What better way to reflect upon your own practices than by having an aspiring teacher in your room? Not only must Refinement-stage teachers model exemplary instructional practices and strategies; they also have a responsibility to mentor and coach the student-teacher through observation and feedback. In a culture of reflective practice, this strategy must place heavy emphasis on the Refinement-stage teacher modeling *thinking* as much as modeling *doing.* This plan of action fosters ongoing self-reflection in both mentor and mentee.

Encourage conference participation and publication submission. Teachers operating in the Refinement stage have expertise and reflective experiences to share. Identify a specific area of strength and encourage this teacher to submit a proposal to present at a conference or write an article for an educational publication. (Ask teachers to copresent with colleagues—or with an administrator or a coach—if they are hesitant.) Organize a mini–educational conference within your building, and ask Refinement-stage teachers to lead a session. By doing so, you can encourage and challenge these folks to become educational leaders and influence student achievement outside their classroom walls.

Engage in interactive journaling. Writing down one's thoughts is perhaps the most powerful form of self-reflection. Writing, itself, is the great synthesizer of knowledge, learning, and understanding. Ask teachers in the Refinement stage to note how their thinking drives their instruction and, subsequently, student learning. Then collect the journals and respond with thoughts and questions, as well as the encouragement to articulate these "think-alouds" with their peers. If your teachers have a copy of our parallel teacher-text, *Teach, Reflect, Learn: Building Your Capacity for Success in the Classroom* (Hall & Simeral, 2015), discuss their reflections and journal entries related to the many tasks and scores of reflective questions we offer to encourage reflective growth. (And for bonus points, ask them to submit their reflections to one of our blog posts at http://bycfs.edublogs.org.)

The Refinement Stage in Real Life

Remember the three vignettes we presented earlier in this chapter? Those three teachers, though fictional, are amalgams of actual teachers with whom we've worked as administrators, coaches, teachers, or consultants over the years. We'd like to return to one of them now, to show you how that teacher's particular capacity-builders might come together to provide comprehensive support. In the scenario that follows, we'll provide some detail about their plan, share how the work unfolded, and identify their preliminary results as their teacher grew as a reflective practitioner. And even if the scenario stems from a different grade level than one you support directly, there are lessons to be gleaned from the interactions, the collaboration, and the focus on the *thinking* behind the doing. Remember, self-reflection is context-independent: our brains are the common denominator.

Vignette, Part 2: Mrs. Phung

Mrs. Phung's principal and instructional coach were sitting down for their weekly state-of-the-school discussion. Their conversation marched up from kindergarten to 1st grade and then to 2nd, 3rd, 4th, and 5th, and eventually the conversation turned to the school's instructional focus for this year: writing. The writing scores had stalled, many students appeared to balk at writing exercises, and teachers reported that instruction in writing was the toughest part of their day.

"What about Mrs. Phung?" asked the principal. "Can't she help?"

"She's definitely a Refinement-stage thinker," replied the coach, "even though she scored herself barely in the Action stage on the self-assessment."

"Right. That's typical of the highly reflective—they always see room for growth," the principal thought aloud. She remembered how she and the coach had discussed Mrs. Phung's powerful reflective habits but were stunned at the results of her self-assessment (found in *Teach, Reflect, Learn* [Hall & Simeral, 2015] and online at www.ascd.org/ASCD/pdf/books/ HallSimeral2017.pdf [password: HallSimeral117006]).

"She's not in a tested grade, but her kids love writing, and it's a strength of hers, instructionally," said the coach.

"Yes, yes. What if she were to engage some of our other teachers in dialogue—nothing formal like teaching lessons or leading PD sessions yet; just talking about writing and how we can make it interesting and fun for kids. Would she do that?" the principal asked excitedly.

That afternoon the coach happened to walk into Mrs. Phung's class right after the students had been dismissed.

"This is no coincidental visit," said Mrs. Phung. "You've got something up your sleeve. What's up?"

For the next 45 minutes, coach and teacher exchanged thoughts about the school's writing focus, the scores, the instruction, and the materials available to teachers. At one point, Mrs. Phung shrugged her shoulders. "I don't really do anything that special," she said. "All we really need is our imagination, our love for ideas, and maybe paper and pencil; but those are really optional."

"So would you be willing to talk about writing with your comrades?" asked the coach.

After another 15 minutes, it was set. Every Friday morning, the coach would host a "Coffee Talk" in her office—an informal, open-invitational gathering where any teacher could drop by, have a cup of coffee (and maybe a donut, but we'd advocate for a healthier choice), and "talk shop" for a half-hour or so before school starts. For the first month, the advertised topic would be "Lovin' Writing." And Mrs. Phung promised to be there each time—not as an expert, but rather as an interested discussant, though she also promised to think up a couple of special insights or lessons she could share to really add value to the dialogues.

As the first couple of weeks went by and teachers engaged in this fun, robust series of conversations, the principal continued her practice of visiting classrooms often to observe teaching and learning and to engage in feedback cycles with her teachers. When she came upon classrooms during writing instruction (which she made every effort to do on purpose, as that was the school's focus), she often wove a comment, question, or invitation in about the Friday morning Coffee Talk sessions.

Mrs. Phung, meanwhile, benefited greatly from the conversations herself. Whereas the coach and principal assumed she would be in a more giving role, she actually found herself soaking up her colleagues' ideas as well, often returning the following week (or sooner, if she couldn't wait) to share the results of her attempts to replicate their strategies. Her enthusiasm about embracing others' ideas was contagious, and teachers all across the building began sharing, borrowing, stealing, and modifying one another's approaches for their own classes.

In the spring, the results of the writing assessment showed modest improvement across the board. Coupled with the staff's excitement and the astounding number of entries in the monthly writing contest for each of the last few months of school, this made for a very promising future for the school's writing program. None of them could wait for the next school year to begin.

The Refinement Stage at a Glance

Most people are unaware that Russian novelist Leo Tolstoy had a keen interest in education. Over the course of his life, he built more than 70 schools and went on to say this about educators in the classroom:

> The best teacher will be he who has, at his tongue's end, the explanation of what it is that is bothering the pupil. These explanations give the teacher the knowledge of the greatest possible number of methods, the ability of inventing new methods and, above all, not a blind adherence to one method but the conviction that all methods are one-sided, and that

the best method would be the one which would answer best to all the possible difficulties incurred by a pupil. That is, not a method, but an art and a talent. (quoted in Schön, 1987, p. 66)

Tolstoy, in all his wisdom, has given us yet another eloquent definition of a teacher in the Refinement stage.

Epilogue

If you've read this book from cover to cover, your head is probably swimming right now. Take a break, have a glass of lemonade, take a nap. Then let's get back to it. It's game time.

You've read about the playing field and the players, and we've attempted to provide you with a pretty thorough playbook. The match (contest, game, derby, event, or whatever you'd like to call it) is scheduled and you've got to prepare yourself.

And now you're probably wondering where to start, yes?

 Every journey begins with the first step.

We expect that you'll have recognized that a culture of reflective practice is not something that descends from the sky via helicopter or drone, à la *The Hunger Games*. Establishing and cultivating a true culture of reflective practice takes a significant amount of forethought, planning, intentionality, and work in the trenches. Fortunately, we believe we've equipped you with the tools to prepare the environment for such work: thorough explanations of Fundamentals 1 through 7 and the Site Assessment (detailed in Chapter 4), which will help you isolate areas of strength and need, which will, in turn, direct your decision making and help you allocate your focus. (See also Appendix B for some frequently asked questions and our responses.)

We also expect you to acknowledge that creating a culture of reflective practice within your school or district is not really something *additional* that anyone will be piling onto your plate. This is work that we're already doing as leaders and as capacity-builders. Or at least it's work that we *should* be doing as leaders and as capacity-builders, in the form of the following big ideas:

- Building strong professional relationships
- Clarifying professional roles and responsibilities
- Setting transparent expectations
- Communicating clearly, specifically, and consistently
- Celebrating our successes
- Calibrating our focus and approaches when necessary
- Setting SMART goals that lead to higher levels of student achievement
- Emphasizing ongoing professional growth
- Following through by supporting one another, providing feedback, and coaching

This list encompasses the content of Fundamentals 1 through 7. Who would argue with these big ideas? This list could have come out of any leadership guide worth its salt. The only real *new* approach we're mixing in is the focus on self-reflection and the *thinking* that drives everything we do. So in a sense, we're simply providing the utensils to help you devour whatever's already on your plate in a really successful, efficient manner. Think about it. We're helping you to work SMART-R in order to refine your reflective habits so you can progress toward excellence in instructional leadership.

And as you embark upon this powerful journey, we commend you.

Appendix A: Building Teachers' Capacity (BTC) Site Assessment

Pete Hall • Alisa Simeral • ASCD Professional Learning Services

Purpose: The Building Teachers' Capacity (BTC) Site Assessment is an assessment tool used to evaluate and examine the level of BTC implementation and guide schools through the process of shifting school culture and climate, growing a reflective mindset, and establishing a culture of reflective practice. The assessment tool can be used through three distinct means:

1. Prior to implementation to gauge readiness for implementing capacity-building approaches and structures.

2. At initial "launch" to set priorities, establish goals, and develop an implementation plan.

3. At any point during implementation to serve as an ongoing formative assessment of progress, identify strengths, and update/revise the implementation plan.

Fundamentals: The BTC Site Assessment assesses the seven fundamentals of building teachers' capacity (below). They are presented in a rough rank/priority order (though each school/district's individual context will determine the priority of these fundamentals):

1. **Relationships, Roles, and Responsibilities**

2. **Expectations and Communication**

3. **Celebration and Calibration**

4. **Goal Setting and Follow-Through**

5. **Strategic PLC and Teacher-Leadership Support**

6. **Transformational Feedback**

7. **Differentiated Coaching**

Vocabulary: Descriptors within the fundamentals and the rubric have been intentionally designed with broad terms in order to encourage and facilitate conversations around vocabulary and meaning and to develop a common understanding around capacity-building practice.

Directions: Analyze the level of implementation, understanding, and/or accepted practice of each of the elements within each of the seven fundamentals. Using the BTC Implementation Rubric as a guide, mark the column that most accurately describes your site's implementation level, adding narrative and evidence as appropriate. This tool can be used in a variety of ways, most commonly one of the following:

1. As a leadership team or as an entire staff, complete the Site Assessment individually; then discuss the composite results.

2. As a leadership team or as an entire staff, discuss each of the components and assign a consensus-designated score; then discuss the composite results.

Building Teachers' Capacity (BTC) Implementation Rubric:

Unaware	Conscious	Action	Refinement
This fundamental is addressed in a cursory manner, if at all. Members of the organization have limited (or no) awareness or understanding of this fundamental's purpose, components, and/or effective implementation.	This fundamental is addressed in a limited manner. Members of the organization have some awareness or understanding of this fundamental's purpose, components, and/or effective implementation, yet the implementation is inconsistent and varies across situations and between individuals.	This fundamental is implemented by most members of the organization. Members of the organization understand the fundamental, attempt to put it into place with some regularity, and have established some practices for affecting the system in a positive manner.	This fundamental is part of the fabric of the organization. Members share ownership of the implementation, connect the fundamental to the organization's vision and mission, determine its effectiveness, and strive to continuously refine the work to affect the system more thoroughly.
Capacity-building Goal: ***Build Awareness*** Develop a clear vision and common understanding of this fundamental.	**Capacity-building Goal:** ***Plan Intentionally*** Strategize and bring consistency to the implementation of this fundamental.	**Capacity-building Goal:** ***Accurately Assess Impact*** Assess the impact of the implementation of this fundamental in order to respond, refine, and/or deepen further work.	**Capacity-building Goal:** ***Become Responsive*** Reflect with increased frequency, accuracy, and depth on this fundamental, and replicate its success within other fundamentals.

BUILDING TEACHERS' CAPACITY (BTC) SITE ASSESSMENT	Unaware	Conscious	Action	Refinement
FUNDAMENTAL 1: Relationships, Roles, and Responsibilities				
a. **Administrator and staff have rapport and trustworthy relationships.**				
Narrative description and/or evidence of implementation/readiness level:				
b. **Coach and staff have rapport and trustworthy relationships.**				
Narrative description and/or evidence of implementation/readiness level:				
c. **Administrator and coach discuss their roles and responsibilities, the nature of their professional partnership, and their common goals as capacity-builders.**				
Narrative description and/or evidence of implementation/readiness level:				
d. **Staff have a clear understanding of the role and responsibilities of coach—and can articulate how they are distinct from those of administrator in order to encourage reflective growth, support effective teaching, and promote student learning.**				
Narrative description and/or evidence of implementation/readiness level:				

BUILDING TEACHERS' CAPACITY (BTC) SITE ASSESSMENT	Unaware	Conscious	Action	Refinement
FUNDAMENTAL 2: Expectations and Communication				
a. School has a written plan for implementing a culture of reflective practice.				
Narrative description and/or evidence of implementation/readiness level:				
b. Staff understand their expectation is to seek ways to grow as reflective practitioners and effective instructors utilizing the Reflective Cycle.				
Narrative description and/or evidence of implementation/readiness level:				
c. Administrator has set the expectation that all teachers will work with a coach to meet their professional goals.				
Narrative description and/or evidence of implementation/readiness level:				

BUILDING TEACHERS' CAPACITY (BTC) SITE ASSESSMENT	Unaware	Conscious	Action	Refinement
FUNDAMENTAL 2: Expectations and Communication *(continued)*				
d. **Administrator articulates the vision for implementing a culture of reflective practice to staff on a regular basis.**				
Narrative description and/or evidence of implementation/readiness level:				
e. **Coach communicates the role of coach and various supportive services available to staff on a regular basis.**				
Narrative description and/or evidence of implementation/readiness level:				
f. **Administrator or coach shares assessment and implementation data with staff and solicits feedback to inform the plan for implementing a culture of reflective practice.**				
Narrative description and/or evidence of implementation/readiness level:				

BUILDING TEACHERS' CAPACITY (BTC) SITE ASSESSMENT	Unaware	Conscious	Action	Refinement
FUNDAMENTAL 3: Celebration and Calibration				
a. **Time is routinely set aside for small and big celebrations of teacher capacity growth, progress toward goals, and other successes.**				
Narrative description and/or evidence of implementation/readiness level:				
b. **Staff review tools (instructional framework, research, data, site assessment and implementation plan, etc.) on a regular basis to calibrate understanding, expectations, vocabulary, and professional practices.**				
Narrative description and/or evidence of implementation/readiness level:				

BUILDING TEACHERS' CAPACITY (BTC) SITE ASSESSMENT	Unaware	Conscious	Action	Refinement
FUNDAMENTAL 4: Goal Setting and Follow-Through				
a. **Administrator meets with each teacher at the beginning of the year to set SMART student achievement goals.**				
Narrative description and/or evidence of implementation/readiness level:				
b. **Staff take the Reflective Self-Assessment Tool to identify their current reflective stage on the Continuum of Self-Reflection.**				
Narrative description and/or evidence of implementation/readiness level:				
c. **Staff identify a personal—SMART-R—goal to grow as reflective practitioners, utilizing the Reflective Cycle.**				
Narrative description and/or evidence of implementation/readiness level:				
d. **Staff work diligently toward their individual goals and strategic action steps in order to continuously grow as reflective practitioners.**				
Narrative description and/or evidence of implementation/readiness level:				
e. **Administrator intentionally follows up with staff on a regular basis to discuss progress toward goals and professional growth.**				
Narrative description and/or evidence of implementation/readiness level:				

BUILDING TEACHERS' CAPACITY (BTC) SITE ASSESSMENT	Unaware	Conscious	Action	Refinement
FUNDAMENTAL 5: Strategic PLC and Teacher-Leadership Support				
a. **Administrator, coach, and teacher-leaders provide differentiated support for grade-level/department teams, using the Continuum of Self-Reflection.**				
Narrative description and/or evidence of implementation/readiness level:				
b. **Staff support one another in the collective pursuit of reflective practice and effective instruction.**				
Narrative description and/or evidence of implementation/readiness level:				
c. **Staff have formal and/or informal opportunities to provide peer-based feedback to one another.**				
Narrative description and/or evidence of implementation/readiness level:				
d. **Teacher-leaders assume a wide range of roles to shape the culture of their school, improve student learning, and influence practice among their peers.**				
Narrative description and/or evidence of implementation/readiness level:				
e. **Teacher-leaders engage in professional learning opportunities that support their professional growth.**				
Narrative description and/or evidence of implementation/readiness level:				

BUILDING TEACHERS' CAPACITY (BTC) SITE ASSESSMENT	Unaware	Conscious	Action	Refinement
FUNDAMENTAL 6: Transformational Feedback				
a. Administrator provides regular feedback to staff to build their reflective tendencies and strengthen technical skill.				
Narrative description and/or evidence of implementation/readiness level:				
b. Coach provides regular feedback to staff to build their reflective tendencies and strengthen technical skill.				
Narrative description and/or evidence of implementation/readiness level:				
c. Clear look-fors, based on best practices, are established at the individual teacher, team/ department, and schoolwide level.				
Narrative description and/or evidence of implementation/readiness level:				
d. Feedback matches individual staff members' needs as reflective practitioners, linked to current stage on Continuum of Self-Reflection.				
Narrative description and/or evidence of implementation/readiness level:				
e. Feedback is growth-oriented, part of a continuous process, accurate, relevant to individual teacher goals, and timely (within 24 hours).				
Narrative description and/or evidence of implementation/readiness level:				

BUILDING TEACHERS' CAPACITY (BTC) SITE ASSESSMENT	Unaware	Conscious	Action	Refinement
FUNDAMENTAL 7: Differentiated Coaching				
a. **Administrator provides regular coaching support to staff to build their reflective tendencies and strengthen technical skill.**				
Narrative description and/or evidence of implementation/readiness level:				
b. **Coach provides regular coaching support to staff to build their reflective tendencies and strengthen technical skill.**				
Narrative description and/or evidence of implementation/readiness level:				
c. **Coaching strategies match individual staff members' needs as reflective practitioners using the Continuum of Self-Reflection.**				
Narrative description and/or evidence of implementation/readiness level:				
d. **Coaching strategies are growth-oriented, part of a continuous process, relevant to individual teacher goals, and provided in a timely manner.**				
Narrative description and/or evidence of implementation/readiness level:				
e. **Staff seek out coach for coaching support of their instructional goals.**				
Narrative description and/or evidence of implementation/readiness level:				

Appendix B: FAQs

To clarify anything we may have missed, we address some Frequently Asked Questions from your colleagues around the world who have launched themselves on this journey already.

Q: How many teachers should I start this process with? And who should I choose?

A: Our advice for this is akin to the old adage asking how to eat an elephant. The classic response is "You don't eat elephants, weirdo!" We say, "One bite at a time." So pick your first teacher wisely. We suggest you begin with a teacher who (1) already reflects in the Action stage and (2) is someone with whom you have a strong professional relationship.

The relationship will speed things up, as you won't have to spend time building and cultivating your interpersonal dynamics. Most likely you can be honest with each other and dig into this process together. The fact that this person is operating in the Action stage also demonstrates a level of commitment to change and growth, so you won't have to spend time instilling motivation and inspiration as much as you would with some other teachers. You can get on with the work at hand.

You might begin by saying to this person, "Hey, I'm learning some new strategies for leadership, coaching, and feedback. Would you be my guinea pig as I try some things out? Most likely, I'll make mistakes along the way, possibly even offend you. All I ask is that you offer me honest and critical feedback and tell me how my approaches help or hinder you, and that we learn together. It's all geared to help you become a more reflective, and therefore more effective, educator. What do you say?"

Q: How do we "tell" teachers about the Continuum of Self-Reflection?

A: Teachers are vital allies in the work to create a culture of reflective practice; therefore, it is necessary to be open, honest, and transparent as we come alongside and elicit them as partners. Remember, this is not work to be done *to* them but *with* them. That being said, we recommend first introducing the Reflective Cycle. Developing understanding around the reflective habits of thought that we want to cultivate is a great place to start—particularly as we work to build relationships with teachers, communicate our expectations about reflection, and celebrate metacognition.

Once Fundamentals 1, 2, and 3 have been established and teachers have a good handle on the Reflective Cycle, we begin our work around Fundamental 4: Goal Setting and Follow-Through. At this point, we can introduce the Continuum of Self-Reflection by way of the reflective self-assessment, using our related text, *Teach, Reflect, Learn: Building Your Capacity for Success in the Classroom* (Hall & Simeral, 2015). The key is to connect the stages of the continuum to the four quadrants on the Reflective Cycle diagram (Figure 2.2, p. 23) and to communicate that the continuum is a tool that drives our growth and reflection.

Q: There are a hundred references to "coach" in this book. What if I have no coach in my building? How do I go about this work without that position?

A: Actually, there are a little over 370 references to coaches in this book. That said, we've tried to provide ample strategies for all capacity-builders to engage in capacity-building work—through relationships, expectations, celebrations, goals, partnering, feedback, and coaching. The actual job title ends up meaning very little, in the big scheme of things.

We have worked with many educational leaders who do not have the privilege of working alongside an instructional coach, because of budget shortages, lack of qualified applicants, or being in a district with one coach for 17 buildings and 219 teachers—that's spread way too thin! The good news is this: there's still a way to build teachers' capacity. Think of the triad diagram (Figure 5.1, p. 71).

Who, in this web of relationships, can engage in coaching strategies to support a given teacher's reflective growth? A better question might be this: Who can't? That particular teacher, right? That leaves the rest of us to serve as capacity-builders!

Most schools have department chairs, team leaders, mentor teachers, or some other sanctioned teacher-leader. Even in the absence of those roles, certainly every teacher has a go-to colleague who provides counsel, advice, guidance, and feedback. Why not add strategic, intentional, differentiated coaching to that menu of support?

And coaching isn't reserved for nonevaluative peers, as we've attempted to state. Administrators can—and regularly should—provide coaching support for their teachers as well. In fact, administrators can be some of the most powerful coaches, due to their level of expertise and connection with so many fantastic educators in varying grade levels, content areas, and settings.

So don't let the lack of an official "coach" become an obstacle. Go ahead—get creative and weave in a steady mix of coaching strategies.

Bibliography

Alliance for Excellent Education. (2014). Teacher attrition costs United States up to $2.2 billion annually, says new Alliance report. Retrieved from http://all4ed.org/press/teacher-attrition-costs-united-states-up-to-2-2-billion-annually-says-new-alliance-report

Archambault, R. D. (Ed.). (1974). *John Dewey on education: Selected writings.* Chicago: University of Chicago Press.

Ashkenas, R. (2012). Seven mistakes leaders make in setting goals. *Forbes.* Retrieved from www.forbes.com/sites/ronashkenas/2012/07/09/seven-mistakes-leaders-make-in-setting-goals/#68f096dfa0f3

Bandura, A. (1977). *Social learning theory.* Englewood Cliffs, NJ: Prentice Hall.

Barber, M., & Mourshed, M. (2007). *How the world's best-performing school systems come out on top.* New York: McKinsey & Company.

Barnes, D. (1992). The significance of teachers' frames for teaching. In T. Russell & H. Munby (Eds.), *Teachers and teaching: From classroom to reflection* (pp. 9–32). New York: Falmer Press.

Barr, A. S. (1958). Characteristics of successful teachers. *Phi Delta Kappan, 39,* 282–284.

Bell, G. (2009). *Water the bamboo: Unleashing the potential of teams and individuals.* Portland, OR: Three Star Publishing.

Bermudez, M. A., & Schultz, W. (2014). Timing in reward and decision processes. *Philosophical Transactions of the Royal Society B: Biological Sciences, 369*(1637). Retrieved from http://rstb.royalsocietypublishing.org/content/369/1637/20120468

Bhardwaj, R. (2016). Celebrate milestone successes to maintain a positive work environment. *Entrepreneur India.* Retrieved from www.entrepreneur.com/article/273004

Blase, J., Blase, J., & Phillips, D. Y. (2010). *Handbook of school improvement: How high-performing principals create high-performing schools.* Thousand Oaks, CA: Corwin.

Boston Globe. (2004). Finally: Red Sox are the champions after 86 years. Boston: Author.

Bottoms, G., & Fry, B. (2009). *The district leadership challenge: Empowering principals to improve teaching and learning.* Retrieved from www.wallacefoundation.org/knowl-edge-center/Pages/District-Leadership-Challenge-Empowering-Principals.aspx

Brame, C. (2013). Flipping the classroom. Vanderbilt University Center for Teaching. Retrieved from http://cft.vanderbilt.edu/guides-sub-pages/flipping-the-classroom

Brookhart, S. (2017). *How to give effective feedback to your students* (2nd ed.). Alexandria, VA: ASCD.

Buckingham, M., & Coffman, C. (1999a). *First, break all the rules: What the world's greatest managers do differently.* New York: Simon & Schuster.

Buckingham, M., & Coffman, C. (1999b). *First, break all the rules: What the world's greatest managers do differently.* [Executive summary]. Concordville, PA: Soundview Executive Book Summaries. Retrieved from www.thetentruths.com.au/Downloads/First_break_all_the_rules_exec_summary.pdf

Buffum, A., Mattos, M., & Weber, C. (2008). *Pyramid response to intervention: RTI, professional learning communities, and how to respond when kids don't learn.* Bloomington, IN: Solution Tree.

Bureau of Labor Statistics, U.S. Department of Labor. (n.d.). *Occupational outlook handbook, 2016–17 edition,* Instructional Coordinators. Retrieved from www.bls.gov/ooh/education-training-and-library/instructional-coordinators.htm

Butzler, K. (2016). The synergistic effects of self-regulation tools and the flipped classroom. *Computers in the Schools: Interdisciplinary Journal of Practice, Theory, and Applied Research 33*(1): 11–23.

Calderhead, J., Denicolo, P., & Day, C. (2012). *Research on teacher thinking: Understanding professional development.* New York: Routledge.

Carucci, R. (2016, August 16). 4 ways to prepare for inevitable career disruption. *Forbes.* Retrieved from www.forbes.com/sites/roncarucci/2016/08/16/4-ways-to-prepare-for-inevitable-career-disruption/#aaa37d3f2ffb

Center for American Progress. (2011). Increasing principal effectiveness: A strategic investment for ESEA. Retrieved from http://files.eric.ed.gov/fulltext/ED535860.pdf

Chappuis, J. (2014). *Seven strategies of assessment for learning* (2nd ed.). Upper Saddle River, NJ: Pearson Education.

Coleman, J. (2012, August 3). Why your company should celebrate more. *Fast Company.* Retrieved from www.fastcompany.com/3000101/why-your-company-should-celebrate-more

Collins, J. (2001). *Good to great: Why some companies make the leap and others don't.* New York: HarperCollins.

Comer, J. (1995). Lecture given at Education Service Center, Region IV. Houston, TX.

Costa, A. (Ed.). (2001). *Developing minds: A resource book for teaching thinking.* Alexandria, VA: ASCD.

Costa, A., & Kallick, B. (Eds.). (2008). *Learning and leading with habits of mind: 16 essential characteristics for success.* Alexandria, VA: ASCD.

Covey, S. (1989). *The 7 habits of highly effective people: Powerful lessons in personal change.* New York: Fireside.

Covey, S. (1990). *Principle-centered leadership.* New York: Fireside.

Covey, S. (1997). *The 7 habits of highly effective families.* New York: Golden Books.

Danielson, C. (2007). *Enhancing professional practice: A framework for teaching* (2nd ed.). Alexandria, VA: ASCD.

Danielson, L. (2009). Fostering reflection. *Educational Leadership, 66*(5). Available online only at www.ascd.org/publications/educational-leadership/feb09/vol66/num05/Fostering-Reflection.aspx

Darling-Hammond, L. (2014–15). Want to close the achievement gap? Close the teaching gap. *American Educator 38*(4), 14–18.

Daudelin, M. W., & Hall, D. T. (1997, December). Using reflection to leverage learning. *Training and Development, 51*(12), 13–14.

David, J. (2008–2009). Collaborative inquiry. *Educational Leadership, 66*(4), 87–88.

Davis, S., Kearney, K., Sanders, N., Thomas, C., & Leon, R. (2011). The policies and practices of principal evaluation: A review of the literature. Retrieved from www.wested.org /online_pubs/resource1104.pdf

Dean, C., Hubbell, E., Pitler, H., & Stone, B. (2012). *Classroom instruction that works: Research-based strategies for increasing student achievement* (2nd ed.). Alexandria, VA: ASCD.

DeVita, C. (2010). Four big lessons from a decade of work. In Wallace Foundation (Ed.), *Education leadership: An agenda for school improvement* (pp. 2–5). Retrieved from www.wallacefoundation.org/knowledge-center/pages/four-big-lessons-education-leadership-an-agenda-for-school-improvement.aspx

Dewey, J. (1910). *How we think.* Boston: D. C. Heath.

Dewey, J. (1916). *Democracy in education.* New York: MacMillan.

Dewey, J. (1933). *How we think: A restatement of the relation of reflective thinking to the education process.* Lexington, MA: Heath.

DuFour, R. (2004). Leading edge: Leadership is an affair of the heart. *Journal of Staff Development, 25*(1), 67–68.

Duhigg, C. (2012). *The power of habit: Why we do what we do in life and business.* New York: Random House

Dweck, C. (2006). *Mindset: The new psychology of success.* New York: Ballantine Books.

Easton, L. (2009). *Protocols for professional learning.* Alexandria, VA: ASCD.

Edwards, J. (2004). *The daffodil principle.* Salt Lake City, UT: Shadow Mountain Publishing.

Eisenberg, E., & Medrich, E. (2013). Make the case for coaching: Bolster support with evidence that coaching makes a difference. *Journal of Staff Development, 34*(5), 48–49.

Elmore, R., & City, E. (2007). The road to school improvement: It's hard, it's bumpy, and it takes as long as it takes. *Harvard Education Letter, 23*(3).

Ende, F. (2016). *Professional development that sticks: How do I create meaningful learning experiences for educators?* Alexandria, VA: ASCD.

Ericsson, K. A., Krampe, R. T., & Tesch-Römer,C. (1993). The role of deliberate practice in the acquisition of expert performance. *Psychological Review, 100*(3), 363–406.

Eyler, J., Giles, D. E., & Schmeide, A. (1996). *A practitioner's guide to reflection in service-learning: Student voices and reflections.* Nashville, TN: Vanderbilt University.

Fielding, L., Kerr, N., & Rosier, P. (2004). *Delivering on the promise of the 95% reading and math goals.* Kennewick, WA: New Foundation Press.

Fisher, D., & Frey, N. (2010). *Enhancing RTI: How to ensure success with effective classroom instruction and intervention.* Alexandria, VA: ASCD.

Fullan, M. (1993). *Change forces: Probing the depth of educational reform.* London: Falmer Press.

Fullan, M. (2001). *Leading in a culture of change.* San Francisco: Jossey-Bass.

Fullan, M. (2008). *The six secrets of change: What the best leaders do to help their organizations survive and thrive.* San Francisco: Jossey-Bass.

Fullan, M. (2010). *Motion leadership: The skinny on becoming change savvy.* Thousand Oaks, CA: Corwin.

Furlong, J., & Maynard, T. (1995). *Mentoring student teachers: The growth of professional knowledge.* London: Routledge.

Gabriel, J. (2005). *How to thrive as a teacher leader.* Alexandria, VA: ASCD.

Geller, E. S. (2016). *The psychology of safety handbook.* Boca Raton, FL: CRC Press.

Gladwell, M. (2008). *Outliers: The story of success.* New York: Little, Brown.

Glatthorn, A. (1997). *Differentiated supervision* (2nd ed.). Alexandria, VA: ASCD.

Glickman, C. (1990). *Supervision of instruction.* Boston: Allyn & Bacon.

Goodwin, B. (2011). *Simply better: Doing what matters most to change the odds for student success.* Alexandria, VA: ASCD.

Goodwin, B. (2014). Curiosity is fleeting, but teachable. *Educational Leadership, 72*(1), 73–74.

Goodwin, B., & Hubbell, E. R. (2013). *The 12 touchstones of good teaching: A checklist for staying focused every day.* Alexandria, VA: ASCD.

Greenleaf, R., & Spears, L. C. (2002). *Servant leadership: A journey into the nature of legitimate power and greatness.* Mahwah, NJ: Paulist Press.

Guskey, T. R. (2014). Planning professional learning. *Educational Leadership, 71*(8), 10–16.

Guskin, A. (1994). Reducing student costs and enhancing student learning: Restructuring the role of the faculty. *Change, 26*(5), 16–25.

Hall, D. (2011, May 6). Speech delivered at the Senior Assembly. Retrieved from www.amherst.edu/news/specialevents/commencement/speeches_multimedia/2011/senior_assembly

Hall, P. (2005). A school reclaims itself. *Educational Leadership, 62*(5), 70–73.

Hall, P., Childs-Bowen, D., Cunningham-Morris, A., Pajardo, P., & Simeral, A. (2016). *The principal influence: A framework for developing leadership capacity in principals.* Alexandria, VA: ASCD.

Hall, P., & Simeral, A. (2008). *Building teachers' capacity for success: A collaborative approach for coaches and school leaders.* Alexandria, VA: ASCD.

Hall, P., & Simeral, A. (2015). *Teach, reflect, learn: Building your capacity for success in the classroom.* Alexandria, VA: ASCD.

Hargreaves, A., & Fink, D. (2004). The seven principles of sustainable leadership. *Educational Leadership, 61*(7), 8–13.

Harris, S. (2005). *Best practices of award-winning elementary school principals.* Thousand Oaks, CA: Corwin.

Harvey, T. R. (1995). *Checklist for change: A pragmatic approach to creating and controlling change* (2nd ed.). Boston: Allyn & Bacon.

Hattie, J. (2009). *Visible learning: A synthesis of over 800 meta-analyses relating to achievement.* New York: Routledge.

Hattie, J. (2015). High-impact leadership. *Educational Leadership, 72*(5), 36–40.

Henderson, J. G. (1992). *Reflective teaching: Becoming an inquiring educator.* New York: Macmillan.

Henderson, J. G. (1996). *Reflective teaching: The study of your constructivist practices.* Englewood Cliffs, NJ: Merrill Prentice Hall.

Henson, R. K. (2001). *Teacher self-efficacy: Substantive implications and measurement dilemmas.* Paper presented at the Annual Meeting of the Educational Research Exchange, College Station, TX.

Hirsch, E., Sioberg, A., & Germuth, A. (2010). *TELL Maryland: Listening to educators to create successful schools.* Retrieved from www.governor.maryland.gov/documents/TELLMDreport.pdf

Hunter, M. (1979). Teaching is decision making. *Educational Leadership, 37*(1), 62–67.

Inc. (2014). These 7 motivational Navy SEAL sayings will kick your butt into gear. Retrieved from www.inc.com/brent-gleeson/7-motivational-navy-seal-sayings-will-kick-your-butt-into-gear.html

Iso-Ahola, S., & Dotson, C. (2014, March). Psychological momentum: Why success breeds success. *Review of General Psychology, 18*(1), 19–33.

Iso-Ahola, S., & Mobily, K. (1980). "Psychological momentum": A phenomenon and empirical (unobtrusive) validation of its influence in sport competition. *Psychological Reports, 46*(2), 391–401.

Joyce, B., & Showers, B. (1982, October). The coaching of teaching. *Educational Leadership, 40*(1), 4–10.

Kanold, T. (2011). *The five disciplines of PLC leaders.* Bloomington, IN: Solution Tree.

Keller, B. (2008). Drive on to improve evaluation systems for teachers. *Education Week, 27*(19), 8.

King, P. M, & Kitchener, K. S. (1994). *Developing reflective judgement: Understanding and promoting intellectual growth and critical thinking in adolescents and adults.* San Francisco: Jossey-Bass.

Kolb, D. A. (1984). *Experiential learning: Experience as the source of learning and development.* Englewood Cliffs, NJ: Prentice Hall.

Laloux, F. (2014). *Reinventing organizations.* Millis, MA: Parker Nelson.

Landsdowne, J. (1944). Only a few were teachers. *Educational Leadership 1*(6), 332–336.

Layden, T. (2016). Closing ceremony. *Sports Illustrated, 125*(5), 30–34.

Learning Forward. (2015). Standards for professional learning: Quick reference guide. Retrieved from https://learningforward.org/docs/pdf/standardsreferenceguide. pdf?sfvrsn=0

Lortie, D. (2002). *Schoolteacher: A sociological study* (2nd ed.). Chicago: University of Chicago Press.

Louis, K. S., Leithwood, K., Wahlstrom, K., & Anderson, S. (2010). *Investigating the links to improved student learning: Final report of research findings.* Retrieved from www. wallacefoundation.org/knowledge-center/Documents/Investigating-the-Links-to-Improved-Student-Learning.pdf

Marsh, J., McCombs, J. S., & Martorell, F. (2012). Reading coach quality: Findings from Florida middle schools. *Literacy Research and Instruction, 51*(1), 1–26.

Martinez, A. R. (2010). The improvisational brain. *Seed Magazine.* Retrieved from http:// seedmagazine.com/content/article/the_improvisational_brain/P1

Marzano, R. (2003). *What works in schools: Translating research into action.* Alexandria, VA: ASCD.

Marzano, R. (2007). *The art and science of teaching: A comprehensive framework for effective instruction.* Alexandria, VA: ASCD.

Marzano, R. (2012). *Becoming a reflective teacher.* Bloomington, IN: Marzano Research Laboratory.

Marzano, R., Frontier, T., & Livingston, D. (2011). *Effective supervision: Supporting the art and science of teaching.* Alexandria, VA: ASCD.

Marzano, R. J., Pickering, D. J., & Pollock, J. E. (2001). *Classroom instruction that works: Research-based strategies for increasing student achievement.* Alexandria, VA: ASCD.

Mass Insight Education. (2012). Successful principals speak out. Retrieved from www. massinsight.org/cms_page_media/201/STG%20Turnaround%20Brief%20-%20 March%202012%20-%20 Successful%20Principals.pdf

Matsumura, L. C., Garnier, H. E., & Spybrook, J. (2013). Literacy coaching to improve student reading achievement: A multi-level mediation model. *Learning and Instruction, 25,* 35–48.

McCarthy, M. D. (1996). One-time and short-term service learning experiences. In B. Jacoby & Associates (Eds.), *Service-learning in higher education* (pp. 113–134). San Francisco: Jossey-Bass.

McIver, M. C., Kearns, J., Lyons, C., & Sussman, M. (2009). *Leadership: A McREL report prepared for Stupski Foundation's Learning System.* ERIC No. ED544625

McREL International. (2013). *McREL's teacher evaluation system: CUES framework.* Denver, CO: Author.

Medina, J. (2008). *Brain rules: 12 principles for surviving and thriving at work, home, and school.* Seattle, WA: Pear Press.

Mendels, P. (2012). The effective principal: 5 pivotal practices that shape instructional leadership. *Journal of Staff Development, 33*(1), 54–58.

Moon, J. (1999). *A handbook of reflective and experiential learning.* London: Routledge.

Moxley, J. H., Ericsson, K. A., Charness, N., & Krampe, R. T. (2012). The role of intuition and deliberative thinking in experts' superior tactical decision-making. *Cognition, 124*(1), 72–78.

New Teacher Project. (2009). The widget effect: Our national failure to acknowledge and act on differences in teacher effectiveness. Retrieved from http://tntp.org/publications/view/the-widget-effect-failure-to-act-on-differences-in-teacher-effectiveness

New Teacher Project. (2015). The mirage: Confronting the hard truth about our quest for teacher development. Retrieved from http://tntp.org/publications/view/the-mirage-confronting-the-truth-about-our-quest-for-teacher-development

Nwogbaga, D.M.E., Nwankwo, O. U., & Onwa, D. O. (2015). Avoiding school management conflicts and crisis through formal communication. *Journal of Education and Practice, 6*(4), 33–36.

Organisation for Economic Co-operation and Development. (n.d.). OECD Teaching and Learning International Survey (TALIS): Teacher Questionnaire. Retrieved from www.oecd.org/edu/school/43081350.pdf

Peale, N. V. (1952). *The power of positive thinking.* Englewood, NJ: Prentice Hall.

Perry, W. G. (1998). *Forms of intellectual and ethical development in the college years: A scheme.* New York: Holt, Rinehart, & Winston.

Pfeffer, J., & Sutton, R. (2000). *The knowing-doing gap: How smart companies turn knowledge into action.* Boston: President and Fellows of Harvard College.

Pink, D. (2009). *Drive: The surprising truth about what motivates us.* New York: Riverhead Books.

Rabinowitz, P. (n.d.). *Building teams: Broadening the base for leadership.* Community Tool Box. Retrieved from http://ctb.ku.edu/en/table-of-contents/leadership/leadership-ideas/team-building/main.

Reeves, D. B. (2009). *Leading change in your school: How to conquer myths, build commitment, and get results.* Alexandria, VA: ASCD.

Reeves, D. B. (2010). *Transforming professional development into student results.* Alexandria, VA: ASCD.

Rosenthal, R., & Babad, E. (1985). Pygmalion in the gymnasium. *Educational Leadership, 43*(1), 36–39.

Sandomir, R. (2015, July 6). Women's World Cup final was most-watched soccer game in U.S. history. Retrieved from www.nytimes.com/2015/07/07/sports/soccer/womens-world-cup-final-was-most-watched-soccer-game-in-united-states-history.html?_r=0

Schaffer, R. H. (1991, March–April). Demand better results—and get them. *Harvard Business Review.* Retrieved from https://hbr.org/1991/03/demand-better-results-and-get-them

Schmidt-Davis, J., & Bottoms, G. (2011). *Who's next? Let's stop gambling on school performance and plan for principal succession.* Retrieved from http:// publications.sreb. org/2011/11V19_Principal_Succession_Planning.pdf

Schmoker, M. (2006). *Results now: How we can achieve unprecedented improvements in teaching and learning.* Alexandria, VA: ASCD.

Schön, D. A. (1983). *The reflective practitioner: How professionals think in action.* New York: Basic Books.

Schön, D. A. (1987). *Educating the reflective practitioner.* San Francisco: Jossey-Bass.

Simeral, A. (2016, June 20). Mediocrity versus excellence: What's the difference? ASCD INservice blog. Retrieved from http://inservice.ascd.org/mediocrity-versus-excellence-whats-the-difference/

Sinek, S. (2009). *Start with why: How great leaders inspire everyone to take action.* New York: Penguin.

Smith, J. (2013, October 4). How to create an authentic and transparent work environment. *Forbes.* Retrieved from www.forbes.com/sites/jacquelynsmith/2013/10/04/how-to-create-an-authentic-and-transparent-work-environment/#53523892562c

Straw, S., Quinlan, C., Harland, J., & Walker, M. (2015). *Flipped learning: Research report.* London: Nesta.

Sun, C. (2011). *NASBE discussion guide: School leadership: Improving state systems for leader development.* Retrieved from www.wallacefoundation.org/knowledge-center/Pages/NASBE-Discussion-Guide-School-Leadership-Improving-State-Systems-for-Leader-Development.aspx

Sutcher, L., Darling-Hammond, L., & Carver-Thomas, D. (2016). A coming crisis in teaching? Teacher supply, demand, and shortages in the U.S. *Learning Policy Institute.* Retrieved from https://learningpolicyinstitute.org/product/coming-crisis-teaching

Thomas, E. E., Bell, D. L., Spelman, M., & Briody, J. (2015). The growth of instructional coaching partner conversations in a preK–3rd grade teacher professional development experience. *Journal of Adult Education, 44*(2), 1–6.

Tomlinson, C. (2014). *The differentiated classroom: Responding to the needs of all learners* (2nd ed.). Alexandria, VA: ASCD.

U.S. Joint Forces Command. (2010). Commander's Handbook for Strategic Communication and Communication Strategy. Retrieved from www.dtic.mil/doctrine/doctrine/jwfc/sc_hbk10.pdf

Wahlstrom, K., Louis, K. S., Leithwood, K., & Anderson, S. E. (2010). *Investigating the links to improved student learning: Executive summary of research findings.* Retrieved from http://conservancy.umn.edu/bitstream/handle/11299/140884/Executive%20Summary%20Report-Web%20%282%29.pdf?sequence=1&isAllowed=y

Wallace Foundation. (2011). *The school principal as leader: Guiding schools to better teaching and learning.* Retrieved from www.wallacefoundation.org/knowledge-center/Pages/overview-the-school-principal-as-leader.aspx

Waters, J. T., Marzano, R. J., & McNulty, B. A. (2003). *Balanced leadership: What 30 years of research tells us about the effect of leadership on student achievement.* Aurora, CO: Mid-continent Research for Education and Learning.

Wolcott, S. K., & Lynch, C. L. (1997). Critical thinking in the accounting classroom: A reflective judgment developmental process perspective. *Accounting Education: A Journal of Theory, Practice and Research, 2*(1), 59–78.

Wong, H., & Wong, R. (1998). *The first days of school: How to be an effective teacher* (2nd ed.). Mountain View, CA: Harry K. Wong Publications.

York-Barr, J., Sommers, W., Ghere, G., & Montie, J. (2006). Reflective practice to improve schools: An action guide for educators (2nd ed.). Thousand Oaks, CA: SAGE.

Zeidler, E. (Ed.), & Hunt, B. (Trans.). (2004). *Oxford users' guide to mathematics.* Oxford: Oxford University Press.

Index

The letter *f* following a page number denotes a figure.

About the Authors

Pete Hall

Veteran school administrator and leadership expert Pete Hall has dedicated his career to supporting the improvement of our education systems. In addition to his teaching experiences in three states, he served as a school principal for 12 years in Nevada and Washington. This is his seventh book—and his fourth coauthored with Alisa Simeral—to accompany over a dozen articles on school leadership. Pete currently serves as a professional development agent, motivational speaker, coach, and mentor for educators worldwide. If he's not competing in (or training for) a triathlon, you can reach him at PeteHall@EducationHall.com or on Twitter at @EducationHall.

Alisa Simeral

Alisa Simeral has guided school-based reform efforts as instructional coach, school dean, professional developer, and leadership mentor. Her focus is, and always has been, empowering educators to take charge of their own professional growth. If how we *think* drives what we *do*, then developing and refining strong metacognitive habits is at the heart of all capacity-building work, leading directly to both teacher and student success.

Alisa's commitment to this mission has been the focus of her research, writing, speaking, and teaching. This is her fourth book; and she now works as consultant and professional speaker to schools—both nationally and internationally—focused on cultivating reflective practice and shifting from cultures of compliance to cultures of commitment. Her mantra is "When our teachers succeed, our students succeed." She can be reached at Alisa@ AlisaSimeral.com or on Twitter at @alisasimeral.